Early Praise for *Genetic Algorithms in Elixir*

A thorough coverage of genetic algorithms and Elixir from the ground up. Two books for the price of one.

➤ **Frances Buontempo**
   Director, Buontempo Consulting Ltd

A comprehensive guide to anyone interested in genetic algorithms and Elixir. Sean does an amazing job at breaking down even the most complicated topics and presenting them in a way that's practical and easy to understand. His unique approach to building genetic algorithms using Elixir is game-changing.

➤ **Svilen Gospodinov**
   Freelance software engineer and consultant

Genetic Algorithms in Elixir is a fantastic resource for a programmer interested in learning a growing new language and fascinating topic at the same time.

➤ **Charlie Wasaff**
   Freelance software developer

Genetic Algorithms in Elixir

Solve Problems Using Evolution

Sean Moriarity

The Pragmatic Bookshelf

Raleigh, North Carolina

Many of the designations used by manufacturers and sellers to distinguish their products are claimed as trademarks. Where those designations appear in this book, and The Pragmatic Programmers, LLC was aware of a trademark claim, the designations have been printed in initial capital letters or in all capitals. The Pragmatic Starter Kit, The Pragmatic Programmer, Pragmatic Programming, Pragmatic Bookshelf, PragProg and the linking *g* device are trademarks of The Pragmatic Programmers, LLC.

Every precaution was taken in the preparation of this book. However, the publisher assumes no responsibility for errors or omissions, or for damages that may result from the use of information (including program listings) contained herein.

Our Pragmatic books, screencasts, and audio books can help you and your team create better software and have more fun. Visit us at *https://pragprog.com*.

The team that produced this book includes:

Publisher: Andy Hunt
VP of Operations: Janet Furlow
Executive Editor: Dave Rankin
Development Editor: Tammy Coron
Copy Editor: L. Sakhi MacMillan
Indexing: Potomac Indexing, LLC
Layout: Gilson Graphics

For sales, volume licensing, and support, please contact *support@pragprog.com*.

For international rights, please contact *rights@pragprog.com*.

ISBN-13: 978-1-68050-794-2
Book version: P1.0—January 2021

Contents

Disclaimer ix
Acknowledgments xi
Preface xiii

1. Writing Your First Genetic Algorithm 1
   Understanding Genetic Algorithms   2
   Introducing the One-Max Problem   5
   Initializing the Population   6
   Understanding the Flow of Genetic Algorithms   7
   Selecting Parents   9
   Creating Children   10
   Running Your Solution   11
   Adding Mutation   13
   What You Learned   14

2. Breaking Down Genetic Algorithms 15
   Reviewing Genetic Algorithms   15
   Looking Deeper into Genetic Algorithms   16
   Using Mix to Write Genetic Algorithms   22
   Building a Framework for Genetic Algorithms   23
   Understanding Hyperparameters   27
   Solving the One-Max Problem Again   29
   What You Learned   31

3. Encoding Problems and Solutions 33
   Using Structs to Represent Chromosomes   33
   Using Behaviours to Model Problems   37
   Understanding and Choosing Genotypes   43
   Solving One-Max for the Last Time   46

Spelling Words with Genetic Algorithms 47
What You Learned 50

4. **Evaluating Solutions and Populations** 51
Optimizing Cargo Loads 52
Introducing Penalty Functions 55
Applying a Penalty to the Shipping Problem 56
Defining Termination Criteria 57
Applying Termination Criteria to Shipping 61
Crafting Fitness Functions 62
Exploring Different Types of Optimization 65
What You Learned 69

5. **Selecting the Best** 71
Exploring Selection 72
Customizing Selection in Your Framework 75
Implementing Common Selection Strategies 78
What You Learned 85

6. **Generating New Solutions** 87
Introducing N-Queens 87
Solving N-Queens with Order-One Crossover 91
Exploring Crossover 95
Implementing Other Common Crossover Strategies 95
Crossing Over More Than Two Parents 102
Implementing Chromosome Repairment 103
What You Learned 105

7. **Preventing Premature Convergence** 107
Breaking Codes with Genetic Algorithms 108
Understanding Mutation 113
Customizing Mutation in Your Framework 115
Implementing Common Mutation Strategies 117
Other Methods to Combat Convergence 122
What You Learned 123

8. **Replacing and Transitioning** 125
Creating a Class Schedule 126
Understanding Reinsertion 129
Experimenting with Reinsertion 133
Growing and Shrinking Populations 135

Local Versus Global Reinsertion 136
What You Learned 137

9. **Tracking Genetic Algorithms** 139
Using Genetic Algorithms to Simulate Evolution 139
Logging Statistics Using ETS 144
Tracking Genealogy in a Genealogy Tree 150
What You Learned 155

10. **Visualizing the Results** 157
Visualizing the Genealogy of the Tiger Evolution 157
Visualizing Basic Statistics 160
Playing Tetris with Genetic Algorithms 162
Installing and Compiling ALEx 163
What You Learned 168

11. **Optimizing Your Algorithms** 169
Benchmarking and Profiling Genetic Algorithms 170
Writing Fast Elixir 175
Improving Performance with Parallelization 177
Improving Performance with NIFs 183
What You Learned 185

12. **Writing Tests and Code Quality** 187
Understanding Randomness 188
Writing Property Tests with ExUnit 189
Cleaning Up Your Framework 192
Writing Type Specifications 195
What You Learned 198

13. **Moving Forward** 199
Learning with Evolution 199
Designing with Evolution 200
Trading with Evolution 201
Networking with Evolution 202
Evolving Neural Networks 203
Where to Go Next 204

Bibliography 205
Index 207

Disclaimer

This publication was privately produced and is not the product of an official in the United States Army acting in an official capacity. The contents of this publication, including words, images, and opinions, are unofficial and not to be considered as the official views of the United States Military Academy, United States Army, or Department of Defense. Neither this publication nor its content are endorsed by the United States Military Academy, United States Army, or Department of Defense.

Acknowledgments

Thank you, Dave Rankin, for helping me work through the initial idea for this book and for helping me through the proposal process. This book would have never happened without your willingness to help me out in those early stages.

Thank you, Tammy Coron, for being such a pleasure to work with and guiding me through this entire process. You kept me organized and on track, your suggestions were always spot on, and my writing has improved significantly just from working with you.

Thank you, Charlie, Frances, Matt, and Svilen, for taking the time to offer your feedback and making this book the best it can be.

Thank you to my family, who was always there for me with support and encouragement.

Thank you to all of my friends, who challenged me to be better everyday with their examples.

Finally, thank you to the entire PragProg team that made this book possible. I never imagined I'd become an author. My experience working with PragProg has been incredible. I am forever grateful for those who believed in me and this book and worked hard to turn it into a finished product.

Preface

Genetic algorithms are a powerful and often overlooked tool for solving difficult problems. Some of the most beautiful solutions to practical problems are inspired by or modeled after solutions found in mother nature. Genetic algorithms are no exception. Inspired by the original optimization algorithm—evolution—genetic algorithms can be used to solve a variety of problems in a variety of fields. As you'll see in this book, genetic algorithms have applications in finance, logistics, artificial intelligence, and more.

Unfortunately, despite being one of the first "artificial intelligence" algorithms, there's a surprising lack of resources available for programmers to explore the ins and outs of using evolution to solve problems. Even still, there are no books designed specifically with Elixir programmers in mind.

My goal in writing this book is to introduce Elixir programmers to a field of programming they might have never been exposed to or were too intimidated to try. Technology evolves rapidly, and programmers need to constantly seek out and learn about new fields and new technologies. While Elixir may not be the ideal language for solving computationally expensive problems, a programmer shouldn't be forced to learn a new language just to learn about genetic algorithms.

In this book, you'll learn everything you need to know to start working with genetic algorithms. As you work through the book, you'll build a framework for problems using genetic algorithms. By the end, you'll have a full-featured, customizable framework complete with statistics, genealogy tracking, and more, and you'll have learned everything you need to solve practical problems with genetic algorithms. You'll do all of this using Elixir. Along the way, you'll learn some Elixir-specific tips and tricks to idiomatically encode problems and solutions, speed up your code, and verify the correctness of the algorithms you implement.

I hope this book forces you to think outside the box and inspires you to further explore the beauty of genetic algorithms.

Who This Book Is For

This book is for programmers with some experience or familiarity working with Elixir, who are looking to expand their knowledge into the field of genetic algorithms. While not traditionally thought of as a language suited for computationally expensive problems, Elixir's simple syntax and functional style make for the creation of idiomatic solutions to optimization problems with genetic algorithms. These solutions gently introduce the user to genetic algorithms and optimization problems without the overhead of learning a completely new programming language.

If you have no experience with Elixir, you might find this book difficult to follow at times. Before getting started, I recommend checking out Elixir School[1] or the Elixir Guides[2] to get some familiarity with the language.

What's in This Book

In Chapter 1, Writing Your First Genetic Algorithm, on page 1, you'll learn the basics of the genetic algorithm by solving an introductory optimization problem. You'll learn about the core concepts of a genetic algorithm by writing an Elixir script. By the end of the chapter, you'll get to see a genetic algorithm in action, and you'll begin to understand the kinds of problems best suited for using genetic algorithms.

In Chapter 2, Breaking Down Genetic Algorithms, on page 15, you'll dive deeper into the core concepts you learned about in the first chapter and you'll use some of Elixir's code constructs to turn the script you wrote in Chapter 1, Writing Your First Genetic Algorithm, on page 1, into a reusable framework for solving optimization problems. You'll learn more about each step in the evolutionary process of a genetic algorithm and, by the end of the chapter, have a barebones framework for using genetic algorithms.

In Chapter 3, Encoding Problems and Solutions, on page 33, you'll learn about how to use Elixir to represent optimization problems and solutions to optimization problems. You'll learn about how genetic algorithms represent solutions and how you can use a variety of strategies to represent real-world solutions using code. Finally, you'll create a program that learns how to spell in order to see how you can use Elixir behaviours to represent any optimization problem imaginable.

---

1. https://elixirschool.com/en/
2. https://elixir-lang.org/getting-started/introduction.html

In Chapter 4, Evaluating Solutions and Populations, on page 51, you'll explore how genetic algorithms learn to find better and better solutions by evaluating a set of solutions. You'll learn more about the concept of fitness. You'll also learn about how to write different fitness functions and termination criteria for different types of problems, including shipping optimization, portfolio optimization, and website optimization.

In Chapter 5, Selecting the Best, on page 71, you'll learn about the first operator in a genetic algorithm—selection. You'll learn about why selection is important, how selection rate affects your algorithms, and how to write different types of selection strategies. You'll learn about how different selection strategies apply best to different types of problems, and you'll learn how to customize them within your genetic algorithms.

In Chapter 6, Generating New Solutions, on page 87, you'll learn about how genetic algorithms create new solutions from existing ones using crossover. You will learn about different types of crossover strategies and how to implement them in Elixir. You'll learn how to solve the N-queens problem to see how crossover strategies can affect the solutions produced by your genetic algorithm.

In Chapter 7, Preventing Premature Convergence, on page 107, you'll learn about a common problem in genetic algorithms—premature convergence—and how to solve it using mutation. You'll create a basic password cracker to demonstrate premature convergence. You'll learn how to implement several different types of mutation strategies, and you'll learn which ones apply best to different problems.

In Chapter 9, Tracking Genetic Algorithms, on page 139, you'll learn about the different metrics and statistics you can track while running your genetic algorithms. You'll learn how to implement an evolutionary simulation using genetic algorithms, and you'll build statistics and genealogy tracking mechanisms around that problem.

In Chapter 10, Visualizing the Results, on page 157, you'll use the statistics collected in Chapter 9, Tracking Genetic Algorithms, on page 139, to create visualizations using different plotting tools. Next, you'll create a genetic algorithm that learns how to play Tetris, and you'll learn how to use different tools to watch your algorithm in action.

In Chapter 11, Optimizing Your Algorithms, on page 169, you'll work through a general optimization process to learn how to get the most performance out of your code. You'll learn how to use Elixir tools to benchmark and profile your algorithms. You'll learn how to write faster Elixir and faster algorithms.

You'll learn how to parallelize your algorithms and how to implement NIFs that run faster than pure Elixir code.

In Chapter 12, Writing Tests and Code Quality, on page 187, you'll learn how to use Elixir features and packages to test and type check your code. You'll learn a bit about writing tests that work well with randomness. You'll then learn how to write typespecs and how to verify your typespecs are correct.

In Chapter 13, Moving Forward, on page 199, you'll be introduced to a variety of practical applications of genetic algorithms. From artificial intelligence to finance to advertising, you'll learn how genetic algorithms are applied in practice, and you'll learn about how you can use them in almost any field.

How to Use This Book

Each chapter in this book builds on the last by making additions to a genetic algorithm framework in some meaningful way. You should read this book in successive order and follow along with the code examples as they are presented to you. If, for some reason, you want to skip around, you can download the code from each chapter on the book's web page.

How Does Elixir Fit In?

Before you start reading this book, you're likely wondering two things:

- Why would I do this in Elixir?
- How does Elixir fit in the bigger picture of genetic algorithm design?

Elixir is certainly not a popular choice for genetic algorithm design; however, that doesn't mean it's not a good choice.

First, the significant increases in available computing power over the last decade have meant the need for incredibly efficient code has diminished. That's not to say you shouldn't pay attention to efficiency and writing efficient code; however, the need to optimize code for low-power hardware has significantly decreased.

Second, as you'll see in Chapter 11, Optimizing Your Algorithms, on page 169, parallelism in Elixir is a straightforward task. The BEAM is especially optimized for running numerous processes at once, so writing and running parallel code is easy. Genetic algorithms are by nature very parallel. A portion of research[3] into genetic algorithms takes advantage of the parallelism offered by Erlang to experiment with parallel genetic algorithms.

---

3. http://personal.denison.edu/~lalla/MCURCSM2011/6.pdf

Finally, Elixir's syntax and design patterns lend themselves nicely to writing idiomatic genetic algorithms. As you'll see throughout this book, Elixir offers a number of useful features for creating a general framework for genetic algorithm design. This is not only excellent for learning but also for rapid prototyping of new ideas.

You might not choose to implement a production-level genetic algorithm in Elixir, but using Elixir to prototype and experiment can save you significant amounts of time and effort.

Now, it's time to get started writing your first genetic algorithm.

## CHAPTER 1

Writing Your First Genetic Algorithm

In a world of competition, people are always searching for the best. The best job, the best diet, the best financial plan, and so on. Unfortunately, with so many options, it's impossible to make the best decisions all the time. Fortunately, humans have evolved to navigate the complexity of everyday life and make informed decisions that ultimately lead to success.

While your brain is naturally wired to make informed decisions, computers are not. Computers are naive—they can only do what you program them to do. So how do you program a computer to make informed decisions, and why is this even necessary?

Consider this example: you're tasked with designing the shipping route for a large shipping company. You're given a list of fifteen cities and your job is to pick the shortest route between them to save the company money on gas and travel expenses. At first, you might think it's best to calculate every possible path between the cities—there're only fifteen. Unfortunately, the number of possible paths is 130,766,744,000,000—that's 130 *trillion*. This problem is an example of the *traveling salesman problem*. The goal of the traveling salesman problem is to find the shortest route between a designated number of cities.

The number of possible paths grows at a *factorial* rate. A factorial is the product of every integer up to a certain integer. In the shipping example with fifteen cities, you can calculate the number of paths by multiplying every integer from 1 to 15.

Nobody has enough time to calculate the distance of 130 trillion paths. You have to take a better, more informed approach. You could choose a random start point and choose to travel to the next closest city after every stop. This strategy might produce the shortest path—you could even calculate the distance of the paths produced from starting at every city and choose the shortest one from that. You'd then only have to calculate the distance of fifteen paths. Unfortunately, experimenting with different strategies is still time consuming, and without a calculated approach you might miss the best strategy.

So how can you make the best decisions and teach a computer to do the same?

The answer is *optimization.* Optimization is the practice of making the best possible decisions in a situation. You can think of optimization as the search for the best. Humans are great at optimizing—it's natural for us to find and make the best decisions for ourselves. Computers can be great at optimizing too; they just need a little help.

Optimization *algorithms* are techniques for solving optimization problems— problems where your goal is to find the best of something. An algorithm is a series of instructions. An optimization algorithm is a set of instructions for finding the best solution to a problem. While there are countless optimization algorithms, one of the oldest and most common is the *genetic algorithm.*

Understanding Genetic Algorithms

Genetic algorithms are a class of optimization algorithms based on evolution and natural selection. They use strategies loosely based on genetics and biology to produce optimal—think "best"—or near-optimal solutions to complicated problems. Initially conceived in the 1960s, the intended use for genetic algorithms was simply a technique for creating adaptable programs. Today, genetic algorithms are used in numerous applications in fields like artificial intelligence and finance. They're great at solving difficult optimization problems and lend themselves nicely to parallel computing and distributed architectures. They can even yield solutions to the shipping problem mentioned earlier.

The First Genetic Algorithm

The first genetic algorithm was introduced by John Holland at the University of Michigan in the 1960s; however, evolutionary algorithms had been around long before that. Early artificial intelligence researchers believed evolution was the key to creating truly intelligent programs. Today, the field of evolutionary computation has many, somewhat loosely defined, branches of research, such as evolution strategies, genetic programming, and genetic algorithms.

At their core, optimization problems are *search problems.* Search problems require you to navigate an area, like a maze, to find an objective, like the end of the maze. Optimization problems are basically the same thing, only there are multiple possible solutions. Imagine a maze with multiple exits. Your goal is to exit the maze as quick as possible—this means your goal is to find the shortest path to any of the maze exits.

Two basic approaches are used for search problems: *brute-force search* and *informed search*. It's important to understand the difference to understand why optimization and genetic algorithms are so useful.

Understanding Informed Search

An informed search relies on a search strategy. In an informed search, you make smart decisions based on the available information. In a brute-force search, you iterate over every possible solution linearly. Brute-force searches use no knowledge of the search area to make decisions. In a maze, a brute-force solution would try every possible path—never stopping to consider whether or not the paths are getting smaller or larger, or if the paths will even lead to an exit. Brute-force searches are naive. Eventually you'll find a solution, but it might take a long time, and it might not even be the best one.

The key to informed search and thus optimization techniques, like genetic algorithms, lies in how they balance *exploration versus exploitation*. Imagine you find yourself lost in the woods without a map or compass. How would you navigate out of the woods?

Using Crossover to Exploit

One option is to use a brute-force strategy—walk in circles around every tree, hoping you make it back to civilization before you get too tired. Of course, if the woods are large, the brute-force strategy becomes especially difficult. Another option is to use the information around you. With this strategy, you *exploit* or take advantage of the information available to you to determine which direction to head next. To exploit in search means to use what you already know to navigate. In this example, perhaps you know that the nearest town is north, and you can tell where north is because of the position of the sun. This, in essence, is what genetic algorithms do. They use the data around them to make correct decisions.

Crossover is how genetic algorithms exploit in search. Crossover is the process of creating new *child* solutions from *parent* solutions. The idea is that the strongest solutions have characteristics that make them strong. These characteristics are called *schemas*. Schemas are building blocks of fit solutions—you'll learn more about them in Chapter 4, Evaluating Solutions and Populations, on page 51.

The term crossover is a loose analogy to genetic reproduction. While the analogy is weak and crossover in genetic algorithms isn't remotely the same as crossover in biology, it can better help you understand what's going on under the hood. Crossover is a part of how genetic algorithms make good decisions. In the woods example, you choose where to go next based on your current position. Your next step is a product of where you were last. The idea is to build progressively better solutions over time, until you reach your goal.

Using Mutation to Explore

Now, imagine that some of the information available to you is misleading. Perhaps somebody tells you there's a road that leads to the nearest town, but the road just takes you in circles around the woods. Would you continue to repeatedly follow the road, never realizing that the path you're on isn't correct? No, you'd *explore* other paths in the woods, hoping that one would eventually lead you out. To explore in search is to try new, random paths to see if they produce a better outcome. This concept of getting stuck in the same place in the search space is parallel to a common pitfall in optimization problems known as *premature convergence*. It's easy for genetic algorithms to get stuck in one part of a search space because some solutions *appear* to be good enough—even though better solutions exist. You'll learn more about premature convergence in Chapter 7, Preventing Premature Convergence, on page 107.

Mutation is how genetic algorithms explore. It's not enough to simply keep trying to build new solutions from previous ones, which is essentially the same as trying the same path over and over again. Mutation introduces randomness into your genetic algorithms. The goal is to slightly alter some aspect of the previous solutions to create newer solutions, which may lead to newer, better paths.

The effectiveness of genetic algorithms largely relies on how you balance exploitation versus exploration. Favoring one over the other has merits. Oftentimes, if you don't know much about a search space, it's best to favor exploration first and then slowly shift toward exploiting the information you already know. This is similar to how you might learn to navigate a new town—try new things until you have enough information to take the best routes.

The best way to understand how genetic algorithms work is to create one. In this next section, you'll learn the basics of genetic algorithms by solving a very simple problem known as the *One-Max problem*.

Introducing the One-Max Problem

The One-Max problem is a trivial problem often used to introduce the concept of genetic algorithms. It's incredibly simple, but it's great for introducing many of the critical aspects of a genetic algorithm. The problem boils down to one question: what is the maximum sum of a bitstring (a string consisting of only 1s and 0s) of length N?

Of course, you know that the maximum sum of a bitstring of length N is N. However, if you wanted to prove this using a brute-force search, you'd end up needing to search through 2^N different solutions. As with any search problem, this isn't too difficult with relatively small bitstrings. But what happens if you want to use this technique for bitstrings of length 40? You'd have to search over one trillion possible bitstrings. To avoid this, you'll create a genetic algorithm that produces an optimal solution without iterating over every possible solution in the search space.

To get started, open a terminal or command prompt. This book presents Unix commands, but you won't need to do anything more difficult than create files and directories or work with Elixir and Mix. With a terminal open, run the following commands:

```
$ mkdir genetic && mkdir genetic/scripts
$ cd genetic/scripts
$ touch one_max.exs
```

This creates a new directory named genetic and a directory within that directory named scripts. It then creates a file within scripts titled one_max.exs. The one_max.exs is where you'll write your genetic algorithm.

Genetic algorithms work via *transformations* on *populations* of *chromosomes* over some number of *generations*. Imagine you're playing a card game where your goal is to get the highest possible card after some number of turns. You are initially given five cards and you can choose to keep any number of cards at the end of every turn.

In this example, a single card is a chromosome. It represents one solution to your problem. Your entire hand is the population; it's a collection of possible solutions. The changes you make to your hand after every turn are transformations. Finally, every turn represents one generation—one transformation of the population.

The figure on page 6 illustrates the basic structure of a genetic algorithm.

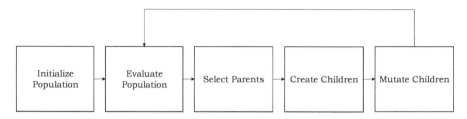

Each step depicted in the image performs a transformation on the population that brings you closer to finding a solution. The process is repeated until a solution is found.

Most genetic algorithms follow a structure similar to the one in the figure, which is easily translated into equally structured code. Your genetic algorithm will also follow these same steps—with code that mirrors each step in the process.

Initializing the Population

You need to start by initializing a population. Remember, the problem wants the maximum sum of bitstrings of length N. So your population will consist of some number of N-length bitstrings. For this example, N is 1000, so you need a population of 1000-length bitstrings.

The number of chromosomes in your population is irrelevant. A larger population means you're currently looking at a larger area of the search space. Typically, the more chromosomes you have, the longer it takes to perform transformations on the entire population. Conversely, the fewer chromosomes you have, the longer it takes to produce a viable solution to your problem and the more susceptible your population is to premature convergence. For this example problem, a population size of 100 strikes a nice balance between the two.

Understanding Population Size

 In a traditional search method like depth-first search or breadth-first search, you examine one solution at a time and determine where to go next. Even in other informed search algorithms like A* or uniform-cost search, you examine one solution at a time. Genetic algorithms examine many solutions at once, ruling out large areas of the search space after every generation. The population size dictates the size of the area of the search space you're looking at.

At the top of the one_max.exs file, define a population consisting of 100, 1000-length bitstrings, like this:

```
population = for _ <- 1..100, do: for _ <- 1..1000, do: Enum.random(0..1)
```

This is a nested list comprehension. You create a list of size 100 consisting of lists of size 1000.

Enum.random/1 takes an *enumerable* and selects a random value from the enumerable. Enumerables are data structures that implement the Enumerable protocol, and that can take advantage of Elixir's Enum library. This book makes extensive use of Enum and the Enumerable protocol. You can read more about both in the Elixir documentation.[1]

The 0..1 syntax is a generator that creates a *Range* from 0 to 1. You don't need to understand what a Range is—you just need to understand that when fed into Enum.random/1, this function will select a 0 or a 1 at random. This is done to produce variation in the population of 1000-length bitstrings. Starting with a random distribution of bitstrings introduces solutions with sufficiently different characteristics. This helps to avoid premature convergence.

Understanding the Flow of Genetic Algorithms

You're now ready to start writing your algorithm. But, before you begin, what do you notice about the structure of the genetic algorithm previously described? Specifically, what happens after children are mutated?

The answer: the process repeats itself. Genetic algorithms are recursive meaning the algorithm repeats itself over and over until it hits a termination point.

Below the initial population, add the following:

```
algorithm =
  fn population, algorithm ->
    # Algorithm here
  end
```

The algorithm is an anonymous function that takes two parameters: population represents the current generation's population, and algorithm is a reference to itself. This is a trick used to implement a recursive anonymous function. It's not essential to understand why this works or why this is necessary. All you need to know is that algorithm is a reference to your algorithm function.

In other languages, you'll likely see genetic algorithms implemented using loops instead of recursion. You need to use recursion because Elixir doesn't support loops. But remember, a recursive function is just as powerful as a loop.

Recursive functions usually have two branches: a base-case and a recursive case. The base case produces the solution to your problem. You should think of this

---

1. https://hexdocs.pm/elixir/Enum.html

as the *termination criteria*. Your termination criteria are the measurements you use to determine when to stop your algorithm. Because you already know what your final solution should look like—a bitstring with a sum of 1000—you can tell your algorithm to stop when this solution appears. You'll learn more about other strategies for telling your algorithm when to stop in Chapter 4, Evaluating Solutions and Populations, on page 51. Replace the # Algorithm here with the following:

```
best = Enum.max_by(population, &Enum.sum/1)
IO.write("\rCurrent Best: " <> Integer.to_string(Enum.sum(best)))
if Enum.sum(best) == 1000 do
  best
else
  # Rest of algorithm here
end
```

The first line extracts the current best solution from the population. The *best* solution is the one with the largest sum. Next, the algorithm prints out the value of the largest sum. Finally, you define your termination criteria—telling the algorithm to stop and return the best solution when the maximum sum has reached 1000.

Now, once again, refer to the steps in a genetic algorithm. The first step is to initialize a population. You already have a population; now you need to do everything else. Replace # Rest of algorithm here with the following:

```
population              # Initial Population
|> evaluate.()          # Evaluate Population
|> selection.()         # Select Parents
|> crossover.()         # Create Children
|> algorithm.(algorithm)  # Repeat the Process with new Population
```

Notice how the algorithm is defined as a series of transformations on the initial population. The population starts as a random list of 1000-length bitstrings. It's then passed into a set of functions that do some work on the population to produce a new, hopefully better population.

This is a pattern you'll see throughout this book. You start with a population, do some predefined work on the population, and then pass the population on to the next generation. A single step in the pattern is called an *evolution*. Genetic algorithms work via evolutions over multiple generations.

Now you need to go about implementing these transformations. Start by adding the following below your population definition:

```
evaluate = fn population -> ... end
selection = fn population -> ... end
crossover = fn population -> ... end
```

Here, you create stubs for three anonymous functions: evaluate, selection, and crossover. Each of these functions represents a step in the genetic algorithm. Each function takes a population and returns a transformed version of the population.

Evaluating the Population

Start by writing the first function—evaluate. This function represents Step #2 in the genetic algorithm. This function takes a population, evaluates each chromosome based on a *fitness function*, and sorts the population based on each chromosome's *fitness*. Fitness is simply a heuristic that tells you how good or bad a solution is—a fitness function calculates this fitness for you. In this problem, the fitness of a chromosome is represented by the sum of the bitstring.

Replace the stub of the the evaluate function with this:

```
evaluate =
  fn population ->
    Enum.sort_by(population, &Enum.sum/1, &>=/2)
  end
```

The evaluate function uses the Enum.sort_by/3 function to sort the population by the sum in descending order. This means that better solutions will exist at the top of the population. It also means that better solutions will be grouped together. Sorting your population is important for the next step.

Selecting Parents

You now have a list of chromosomes sorted by sum. You want to produce parents for reproduction. This step is referred to as *selection*. Selection is the process of picking the parents that will be combined to create new solutions. The goal of selection is to pick some parents that can easily be combined to create better solutions.

For this step, you'll want the result of the selection function to be formatted nicely for crossover. Your selection function should return a list of tuples consisting of a pair of parents to be combined. Inside the selection function, add the following:

```
selection =
  fn population ->
    population
    |> Enum.chunk_every(2)
    |> Enum.map(&List.to_tuple(&1))
  end
```

In this function, you use Enum.chunk_every/2 to create a list of pairs. These pairs are parents that are selected for combination in the crossover step. Sometimes, the population you're working with isn't necessarily a friendly number like 100. You can also use Enum.chunk_every/3 and tell Elixir what to do with the leftover elements in your list.

The result of Enum.chunk_every/2 is passed to Enum.map/2, which iterates over the list and transforms the values using List.to_tuple/1. This function transforms the list of lists to a list of tuples. This is done because tuples are much easier to work with in the next step.

Notice how the last two steps have created pairs of parents of approximately equal fitness. The list is sorted by the maximum sum in descending order. This means that the selection function will automatically pair more fit chromosomes with other fit chromosomes and vice versa with unfit chromosomes. This isn't always the best strategy, but you'll learn more about this in Chapter 5, Selecting the Best, on page 71.

Creating Children

With a population of parents prepared for crossover, it's time to implement the crossover function.

Crossover is analogous to reproduction. It's a genetic operator that takes two or more parent chromosomes and produces two or more child chromosomes. Thus far, the transformations have produced a list of tuples consisting of two 1000-length bitstrings. You want to produce a population you can pass back into the algorithm function. Implement the crossover function like this:

```
crossover =
  fn population ->
    Enum.reduce(population, [],
      fn {p1, p2}, acc ->
        cx_point = :rand.uniform(1000)
        {{h1, t1}, {h2, t2}} =
          {Enum.split(p1, cx_point),
           Enum.split(p2, cx_point)}
        [h1 ++ t2, h2 ++ t1 | acc]
      end
    )
  end
```

First, take note of the first argument passed to the anonymous function in Enum.reduce/3. Elixir has a rich set of pattern-matching features. In the selection step, the list of chromosomes was turned into a list of tuples of adjacent pairs. Because of this, you can use pattern-matching to extract the individual chromosomes—denoted p1 and p2 for Parent 1 and Parent 2—and perform some operation on them.

Enum.reduce/3 requires the anonymous function to also accept an accumulator—denoted acc—which takes an initial value and builds from the return value of the function. The initial value here is the empty list shown in the second parameter. The function returns two new chromosomes prepended to the accumulator.

So, how are the new chromosomes created? A random crossover point is selected using Erlang's rand module. The :rand.uniform/1 function produces a uniform integer between 0 and N-1 where N is the integer parameter it receives. Passing 1000 to this function means you'll receive a random integer between 0 and 1000.

Enum.split/2 returns a tuple of two enumerables. The enumerables are split at the random point selected earlier. The chromosomes are then recombined with the tails swapped. This is known as *single-point crossover* and is one of the simplest crossover methods used. You'll learn more about single-point crossover and other crossover techniques in Chapter 6, Generating New Solutions, on page 87.

Running Your Solution

Your genetic algorithm will now look something like this:

```
population = for _ <- 1..100, do: for _ <- 1..1000, do: Enum.random(0..1)

evaluate =
  fn population ->
    Enum.sort_by(population, &Enum.sum/1, &>=/2)
  end

selection =
  fn population ->
    population
    |> Enum.chunk_every(2)
    |> Enum.map(&List.to_tuple(&1))
  end

crossover =
  fn population ->
    Enum.reduce(population, [],
      fn {p1, p2}, acc ->
        cx_point = :rand.uniform(1000)
        {{h1, t1}, {h2, t2}} =
          {Enum.split(p1, cx_point),
           Enum.split(p2, cx_point)}
```

```
          [h1 ++ t2, h2 ++ t1 | acc]
        end
    )
  end
algorithm =
  fn population, algorithm ->
    best = Enum.max_by(population, &Enum.sum/1)
    IO.write("\rCurrent Best: " <> Integer.to_string(Enum.sum(best)))
    if Enum.sum(best) == 1000 do
      best
    else
      population
      |> evaluate.()
      |> selection.()
      |> crossover.()
      |> algorithm.(algorithm)
    end
  end
```

Your algorithm now has all of the necessary components it needs to produce a solution; however, you might be wondering why the mutation step was left out. You'll find out in a minute—before then, try running your algorithm to ensure that everything works correctly.

Remember, the algorithm function takes a population and a reference to itself as input. Additionally, remember that it returns a solution when a maximum sum of 1000 is achieved. Add the following lines to the end of the one_max.exs file:

```
solution = algorithm.(population, algorithm)

IO.write("\n Answer is \n")
IO.inspect solution
```

Here, you assign the result of the completed algorithm (that is, the solution) to a variable named solution. You then output some text to the screen to show what your algorithm has come up with.

Next, go back to your terminal and navigate to the scripts folder. Then run the following command:

```
$ elixir one_max.exs
Current Best: 982
```

But wait, what's going on here? Why is the algorithm stopping on a best fitness below 1000? It's likely that, no matter how many times you run it, the algorithm's improvement will almost certainly slow near 1000. You may even find it difficult for the problem to ever reach 1000. The problem is premature convergence.

Adding Mutation

Despite initializing your population to a seemingly random distribution, eventually the parents got too genetically similar to make any improvements during crossover. This illustrates the importance of including the mutation step in your algorithm and how vital exploration is to informed search techniques.

After the crossover function in the algorithm, add the following:

```
|> mutation.()
```

Now, the structure of the algorithm looks like this:

```
population
|> fitness.()
|> selection.()
|> crossover.()
|> mutation.()
|> algorithm.(algorithm)
```

Mutation is similar to the other functions in that it accepts a population as a parameter. You only want to mutate a small percentage of your population as well—this is to preserve the progress that's already been made. Below your crossover definition, add the following:

```
mutation =
  fn population ->
    population
    |> Enum.map(
      fn chromosome ->
        if :rand.uniform() < 0.05 do
          Enum.shuffle(chromosome)
        else
          chromosome
        end
      end)
  end
```

This function iterates over the entire population and randomly shuffles a chromosome with a probability of 5%. The :rand.uniform() < 0.05 condition is a pattern that emerges a lot throughout this book. It's one way of simulating a random event in Elixir.

Enum.shuffle/1 takes in an enumerable and randomizes the elements in the enumerable. Think of it like shuffling a deck of cards. Doing this actually preserves the fitness of the chromosome; however, it also prevents the parents from becoming too similar before they crossover. You'll learn more about this technique and others in Chapter 7, Preventing Premature Convergence, on page 107.

With the mutation function implemented, you're ready to try running your algorithm again, like this:

```
$ elixir one_max.exs
Current Best: 1000
Answer is
[1,1,1...,1]
```

Congratulations, you've just written your first genetic algorithm.

What You Learned

In this chapter, you learned about informed search and why it's superior to brute-force search for finding solutions to difficult problems. You also learned about the types of problems, like finding an optimal shipping route between cities, that are nearly impossible to solve using brute-force search. Most importantly, you learned what genetic algorithms are and how to implement a basic genetic algorithm to solve the One-Max problem.

In the next section, you'll take the genetic algorithm you created here and use it to start implementing a general framework that you can apply to numerous other problems.

## CHAPTER 2

Breaking Down Genetic Algorithms

In the previous chapter, you learned about informed search and why it's superior to brute-force search. You were introduced to genetic algorithms and saw how they balance exploitation and exploration for different problems. You used this knowledge to tackle the One-Max problem, which is an introductory optimization problem.

While your previous solution to the One-Max problem was effective, it's difficult to both tweak and expand. More advanced applications of genetic algorithms will require extensive fine-tuning and experimentation to achieve the best results, which means you need to create modular and easily customizable solutions.

In this chapter, you'll once again attack the One-Max problem; but your goal this time around is to use the One-Max problem to help you design and build a framework you can use to create genetic algorithms. You can then apply this framework and structure to other problems—making it easier to tweak the different aspects of your algorithms.

Reviewing Genetic Algorithms

Recall from the previous chapter that genetic algorithms work via a series of transformations on populations of chromosomes over some number of generations. One generation represents one complete series of transformations. Ideally, the population that results from subsequent generations have better solutions than previous ones.

The structure of a genetic algorithm provides a generic framework on which to build. For example, every step in the process takes a population and produces a population for the next step. Because you know what every step expects, you can easily generalize your genetic algorithms to all types of problems. While some parts of the algorithm—such as encoding, evaluation, and termination—pertain only to specific problems, most aspects of a genetic algorithm are common to all problems.

You can use this structure to plan out how your framework will look. You'll ask yourself questions like: what parts of the algorithm are common to all problems? What parts are unique? How can I best split each step for easy customization? How can I take advantage of Elixir's features to make my algorithms as idiomatic, customizable, and modular as possible?

Think about these questions as you continue through the rest of this chapter.

Looking Deeper into Genetic Algorithms

Based on what you've learned so far, you should understand that every genetic algorithm follows the same basic steps. While different algorithms for different problems may use different techniques, probabilities, or strategies, they all share the same structure. As a programmer, you want to take advantage of this.

One of the golden rules of programming is Don't Repeat Yourself (DRY), which essentially boils down to not rewriting unnecessary code. You can exploit the shared structure of genetic algorithms to avoid rewriting code that remains the same from algorithm to algorithm. Unfortunately, you have to start from scratch.

So how do you go about designing a versatile framework from the ground up? Start with the basics. All genetic algorithms follow the same structure. They all use chromosomes and populations, and they all require similar inputs. You can use this to your advantage and begin designing from the ground up.

Chromosomes and Populations

Chromosomes represent solutions to problems. In the One-Max problem, your solutions consisted of a series of 1s and 0s; however, that won't be the case for every problem. Some problems are encoded using real values, some as permutations, and some using characters. Also, some problems require that you use a data structure other than a list to encode solutions.

All of this means that specific encoding schemes are unique and vary from problem to problem. To ensure your framework is as general as possible and works for all of your encoding schemes, you can use the Enumerable protocol.

In Elixir, protocols allow you to implement polymorphism within your libraries. Data structures that implement the Enumerable protocol can be passed into any function within the Enum library. That means you can encode your chromosomes using any data structure that implements Enumerable—even ones you build yourself.

A population, on the other hand, is simply a collection of chromosomes. The following image demonstrates the difference between a chromosome and a population:

Single Chromosome in Search Space

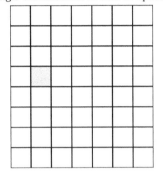

Population of Chromosomes in Search Space

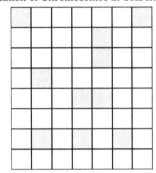

For the most part, how you encode a population won't change—as long as the population is a series of chromosomes, it doesn't matter what data structure you use. For simplicity, this book uses lists to contain chromosomes.

Also, the size of your population doesn't matter. Bigger populations take longer to transform, but they may converge on a solution faster, whereas smaller populations are easier to transform, but they may take longer to converge.

Based on what you know now, you can begin to define some rules your framework must enforce, such as:

- To use polymorphism, you must encode chromosomes using a data structure that implements the Enumerable protocol.

- Because populations are stored as lists, you can use any function in the Enum or List library to implement transformations.

- Your algorithm should work on any population size.

By enforcing each of these rules, you'll be able to expand your framework for a variety of problems.

Initializing the Population

The first step in every genetic algorithm is initializing a population. Typically, the first population is random—it's like a shotgun blast onto the search space.

The idea is to start out examining many different solutions and slowly work toward the best ones.

You've already determined that a population is a list, which means the function you implement for this step must return a list of chromosomes. But you need to ensure that your function can apply to all types of problems and doesn't include specifics about how chromosomes are encoded. To do this, you can take a function that generates chromosomes as input.

Elixir allows you to pass functions as arguments to other functions. You can ensure one of the parameters is a function that produces a chromosome. You don't care about the specifics of how this function is implemented; you only care that this function returns a chromosome.

With this step, you have two main goals:

- The initialization step must produce an initial population—a list of possible solutions.

- The function which initializes the population should be agnostic to how the chromosome is encoded. You can achieve this by accepting a function that returns a chromosome.

Evaluating the Population

The evaluation step is responsible for evaluating each chromosome based on some fitness function and sorting the population based on this fitness. This makes it easy to extract the best chromosome from the population. It also makes it easier to work with the population in the selection step.

Just like encoding schemes vary from problem to problem, so does fitness. Different problems require different measures of how good a solution is. If you were trying to find the shortest path between two points, you'd evaluate your solutions based on the distance of the path they produce. If you were trying to optimize a portfolio full of stocks, you'd evaluate the portfolio based on potential return. Essentially, you don't care how the fitness function is implemented or even what it returns—you just need a measure that allows you to compare the fitness of each chromosome against the rest of the chromosomes in the population.

This leaves you with the following goals or requirements of the evaluation step:

- The evaluation step must take a population as input.

- The evaluation step must produce a population sorted by fitness.

- The function which evaluates the population should take a parameter that is a function that returns the fitness of each chromosome.

- The fitness function can return anything, as long as the fitness can be sorted.

Selecting Parents

With a sorted population, you can begin to select parents for reproduction. Remember, selection is responsible for matching parents that will produce strong children. Later on, you'll implement different selection methods to achieve this effect. For now, the selection method should only pair adjacent chromosomes in the population. Because the population is sorted, the strongest chromosomes will reproduce with other strong chromosomes. This is referred to as *elitism selection*.

One additional goal of the selection function is to make it easy for the crossover function to transform the population into a new population. You can do this by transforming the population of chromosomes into tuples—as you did in the previous chapter.

Therefore, the rules for selection are:

- The selection step must take a population as input.
- The selection step must produce a transformed population that's easy to work with during crossover—say by returning a list of tuples which are pairs of parents.

Creating Children

Remember that crossover is analogous to reproduction. The goal of crossover is to exploit the strengths of current solutions to find new, better solutions. Crossover is one of the last steps before starting a new generation and should create a population that looks and feels identical to the one you started with—albeit with new solutions.

In Chapter 6, Generating New Solutions, on page 87, you'll learn a variety of crossover methods to use in different circumstances. Remember from the last step that the transformed population is a list of tuples, which are pairs of adjacent parents. You need to take these parents and transform the population into a brand-new population.

This image might help you understand this step better:

1	0	1	1	1

0	1	0	0	1

⟹

1	1	1	1	1

0	0	1	0	1

0	1	0	0	1

1	0	1	1	1

⟹

0	1	0	0	1

1	1	1	1	1

1	1	0	1	0

1	1	0	1	1

⟹

0	0	1	1	0

1	1	0	1	1

0	0	1	1	1

0	1	1	0	1

⟹

1	1	1	1	1

0	1	1	0	1

Parents   Children

Notice how you combine each pair of parents to create a new pair of children. After this step, you should be left with a population that is identical in size to your original one.

With that in mind, the crossover step should:

- Take a list of 2-tuples as input.

- Combine the 2-tuples, which represent pairs of parents. For now, use single-point crossover.

- Return a population identical in size to the initial population.

Creating Mutants

Mutation is the last step before the next generation. Remember, the goal of mutation is to prevent premature convergence by transforming some of the chromosomes in the population. There are a number of mutation strategies. For now, you can keep your mutation function the same as the one you used in Chapter 1, Writing Your First Genetic Algorithm, on page 1. In Chapter 7, Preventing Premature Convergence, on page 107, we'll introduce other types of mutation functions. The mutation rate should be kept relatively low—typically somewhere around 5%.

So what can you gather from this?

- The mutation step should accept a population as input.

- The mutation step should mutate *only some* of the chromosomes in the population—the percentage should be relatively small.

- The mutation strategy should be identical to the mutation function from the previous chapter.

Termination Criteria

In Chapter 1, Writing Your First Genetic Algorithm, on page 1, you told your genetic algorithm to stop when the solution reached a maximum. Will you always know the maximum? Is there always a maximum? What if your algorithm can never achieve a maximum? Do you want it to run forever?

You can gather from this that termination criteria vary from problem to problem. Sometimes you know the answer; you just need to get there. Other times you want to see how good you can get your population, but you don't want to waste time evolving over millions of generations. You'll learn various termination criteria in Chapter 4, Evaluating Solutions and Populations, on page 51. What you need to know right now is that termination criteria are defined by the problem you're working with.

What does this mean? It means you need to accept some kind of termination criteria. To keep things simple, assume that you're only ever working with the One-Max problem with strictly positive, integer fitnesses. When does the One-Max problem terminate? When the maximum is found.

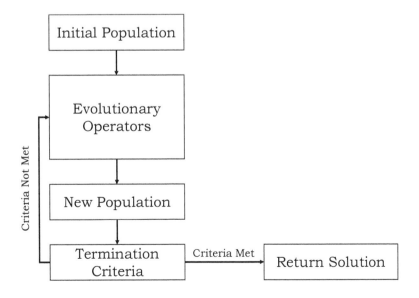

What rules can you generate from this?

- Termination criteria must be defined by the problem—the framework must accept some problem-defined criteria to stop the algorithm.

- Termination criteria, for now, must be just an integer—the maximum value needed to stop evolution.

Using Mix to Write Genetic Algorithms

Elixir projects are created, built, and tested using *Mix*. You'll use Mix for managing dependencies, testing your libraries, and running your genetic algorithms. For now, you'll create a Mix project that contains a framework for writing genetic algorithms.

Start by opening a terminal and navigating to the genetic directory you created in the previous chapter, like this:

```
$ cd genetic
```

Inside the genetic directory, create a new Mix project using the new command:

```
$ mix new genetic
```

genetic is the name of your Mix project. You can choose whatever name you'd like, so long as it's a valid name for a Mix project.

Navigate to the genetic directory and inspect its contents, like so:

```
$ cd genetic && ls
lib mix.exs README.md test
```

lib will contain all of the contents of your genetic algorithm framework. It should only contain genetic.ex.

test will contain all of your tests. Don't worry about the contents of the directory for now.

mix.exs will contain dependencies and other project configurations. The default configuration is sufficient for now.

In addition to the default directories and files, you'll need a directory named scripts. This directory will contain your solutions to various optimization problems. In a terminal inside of your Mix project, create a new directory, like this:

```
$ mkdir scripts
```

With the project set up, it's time to create your framework.

Building a Framework for Genetic Algorithms

You now have an empty project and an idea of what your genetic algorithm framework should look like. It's time to start implementing each step.

Start by opening the genetic.ex file. The file is populated with some default code and will look something like this:

```
defmodule Genetic do
  ...documentation...
  def hello do
    :world
  end

end
```

You can delete the default documentation and Hello World function. This module will contain the most basic parts of your genetic algorithm. This is where you'll define each step of the algorithm based on the rules you determined earlier.

Creating an Initial Outline

In genetic.ex, start by creating a function named run, like this:

```
def run(...) do
  population = initialize()
  population
  |> evolve()
end
```

This function calls the initialize function, which is responsible for creating the initial population. You might be wondering why the parameters of run are left blank. You'll worry about them later. For now, concentrate on the overall structure of the code.

After you initialize the population, you pass the population into a function named evolve. evolve is designed to model a single evolution in your genetic algorithm. Below the run function, define evolve, like this:

```
def evolve(population, max_fitness) do
  population = evaluate(population, ..., opts)
  best = hd(population)
  IO.write("\rCurrent Best: ...")
  if ... == max_fitness do
    best
  else
    population
    |> select()
    |> crossover()
```

```
      |> mutation()
      |> evolve()
   end
end
```

For now, disregard the blank parts of the code. You'll fill these in at the end. This function evaluates the population and then extracts the "best" solution from the population. You can do this using the hd/1 function because one of the rules for evaluate was that it returns a sorted population. This means the fittest chromosome will always be the first one in the population.

This function also implements the recursion you need. It defines the base or termination case. Part of the termination criteria is left blank for now. It checks some blank value versus the maximum desired fitness. The recursive case is essentially identical to the recursive case from Chapter 1, Writing Your First Genetic Algorithm, on page 1.

With the basic outline defined, you can start implementing each step.

Initialization

Remember the rules you defined in the previous section? You'll use them now to implement each step correctly. Start with the initialize function. Based on the design rules discussed previously, you know the function must return a population represented as a list of chromosomes. You also know that it must accept some function which produces an encoding of a single solution.

Above the run function, define the initialize function as follows:

```
def initialize(genotype) do
  for _ <- 1..100, do: genotype.()
end
```

This function is a list comprehension that generates chromosomes using the provided genotype/0 function. You might be wondering why this function is called genotype. You'll learn more about this in Chapter 3, Encoding Problems and Solutions, on page 33. 1..100 is a range that creates a total of 100 chromosomes. Remember, your population can be any size. You can change this depending on your problem. The function returns a list of 100 chromosomes.

Evaluation

The next step is evaluation. Your rules for evaluation require you to create a function that sorts the provided population based on a provided fitness function. Based on how you define the transformations in the outline of your algorithm, the first parameter of the function should be a population.

Below initialize/1, create a new function named evaluate:

```
def evaluate(population, fitness_function) do
  population
  |> Enum.sort_by(fitness_function, &>=/2)
end
```

This function is identical to the evaluate function that you defined in Chapter 1, Writing Your First Genetic Algorithm, on page 1. However, rather than sorting chromosomes by sum, you sort chromosomes based on the provided fitness_function.

Selection

Now that you have a sorted population, you can define the selection step. Remember that your selection function needs to return an enumerable of tuples. For now, it doesn't take any inputs besides population.

Below evaluate/2, define the select/1 function, like this:

```
def select(population) do
  population
  |> Enum.chunk_every(2)
  |> Enum.map(&List.to_tuple(&1))
end
```

This function is identical to the select function you defined in Chapter 1, Writing Your First Genetic Algorithm, on page 1. The resulting population is an enumerable of tuples. This makes it easier to implement crossover.

Crossover

At this point, you performed initialization, evaluation, and selection. The population is transformed and ready for recombination.

Below select/1, add the following:

```
def crossover(population) do
  population
  |> Enum.reduce([],
      fn {p1, p2}, acc ->
        cx_point = :rand.uniform(length(p1))
        {{h1, t1}, {h2, t2}} =
          {Enum.split(p1, cx_point),
           Enum.split(p2, cx_point)}
        {c1, c2} = {h1 ++ t2, h2 ++ t1}
        [c1, c2 | acc]
      end
    )
end
```

This function should look similar to the crossover method in the previous chapter. The only difference is that :rand.uniform/1 accepts the length of one of the parents as input. This is done so the algorithm can work on chromosomes of any length. Other than that, the algorithm is identical. It splits the parents at the crossover point, creates two new children, and prepends them to the population.

Mutation

The final step in the algorithm is mutation. Mutation has no special rules. It should look identical to the mutation function you defined in Chapter 1, Writing Your First Genetic Algorithm, on page 1.

Below crossover/1, add the following:

```
def mutation(population) do
  population
  |> Enum.map(
      fn chromosome ->
        if :rand.uniform() < 0.05 do
          Enum.shuffle(chromosome)
        else
          chromosome
        end
      end
    )
end
```

You iterate over every chromosome in the population, checking to see if some condition is met. The condition is meant to model picking chromosomes at random with a probability of 5%. If a chromosome is picked, its genes are shuffled. If it isn't, it remains the same.

With that, the basic steps of your algorithm are complete.

Filling in the Blanks

Remember the blanks you left in the evolve and run functions? Also, did you notice that none of the functions you called in evolve took parameters? It's time to fill in these blanks.

The functions initialize/2 and evaluate/2 take extra parameters aside from a population. Because you won't be calling these functions individually outside the module, you can take these parameters inside the run and evolve functions and pass them to initialize and evaluate from there. You need to take the following parameters into both run and evaluate: fitness_function, genotype, and max_fitness.

Additionally, with the required parameters in place, you can fill in the blanks left in the outline of the run and evolve functions.

Edit the functions so they look like this:

```
def run(fitness_function, genotype, max_fitness) do
  population = initialize(genotype)
  population
  |> evolve(fitness_function, genotype, max_fitness)
end
def evolve(population, fitness_function, genotype, max_fitness) do
  population = evaluate(population, fitness_function)
  best = hd(population)
  IO.write("\rCurrent Best: #{fitness_function.(best)}")
  if fitness_function.(best) == max_fitness do
    best
  else
    population
    |> select()
    |> crossover()
    |> mutation()
    |> evolve(fitness_function, genotype, max_fitness)
  end
end
```

At this point, all of the blanks are filled. Additionally, the evolve and run functions accept the required problem-specific parameters and pass them to the functions that need them.

You now have a complete, working framework.

Understanding Hyperparameters

In machine learning, *hyperparameters* refer to the parts of the algorithm you set before the algorithm starts training. Internally, the algorithm learns parameters that help it perform a task. Externally, the programmer controls parameters that dictate how the algorithm trains.

In the context of genetic algorithms, hyperparameters refer to things like population size, mutation rate, and so on, that you choose before running the algorithm.

Because your hyperparameters can have a huge impact on the outcome of your algorithms, it's important that you're able to rapidly change them. To ensure you can change hyperparameters without too much of a headache, you need to implement a simple configuration mechanism into your framework that separates the hyperparameters from the overall structure of the algorithm.

To start, change the signature of both run/3 and evolve/4 to accept an additional parameter:

```elixir
def run(genotype, fitness_function, max_fitness, opts \\ []) do
# ...omitted...
end
def evolve(population, fitness_function, max_fitness, opts \\ []) do
# ...omitted...
end
```

opts \\ [] indicates an optional parameter that will default to an empty list if you pass nothing in its place. You can use opts to pass hyperparameters in a Keyword list. Using a parameter like opts is a common paradigm for Elixir programs.

After you add opts to the signatures of run, you need to edit all of your functions to accept opts. Change the function signatures of all of the functions in genetic.ex to accept an optional opts parameter, like this:

```elixir
def initialize(genotype, opts \\ []) do
  # ...omitted...
end

def evaluate(population, fitness_function, opts \\ []) do
  # ...omitted...
end

def select(population, opts \\ []) do
  # ...omitted...
end

def crossover(population, opts \\ []) do
  # ...omitted...
end

def mutation(population, opts \\ []) do
  # ...omitted...
end
```

Finally, pass opts to every function in run and evolve:

```elixir
def run(genotype, fitness_function, max_fitness, opts \\ []) do
  population = initialize(genotype)
  population
  |> evolve(fitness_function, max_fitness, opts)
end
def evolve(population, fitness_function, max_fitness, opts \\ []) do
  population = evaluate(population, fitness_function, opts)
  best = hd(population)
  IO.write("\rCurrent Best: #{fitness_function.(best)}")
  if fitness_function.(best) == max_fitness do
    best
```

```
    else
      population
      |> select(opts)
      |> crossover(opts)
      |> mutation(opts)
      |> evolve(fitness_function, max_fitness, opts)
    end
end
```

For now, the only hyperparameter you'll account for is population size. To do this, edit initialize/2 to look like this:

```
def initialize(genotype, opts \\ []) do
  population_size = Keyword.get(opts, :population_size, 100)
  for _ <- 1..population_size, do: genotype.()
end
```

Keyword.get/3 accepts a Keyword, a key, and a default value if there's no value for the given key. Here you set the default population size to 100, which is sufficient for most genetic algorithms.

In later chapters, you'll be introduced to more hyperparameters and learn to account for them so your algorithms are easily configurable.

Solving the One-Max Problem Again

With your framework built, it's time to apply it to the One-Max problem. Open a terminal and create a new file in the scripts directory named one_max.exs, like this:

```
$ touch scripts/one_max.exs
```

Open the one_max.exs file. Now, think about what your framework already accomplishes for you and what parts of the problem you need to define. What are the problem-specific parameters you need to pass into run?

Once you determine what these parameters are, you'll need to start defining them. Logically, the first one is how you encode chromosomes. Remember, for the One-Max problem, you're looking for the maximum sum of a bitstring of length N. To keep things consistent, your length should be 1000. This means your solutions should be bitstrings of length N.

To define your genotype, at the top of the one_max.exs file, add the following:

```
genotype = fn -> for _ <- 1..1000, do: Enum.random(0..1) end
```

This should look similar to what you did in Chapter 1, Writing Your First Genetic Algorithm, on page 1. All that's missing is the outside for-loop.

However, if you recall, the outside for-loop is taken care of for you in the initialization step, so it's unnecessary now.

The next step is to define your fitness function and termination criteria. How did you evaluate solutions in the previous chapter? Remember, you want a maximum sum, so fitness is just the sum. What's the maximum possible sum you can achieve with a bitstring of length 1000? 1000. Therefore, your termination criteria or max_fitness is 1000.

Below genotype, define your fitness function and termination criteria like this:

```
fitness_function = fn chromosome -> Enum.sum(chromosome) end
max_fitness = 1000
```

You might notice that you can just pass &Enum.sum/1 into the run function. That's perfectly fine; however, it won't always work out like that. It may make more sense to be more verbose so you really understand what's going on.

All you need to do now is call run/4 with your predetermined parameters and extract your solution. Remember that run/4 returns the best solution once it is found. You'll want to assign this to a variable so you can inspect its contents later on.

Below fitness_function, add the following:

```
soln = Genetic.run(fitness_function, genotype, max_fitness)

IO.write("\n")
IO.inspect(soln)
```

Because this file gets run inside of a Mix project, you can call module functions defined in the Mix project. You assign soln to the result of Genetic.run/4 and output its contents to the console. This simply runs the genetic algorithm then inspects the resulting solution.

You'll notice that, for now, nothing was passed in place of opts. That's okay, because you've already defined default configuration options.

The next step is to open a terminal and navigate to your Mix project. Once there, you can run your genetic algorithm like this:

```
$ mix run scripts/one_max.exs
Current Best: 1000
[1,1,1...,1]
```

You should note that you must use mix run and not elixir like in the previous chapter. Using mix ensures your Mix project is compiled and loaded before the script is executed. From this point forward, you'll be using mix to run your algorithms. For every algorithm, you'll be told exactly when you can compile and run your code from a terminal.

What You Learned

In this chapter, you started to create a framework for writing genetic algorithms. You designed the framework by defining criteria that's consistent and different between problems. You defined rules that your framework must enforce to ensure it can be generalized to a number of problems.

You then took the basic framework you created and re-solved the One-Max problem. Notice that the framework did most of the legwork for you. With the framework defined, you can focus on solving more difficult problems using genetic algorithms.

Up next, you'll explore the problem-specific aspects of genetic algorithms and learn how to fit problems into the framework you created in this chapter.

## CHAPTER 3

Encoding Problems and Solutions

Not all problems are created equal. Every optimization problem you face will inevitably have a unique set of challenges. However, this doesn't mean that you should approach every problem differently, as patterns will often arise from one problem to the next.

A key aspect of problem solving is to model problems in a way that makes them easier to understand and thus easier to solve. This might mean translating data into formats that are easier to work with, choosing or creating data structures that simplify solutions, or transforming the problem itself into a form you already know. The steps you take at the beginning when planning your approach to solving a specific problem are vital to finding its solution.

In the previous chapter, you designed a framework for writing genetic algorithms. The framework you designed generalized the steps common to all genetic algorithms. The purpose of this exercise was both to better understand the structure of genetic algorithms and optimization problems and to make it easier for you to write genetic algorithms in the future.

In the process of designing this framework, you separated problem-specific aspects from more general aspects of genetic algorithms. In this chapter, you'll take a closer look at these problem-specific aspects and how to handle them.

Using Structs to Represent Chromosomes

The chromosomes you created in the previous chapters are enumerable objects that represent solutions to a problem. At the most fundamental level, this is correct; however, in practice, this isn't a viable implementation.

Consider this: you're attempting to solve a problem in which the age of the chromosome determines its fitness. One reason you'd do this is to ensure enough variance between generations. Ideally, you'd persist older chromosomes between generations to a certain point, before killing them off once they've reached a certain age. In this respect, you ensure an equal distribution of both old and young chromosomes and, thus, naturally occurring variance in the population. Solving a problem like this using only an Enum type to represent a chromosome creates unnecessary complexity. It's often the case that you need a more robust data structure to keep track of a number of metrics at a time. In Elixir, you can accomplish this task using a *struct*.

A struct is a map with a few additional features. Structs allow you to define default values and required fields. They also cannot take on additional fields after their creation.

The guarantees that structs provide make them a perfect fit for defining custom types—without the fear of breaking your programs. With structs, you can ensure that a predefined chromosome type is initialized with a predefined set of genes—one that won't break your genetic algorithms.

Creating a chromosome struct offers a number of conveniences that you wouldn't have if you simply used an Enum or some other data type to represent a chromosome. For example, if you wanted to calculate the average fitness of a population, you would need to recalculate the fitness of each individual chromosome first, which can be a computationally expensive task. Using a struct, however, you can save time by only calculating the fitness once, and then storing it as a key-value pair within the struct itself.

Understanding Chromosomes

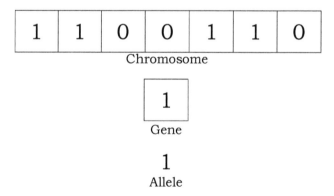

1	1	0	0	1	1	0

Chromosome

1

Gene

1

Allele

Before you're ready to create a struct that models a chromosome, you first need to understand what a chromosome is and what characteristics it has.

At the most basic level, a chromosome is a single solution to your problem. It's a series of genes consisting of values known as *alleles*. Genes can represent any number of things. For example, in the shipping problem introduced in Chapter 1, Writing Your First Genetic Algorithm, on page 1, each gene represents a successive stop in a city. The entire chromosome, then, represents a complete path to every city defined in the problem.

Genes are typically represented using list types or other enumerable data types, like trees, sets, and arrays. In Elixir, the Enum library provides a number of useful functions for manipulating any data type that implements the Enumerable protocol. In fact, the framework you wrote in the previous chapter exclusively uses Enum library functions. Therefore, you can represent genes using any data type that implements the Enumerable protocol—even ones that are not part of the Elixir standard library.

While genes are the most fundamental piece of a chromosome, there are several characteristics you can track for both convenience and functionality. A basic chromosome struct could include fitness, size, and age on top of genes. For simplicity, the chromosome struct in this book will consist of these exact features. In later chapters, you'll see the convenience that tracking these characteristics can provide.

The characteristics you may choose to add to your chromosome struct have no limits. Some problems may require additional features not described in this chapter—the beauty of structs is in their flexibility. Choosing to represent a chromosome in this manner gives you the ability to rapidly adjust what you need for each problem.

Creating a Chromosome Struct

Open a terminal and navigate to the genetic/lib directory. From there, create a new directory named types, as well as a new file named chromosome.ex, like this:

```
$ mkdir types
$ touch types/chromosome.ex
```

You'll create the chromosome struct within types/chromosome.ex. Open the types/chromosome.ex file and add the following code:

```
defmodule Types.Chromosome do

  defstruct [:genes, :size, :fitness, :age]

end
```

This code defines a module Types.Chromosome, which contains a struct consisting of the keys :genes, :size, :fitness, and :age. Remember, defstruct is used to define a new struct. The atoms that follow are the fields the struct contains. You can create a new chromosome struct using the %Types.Chromosome syntax.

This version of the chromosome struct will work, but it lacks a bit of functionality. Currently, none of the fields have default values and there are no required keys. This means that a newly created chromosome struct could technically contain fields with all nil values.

Change the chromosome struct by adding defaults for :size, :fitness, and :age, like this:

```
defstruct [:genes, size: 0, fitness: 0, age: 0]
```

Now, any newly created chromosome will have a default size, fitness, and age of 0. You could technically make the default values whatever you want—it all depends on what you're trying to accomplish.

Finally, all chromosomes must contain genes. If a chromosome doesn't have any genes, it's not really a chromosome. To make this chromosome require genes, add the following code above defstruct:

```
@enforce_keys :genes
```

Your final module will look like this:

```
defmodule Types.Chromosome do
  @enforce_keys :genes
  defstruct [:genes, size: 0, fitness: 0, age: 0]
end
```

You can now create chromosome structs that track the genes, size, fitness, and age of a chromosome in your populations.

Creating a Chromosome Type

Elixir is a dynamically typed language; however, it's often useful to create *typespecs* for custom data types. Typespecs are useful for documentation and static code analysis using tools like dialyzer. This book won't cover the use of dialyzer, but you'll use the types you create in this section later in the chapter.

A typespec is defined using the @type attribute followed by the name and definition of the type. Elixir supports compound types as well as the creation of custom types using structs.

You'll create your chromosome type in the types/chromosome.ex file. Open the types/chromosome.ex file and add the following code above the struct you defined in the previous section:

```
@type t :: %__MODULE__{
  genes: Enum.t,
  size: integer(),
  fitness: number(),
  age: integer()
}
```

This code creates a custom type t, which is an instance of a Types.Chromosome struct. The __MODULE__ keyword is a macro that gets replaced with the name of the module in which it's defined. t is a standard practice for defining module types in Elixir.

The chromosome type also declares specific types for the fields of the chromosome. As mentioned previously, genes must be an Enum type. Size and age are both integers. Fitness is a number, which is a built-in Elixir type representing a float or integer.

The final Chromosome module will look like this:

```
defmodule Types.Chromosome do

  @type t :: %__MODULE__{
    genes: Enum.t,
    size: integer(),
    fitness: number(),
    age: integer()
  }

  @enforce_keys :genes
  defstruct [:genes, size: 0, fitness: 0, age: 0]
end
```

Using Behaviours to Model Problems

Recall that one technique to solving problems is to transform them into a form you already understand. While every problem seems different, and on the surface may require different techniques to solve, they almost always have patterns and similarities between them. This is especially true with the problems you'll solve with genetic algorithms.

The framework you built in Chapter 2, Breaking Down Genetic Algorithms, on page 15, separates a few problem-specific parameters from the common aspects of a genetic algorithm. These parameters are a fitness function, a genotype, and termination criteria. This means that every problem you attempt to solve using a genetic algorithm must implement all three of these functions—the nature of the framework creates a natural *abstraction* for problems.

An abstraction is a simplification of underlying complexities and implementations. The purpose of abstraction is to force you to think of things at different levels of specificity. It gives you an idea of what to look for before you approach a problem. This is especially useful when approaching new problems with genetic algorithms. When you want to approach a new problem, you already know that you need a fitness function, or a way to measure success; a genotype, or a way to represent solutions; and some termination criteria, or a way to tell the algorithm when to stop. While the specifics are the difficult part, you're never starting from scratch with this abstraction in place.

Unfortunately, Elixir doesn't feature abstract classes, interfaces, or traits like other object-oriented languages. Instead, you can implement abstraction using *behaviours*.

Mind the "u"

 Elixir uses the British spelling of "behaviour."

Behaviours Are a Contract

In much the same way that interfaces enforce a specification in object-oriented languages, behaviours enforce specifications in Elixir.

A behaviour is a contract—a means of defining what you want with specifications and ensuring that any module that implements a behaviour does the same. With a behaviour, you can define functions that a module must implement to be valid.

Behaviours consist of a number of *callbacks*. Callbacks are function signatures with an accompanying return type. Callbacks indicate what functions behaviours must implement, with guidelines on what they take and what they return.

A callback looks something like this:

```
@callback function_name(parameter_type, parameter_type, ...) :: return_type
```

To define a behaviour, you define a series of callbacks within a module. A behaviour looks like this:

```
defmodule Behaviour do
  @callback function1(String.t) :: {:ok, String.t}
  @callback function2(List.t) :: {:ok, List.t} | {:error, String.t}
end
```

You would then adopt a behaviour, like so:

```
defmodule Adopt do
  @behaviour Behaviour

  @impl Behaviour
  def function1(string), do: {:ok, string}

  @impl Behaviour
  def function2(list) do
    case list do
      nil -> {:error, "Can't be nil!"}
      _   -> {:ok, list}
    end
  end
end
```

Behaviours are relatively straightforward to implement. You define a module that contains a series of callbacks. Defining a behaviour is the same as defining an outline for a module which adopts that behaviour. When adopting a behaviour, you simply enumerate the name of the behaviour, followed by implementations of the required callbacks.

Note that the @impl keyword is not necessarily required; however, it does generate useful warnings when your functions don't do what they're specified to do.

You'll use behaviours to define a contract for the problems you want to solve using genetic algorithms. The problem behaviour will ensure that the problem-specific parts of your genetic algorithm are implemented correctly and are seamlessly integrated with the framework you designed earlier in Chapter 2, Breaking Down Genetic Algorithms, on page 15.

Creating the Problem Behaviour

To get started writing your behaviour, create a new file within the lib directory named problem.ex.

Now, open the problem.ex file and add a new module named Problem, like this:

```
defmodule Problem do
  alias Types.Chromosome
end
```

This is a barebones module that contains an alias for the Chromosome module you created in the previous section. The alias makes accessing the Chromosome module easier later on.

At this point, it's time to start thinking about what a problem consists of. Remember, you need to define callbacks that modules adopting the Problem behaviour will need to implement. In the previous chapter, the problem-specific functions were a fitness function and a genotype function, which is a good place to start.

Think about what each of these functions took as input and what they needed to do. The genotype function didn't require any input. All it needed to do was return an enumerable which represented a single chromosome. In this chapter, you created a chromosome type that works in place of the original representation of a chromosome. Therefore, all the function needs to do is return a chromosome.

Your genotype callback will look like this:

```
@callback genotype :: Chromosome.t
```

Chromosome.t is the custom type you built in the previous section. This means that genotype/0 must return a chromosome struct.

The next function a problem needs is a fitness function. Remember, a fitness function assesses the fitness of a single chromosome and returns some sort of fitness value. In practice, a fitness function can return any value, so long as the value can be sorted in some way. In this book, you'll only create fitness functions that return positive or negative numbers, so you can simplify the callback to only return numbers. The callback will look like this:

```
@callback fitness_function(Chromosome.t) :: number()
```

The last problem-specific parameter you must implement is a termination criteria. In the previous chapter, this criteria was represented as a max fitness. This was sufficient for the One-Max problem; however, you won't always be able to reach a specific fitness threshold. Sometimes you won't even know what a solid threshold is. You'll need more problem-specific termination criteria.

Most of the time, termination is determined based on information about the population or after a maximum number of steps. In Chapter 4, Evaluating Solutions and Populations, on page 51, you'll learn more about termination criteria. What you need to define at this point is a function that analyzes the population and tells your framework whether to continue evolving or to cease and return the best solution. This function should take an enumerable representing the population and return a Boolean indicating whether the evolution should stop or continue.

Something like this will work:

```
@callback terminate?(Enum.t) :: boolean()
```

The function terminate?/1 takes in a population and returns a Boolean—false means continue evolving and true means stop and return. The question-mark at the end is common to Boolean functions in Elixir.

The problem behaviour will now look like this:

```
defmodule Problem do
  alias Types.Chromosome

  @callback genotype :: Chromosome.t

  @callback fitness_function(Chromosome.t) :: number()

  @callback terminate?(Enum.t) :: boolean()
end
```

This module represents a contract you can use for all of the problems you want to solve using a genetic algorithm. It provides a very simple abstraction from which to start—implementing specifics is difficult, but you know exactly what you need to implement with each problem.

Adjusting the Framework

To insert the Problem behaviour into your framework, you'll need to make a few minor adjustments. Additionally, you'll need to make some changes to account for your new chromosome struct.

First, open the genetic.ex file and add the following at the top:

```
alias Types.Chromosome
```

The alias is necessary to easily access the chromosome struct.

Next, locate the run and evolve functions you defined in the previous chapter, and change them to look like this:

```
def run(problem, opts \\ []) do
  ...
end
def evolve(population, problem, opts \\ []) do
  ...
end
```

Now you need to reference the functions specific to the problem behaviour rather than those passed in as parameters. Change the body of the run and evolve functions to look like this:

```
def run(problem, opts \\ []) do
  population = initialize(&problem.genotype/0)
  population
  |> evolve(problem, opts)
end
def evolve(population, problem, opts \\ []) do
  population = evaluate(population, &problem.fitness_function/1, opts)
  best = hd(population)
  IO.write("\rCurrent best: #{best.fitness}")
  if problem.terminate?(population) do
    best
  else
    population
    |> select(opts)
    |> crossover(opts)
    |> mutation(opts)
    |> evolve(problem, opts)
  end
end
```

Notice that all the references to parameters have been changed to references to the corresponding function in the problem parameter. This is because the termination criteria depends on the population of chromosomes already having an associated fitness. All of the other code is the same.

The next change you need to make is to ensure you're constantly updating your chromosome structs with new ages and fitnesses as you transition between generations. You can do this in the evaluate function. Change it to look like this:

```
def evaluate(population, fitness_function, opts \\ []) do
  population
  |> Enum.map(
    fn chromosome ->
      fitness = fitness_function.(chromosome)
      age = chromosome.age + 1
      %Chromosome{chromosome | fitness: fitness, age: age}
    end
  )
  |> Enum.sort_by(& &1.fitness, &>=/2)
end
```

Finally, you need to adjust the crossover and mutation functions so they work correctly with your chromosome type. Change your functions to look like this:

```
def crossover(population, opts \\ []) do
  population
  |> Enum.reduce([],
      fn {p1, p2}, acc ->
        cx_point = :rand.uniform(length(p1.genes))
        {{h1, t1}, {h2, t2}} =
          {Enum.split(p1.genes, cx_point),
            Enum.split(p2.genes, cx_point)}
        {c1, c2} =
          {%Chromosome{p1 | genes: h1 ++ t2},
            %Chromosome{p2 | genes: h2 ++ t1}}
        [c1, c2 | acc]
      end
    )
end

def mutation(population, opts \\ []) do
  population
  |> Enum.map(
      fn chromosome ->
        if :rand.uniform() < 0.05 do
          %Chromosome{chromosome | genes: Enum.shuffle(chromosome.genes)}
        else
          chromosome
        end
      end
    )
end
```

Notice how these functions now return new chromosomes as well as reference
the genes of old chromosomes rather than working on the chromosomes
directly with Enum. This will give you access to the fields you define for the
Chromosome struct, such as age, fitness, and size.

With these minor adjustments, your framework is now completely compatible
with the work you did in this chapter.

Understanding and Choosing Genotypes

One of the most important decisions you can make when using a genetic
algorithm is the type of *encoding* you use to represent solutions. Encodings
are simply representations of a single solution. A good encoding needs to
contain only the information necessary to represent a complete solution to a
problem. If a solution is a path through a grid, an encoding of a solution
would only need to contain the coordinates of each gridpoint it passes through.

The type of encoding scheme you use is known as a *genotype*. The genotype
of a chromosome tells you what the chromosome should look like. It defines

your search space. For example, if you're trying to create an optimal shipping route through fifteen cities, your genotype is a permutation of all fifteen cities.

While the genotype is the internal representation of solutions, the *phenotype* is the expressed representation of solutions. The following figure illustrates the relationship between genotype and phenotype:

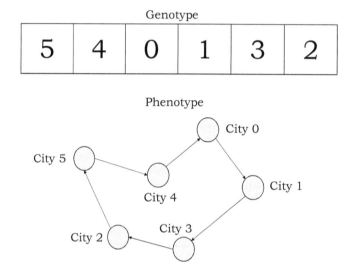

You don't need to understand the distinction between genotype and phenotype. It's just some useful terminology.

Out of a number of different genotypes, this book will use three—binary, permutation, and real-value—because these are the most common and sufficient for fully understanding genetic algorithms. You'll also meet a fourth—tree-based—because it's relatively common, but you won't use any in this book.

Binary Genotypes

1	1	0	0	1	1	0

Binary genotypes, or *bitstrings*, are genes consisting of only 1s and 0s. This is the genotype you used to represent solutions to the One-Max problem. The binary genotype is the most common genotype because you can apply it to such a wide variety of problems. One example of how you can use binary genotypes is in representing different characteristics. Each gene can represent the presence of a single characteristic—either with a 1 or a 0. You can even use binary genotypes to represent continuous values.

Binary Genotypes

The binary genotype or bitstring was the original intended solution representation in the original genetic algorithm. For a long time, the use of a binary genotype is one thing that helped differentiate genetic algorithms from other evolutionary algorithms like evolution strategies. Some might argue that an algorithm can't reasonably be considered a genetic algorithm if solutions aren't encoded as bitstrings. Most of the time, however, this distinction doesn't matter.

Permutation Genotypes

5	4	0	1	3	2	6

The second most common genotype is permutations. Permutations are especially effective for scheduling problems or finding paths in a finite set of points. The types of problems involving permutation genotypes are called *combinatorial optimization*. Combinatorial optimization problems look for ordered solutions. The traveling salesman problem is an example that you can implement using a permutation genotype. Each city is encoded as a number and the path is an order of cities. One limitation of permutations is the type of mutation and crossover that you can use. It's especially difficult to create new chromosomes that maintain the integrity of the permutation.

Real-Value Genotypes

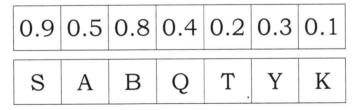

0.9	0.5	0.8	0.4	0.2	0.3	0.1
S	A	B	Q	T	Y	K

The last genotype you'll see in this book is the real-value genotype. Real-value genotypes represent solutions using real values. This "real value" could be a string, a float, a character, and so forth. This is especially common for problems involving weights of some sort or where you need to generate a string. Real-value genotypes are less common, but they prove useful when you need to optimize parameters of some sort.

Why Real-Value Genotypes?

As mentioned before, you can use binary genotypes to represent pretty much anything. So why is it necessary to have real-value genotypes? One reason is *precision*. When you manually encode and decode continuous values as binary genotypes, you lose access to the floating-point precision implemented natively on your machine. Additionally, the use of real-value genotypes can simplify your code, as you don't have to worry about manually encoding and decoding solutions.

Tree/Graph Genotypes

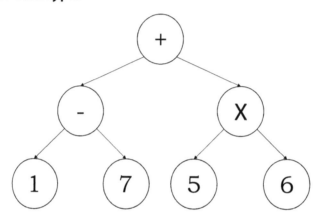

One particularly interesting genotype that you'll encounter is a tree-based or graph genotype. The most common application of tree genotypes is in *genetic programming*. Genetic programming is a branch of evolutionary computation in which one tries to evolve programs to achieve a desired result. The idea is that you can teach a computer to program itself. In these cases, solutions are typically represented as syntax trees representing valid programs. As interesting as they are, there's little evidence that shows genetic programming is of any tangible use. It's difficult to evolve solutions so that they remain valid, and other techniques out there perform better on programming tasks.

Solving One-Max for the Last Time

To get your feet wet with the Problem behaviour you created in this chapter, start small by solving the One-Max problem. You already know what the three problem-specific parameters should look like; all you have to do is fit them into the framework you defined in this chapter.

Open the scripts/one_max.exs file and replace the contents with this:

```
defmodule OneMax do
  @behaviour Problem
  alias Types.Chromosome

  @impl true
  def genotype do
    genes = for _ <- 1..42, do: Enum.random(0..1)
    %Chromosome{genes: genes, size: 42}
  end

  @impl true
  def fitness_function(chromosome), do: Enum.sum(chromosome.genes)

  @impl true
  def terminate?([best | _]), do: best.fitness == 42
end
```

By now, you should be familiar with these functions, as they are identical to the functions you implemented in your previous attempts at solving the One-Max problem. This time, however, they fit within your problem behaviour.

To run your solution, add the following code below your module definition:

```
soln = Genetic.run(OneMax)

IO.write("\n")
IO.inspect(soln)
```

Now, run one_max.exs:

```
$ mix run scripts/one_max.exs
Current Best: 42
%Types.Chromosome{
  age: 1,
  fitness: 42,
  genes: [1, 1,..1],
  size: 42
}
```

Spelling Words with Genetic Algorithms

To illustrate the power of your new framework, you'll use it to solve a new basic problem: spelling. You'll teach your algorithm to spell an impossibly long word: *supercalifragilisticexpialidocious*.

Start by creating a new file called speller.exs in scripts and define a new problem:

```
defmodule Speller do
  @behaviour Problem
  alias Types.Chromosome
```

```
  def genotype, do: # ...

  def fitness_function(chromosome), do: # ...

  def terminate?(population), do: # ...
end
```

Now you need to define a Problem implementation for your tasks. In this chapter, you learned there are three parts to every problem: a genotype, a fitness function, and termination criteria.

The first thing you'll want to decide is the genotype. Your goal is to spell *supercalifragilisticexpialidocious* which is a 34-letter word. That means your search space is all 34-letter words. You can define your genotype like this:

```
def genotype do
  genes =
    Stream.repeatedly(fn -> Enum.random(?a..?z) end)
    |> Enum.take(34)
  %Chromosome{genes: genes, size: 34}
end
```

Stream.repeatedly/1 returns a Stream that will continuously apply a function. In this case, the function you want it to apply is Enum.random/1 over every single alphabetical character. You then take 34 different characters from the stream to produce solutions.

The next thing you need is a fitness function. You want your fitness function to be a measure of how close the guessed word is to the target word. Luckily, Elixir has some functions that implement the desired behavior. Implement your fitness function like this:

```
def fitness_function(chromosome) do
  target = "supercalifragilisticexpialidocious"
  guess = List.to_string(chromosome.genes)
  String.jaro_distance(target, guess)
end
```

String.jaro_distance/2 returns the similarity between the two words, with 1 meaning the words are the same. You need to convert your genes to a string because String.jaro_distance/2 expects two Strings.

Because String.jaro_distance/2 only returns 1 when the words are the same, you can implement your termination criteria like this:

```
def terminate?([best | _]), do: best.fitness == 1
```

That's all you need. Your whole problem should look like:

```elixir
defmodule Speller do
  @behaviour Problem
  alias Types.Chromosome

  def genotype do
    genes =
      Stream.repeatedly(fn -> Enum.random(?a..?z) end)
      |> Enum.take(34)
    %Chromosome{genes: genes, size: 34}
  end

  def fitness_function(chromosome) do
    target = 'supercalifragilisticexpialidocious'
    guess = chromosome.genes
    String.jaro_distance(target, guess)
  end

  def terminate?([best | _]), do: best.fitness == 1
end
```

Now, add the following below your module:

```elixir
soln = Genetic.run(Speller)

IO.write("\n")
IO.inspect(soln)
```

Now run your algorithm:

```
$ mix run scripts/speller.exs
Current Best: 1.0
supercalifragilisticexpialidocious
```

That's all it takes. Spelling a word you can just look up might not be the most impressive task; however, this problem shows the power of your framework. All you need to run a genetic algorithm against a problem is to define a genotype, fitness function, and termination criteria.

"It's Taking Too Long…"

 You might find that your algorithm in the last problem takes awhile to converge. That's OK. You haven't been equipped with the necessary tools to write algorithms that converge quickly on more difficult problems like this one. In the next few chapters, you'll add some tools that will make algorithms like this one a breeze.

As you continue through this book, you'll use this same Problem abstraction to solve progressively more difficult problems.

What You Learned

In this chapter, you learned how to take advantage of Elixir's language features to better represent chromosomes. You also learned about the importance of abstraction to solving difficult problems. You used this principle to create a basic problem behaviour for modeling an optimization problem. You then learned about the different genotypes and how important encoding is.

In the next chapter, you'll take a short detour before diving into more difficult aspects of genetic algorithms. You'll learn about testing with randomness and verifying the correctness of the algorithms you've already written.

## CHAPTER 4

Evaluating Solutions and Populations

Every problem has an objective. The goal of optimization is to maximize or minimize a value. The goal of search is to find a path to an objective. The common thread between optimization and search is an *objective*.

Your objective is your final destination—the end goal of your genetic algorithm. Sometimes, you might not know exactly what your end goal looks like, but you still need a way to know if you're moving in the right direction. If you've ever played the game "Hot or Cold," you understand what this looks like. You search for an object and somebody gives you clues to its location by telling you whether you're "hot"—close to the object—or "cold"—further from the object. "Hot" and "cold" are basic assessments of your current location—they help you continue moving in the right direction without actually knowing where you're going.

In genetic algorithms, fitness functions tell you how "hot" or "cold" you are. You use them as a barometer to measure your progress toward the best solution.

That's why each new generation in a genetic algorithm starts with an evaluation of the current population. The evaluation step is crucial in ensuring your algorithm is progressing toward the best solution. In Chapter 2, Breaking Down Genetic Algorithms, on page 15, you defined the evolve/3 function in lib/genetic.ex. If you recall, that function looks like this:

```
def evolve(population, problem, opts \\ []) do
  population = evaluate(population, &problem.fitness_function/1, opts)
  best = hd(population)
  IO.write("\rCurrent best: #{best.fitness}")
  if problem.terminate?(population) do
    best
  else
    population
    |> select(opts)
```

```
      |> crossover(opts)
      |> mutation(opts)
      |> evolve(problem, opts)
    end
end
```

At two points in this code, the population is being evaluated. The first instance occurs in the first line of the function body, and looks like this:

```
population = evaluate(population, &problem.fitness_function/1, opts)
```

This line of code immediately transforms the population variable passed to the run/2 function by calling the evaluate/2 function to assess the population based on your problem-specific fitness function.

The next point of evaluation is a little less obvious. Take note of the if-condition, which determines when to stop an evolution and return the best solution. The condition calls problem.terminate?/1, which assesses the population based on some problem-specific parameter and decides whether or not to continue.

Fitness functions and termination criteria are two means of assessing solutions in a genetic algorithm. Fitness functions tell you how good a solution is. Termination criteria tells you when to stop the genetic algorithm and return the solution. More often than not, your termination criteria is tied to the best fitness in your population. Both fitness functions and termination criteria are equally important in creating an effective genetic algorithm to solve your problems.

In this chapter, you'll start by examining a new kind of problem to illustrate the importance of crafting a good fitness function and to learn how to craft fitness functions using common techniques for different problems. Additionally, you'll learn how to define termination criteria that stops your algorithms from searching and returns the best possible solutions.

Optimizing Cargo Loads

Suppose you work for a shipping company that has asked you to determine how to properly load cargo with different products so that you maximize profits and don't exceed a specified weight limit. You have ten products, labeled A–J, with corresponding weights: [10, 6, 8, 7, 10, 9, 7, 11, 6, 8]. Each project has an associated profit margin: [6, 5, 8, 9, 6, 7, 3, 1, 2, 6] and the weight limit of the cargo is 40. The image on page 53 shows the loads and their corresponding weights and profit margin.

You need to determine exactly which products to load to maximize profits and not go over the weight limit.

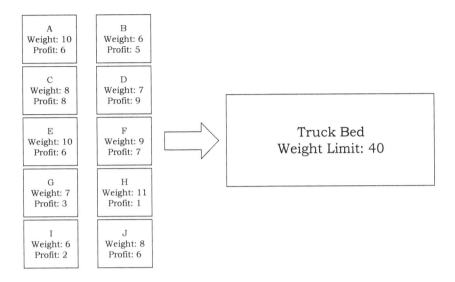

The problem presented here is a modification of the *knapsack* problem. The knapsack problem belongs to a class of optimization problems known as *constraint satisfaction problems*. Constraint satisfaction problems or CSPs are a type of optimization problem in which you're asked to optimize a value under a set of *constraints*. Constraints are some limitation placed on your solutions. For example, in the problem above, your profits are limited by the amount of cargo you can fit in your truck.

To get started solving this problem, create a new file cargo.exs and add a new Problem implementation to it:

```
defmodule Cargo do
  @behaviour Problem
  alias Types.Chromosome

  @impl true
  def genotype, do: # ...

  @impl true
  def fitness_function(chromosome), do: # ...

  @impl true
  def terminate?(population), do: # ...

end
```

The first thing you need to do is determine how to represent your solutions. You have ten classes of cargo you can bring on board. You have two options with each class of cargo: bring it or not bring it. You can represent configurations with a binary genotype of size 10. In this case, the solution 1011000010 means you are bringing Product A, Product C, Product D, and Product I.

Implement the genotype like this:

```
def genotype do
  genes = for _ <- 1..10, do: Enum.random(0..1)
  %Chromosome{genes: genes, size: 10}
end
```

Next, you need to implement a fitness function. Your objective is to maximize profit, so your fitness function needs to somehow relate back to profitability. You need to somehow account for weights, but you can worry about that later.

Your fitness function should sum the total profits gained by the proposed cargo configuration. Implement it like this:

```
def fitness_function(chromosome) do
  profits = [6, 5, 8, 9, 6, 7, 3, 1, 2, 6]
  profits
  |> Enum.zip(chromosome.genes)
  |> Enum.map(fn {p, g} -> p * g end)
  |> Enum.sum()
end
```

Here you multiply the potential profit of a product by 1 or 0 depending whether or not it's present in the cargo configuration. Then you sum the list to receive the total profits.

The final thing you need to implement is the termination criteria. The maximum total profit you can achieve if you fit all the cargo on your truck is 53. For now, your termination criteria will look like this:

```
def terminate?(population), do:
  Enum.max_by(population, &Cargo.fitness_function/1).fitness == 53
```

Now, below your module definition, add the following:

```
soln = Genetic.run(Cargo, population_size: 50)

IO.write("\n")
IO.inspect(soln)

weight =
  soln.genes
  |> Enum.zip([10, 6, 8, 7, 10, 9, 7, 11, 6, 8])
  |> Enum.map(fn {g, w} -> w*g end)
  |> Enum.sum()

IO.write("\nWeight is: #{weight}\n")
```

In this snippet, you run your algorithm with a population of 50 to obtain a solution. Then, you inspect the solution to see what the best configuration is. Finally, you calculate the total weight of this configuration and output the result to the console.

Next, run your problem like this:

```
$ mix run examples/cargo.exs
Current Best: 53
[1, 1, 1, 1, 1, 1, 1, 1, 1, 1]
Weight is: 82
```

While your profits are very high, your weight is through the roof. Your solution doesn't correctly account for the stated constraint. Essentially, you've just implemented One-Max all over again. You need a different technique to account for constraints: *penalty functions*.

Introducing Penalty Functions

You need a way to account for solutions that aren't considered valid—meaning they don't meet the constraints defined by the problem. For example, in your cargo problem, you need a way to penalize solutions that exceed the weight limit so your algorithm doesn't produce an invalid solution. A penalty function is a function applied to constraint satisfaction problems for the purpose of reducing the constraint satisfaction problem into an unconstrained problem. Rather than putting constraints on possible solutions, penalty functions incur a cost on solutions that violate a constraint of the original problem.

In layman's terms, that means you take points away from solutions that aren't valid so they don't get considered better than solutions that are valid.

To better understand penalty functions, consider this: the speed limit changes depending on the road you're driving on. Law enforcement would love it if your car automatically detected the speed limit of a certain road and allowed you to drive only at or below that speed. Of course, implementing this would be impossible—there are too many roads, and speed limits change rapidly between them. Rather than putting constraints on cars, the law introduces a *penalty* for driving over the speed limit. The penalty is a speeding ticket. The cost of speeding outweighs the cost of driving within the speed limit. In this way, the law eliminates the need for explicit constraints and instead punishes drivers who don't obey the rules.

Penalty functions can be simple or complex depending on your problem. Oftentimes, it's useful to make the penalty proportional to how much the constraint was violated. In the speeding example, you could fine somebody $10 for every mile per hour they drove above the speed limit. This means excessive speeders are punished more heavily than those who operate close to the limits.

Penalty Functions

If you research penalty functions outside of this book, you'll find several common penalty functions for optimization problems such as delta penalty, quadratic penalty, or closest valid penalty. It can be useful to know these for advanced problems, but it's not necessary right now. As long as you understand *what* penalty functions are meant to accomplish, you'll be able to understand and apply more complex methods of implementing them.

Applying a Penalty to the Shipping Problem

Now that you understand penalty functions, you need to apply them in the context of your cargo problem. You'll implement a very basic penalty: if a solution exceeds the weight limit, its fitness is 0. Otherwise, its fitness is equal to the profit it yields.

To implement this penalty, change your fitness function to look like this:

```
def fitness_function(chromosome) do
  profits = [6, 5, 8, 9, 6, 7, 3, 1, 2, 6]
  weights = [10, 6, 8, 7, 10, 9, 7, 11, 6, 8]
  weight_limit = 40

  potential_profits =
    chromosome.genes
    |> Enum.zip(profits)
    |> Enum.map(fn {c, p} -> c * p end)
    |> Enum.sum()

  over_limit? =
    chromosome.genes
    |> Enum.zip(weights)
    |> Enum.map(fn {c, w} -> c * w end)
    |> Enum.sum()
    |> Kernel.>(weight_limit)

  profits = if over_limit?, do: 0, else: potential_profits
  profits
end
```

In this snippet, you define problem-specific constants: profits, weights, and weight_limit. Then you calculate the potential profit in the same way you did in your previous fitness function. Next, you calculate the total weight and determine whether or not it exceeds weight_limit. Finally, you return a profit based on your penalty.

Now, you can try running your algorithm again:

```
$ mix run scripts/cargo.exs
Current Best: 39
```

After awhile, you might notice your algorithm stops improving but doesn't stop running. You may have anticipated this. With your new penalty, but old termination criteria, your algorithm will never stop running because it can never reach the maximum possible profits.

Theoretically, you could calculate your new potential max, but that defeats the purpose of using a genetic algorithm. Instead, you need to know when to stop your algorithm, even when you don't know what the best solution looks like.

Defining Termination Criteria

Next to a good fitness function, termination criteria is the most important aspect of your genetic algorithms. If you don't know when to stop and return a solution, you'll never get a solution in the first place. The goal of termination criteria is to stop the algorithm when it has reached maximum fitness. You could write a perfect algorithm, but if it never knows when to stop, it wouldn't matter. Imagine if you successfully managed to get out of the woods and reached civilization, but you kept wandering back into the woods because you didn't know you were back to safety.

Most of the problems you worked with so far have explicit goals. You know what the solution should look like, so you know exactly when to stop. Unfortunately, as you saw with the cargo problem, you'll almost never have all of the information you need. One of the challenges is trying to determine when to stop your evolution and return a solution. The goal is to produce the best solution possible, even when you don't know that it's the absolute best.

In this section, you'll learn three basic techniques for defining termination criteria. Of course, you may find it beneficial to define termination criteria specific to your problem; however, these techniques will work for a majority of the problems you encounter.

Stopping Evolution at a Fitness Threshold

Stopping when your population has reached a certain fitness threshold is the most straightforward approach to terminating your algorithms. This approach is common when you either know what the solution is supposed to be or you've been given specific success criteria.

In the first few chapters, you worked with a maximum fitness threshold—you terminated when the best solution reached a target fitness. You can also terminate your algorithms at a minimum fitness, or even an average fitness. For example, in portfolio optimization, you might want to create a number of possible portfolios that meet an average threshold of success—in this case, you would check the population's average fitness and return when it meets some threshold.

You can apply these techniques to the One-Max problem. Open lib/one_max.exs and experiment with the following termination criteria:

```
defmodule OneMax do
  # ...Genotype/Fitness Function defined...

  # Maximum Fitness Threshold
  def terminate?(population), do:
    Enum.max_by(population, &OneMax.fitness_function/1) == 42

  # Minimum Fitness Threshold
  def terminate?(population), do:
    Enum.min_by(population, &OneMax.fitness_function/1) == 0

  # Average Fitness Threshold
  def terminate?(population) do
    avg =
      population
      |> Enum.map(&(Enum.sum(&1) / length(&1)))
    avg == 21
  end
end
```

Each of these termination criteria will return different solutions. The first will stop when the best chromosome possible is found, the second will stop when the worst chromosome possible is found, and the last will stop when the average chromosome is found.

Fitness-based termination criteria is the most straightforward to implement; however, it's difficult to come across a problem where you're certain about when to stop.

Stopping Evolution after n Generations

Another method for designating termination criteria is to stop after your algorithm has run for a sufficiently long time. With this approach, you need to determine what "sufficiently long" means. The beauty of this approach is the ability to experiment with different numbers of generations. You may initially believe your algorithm will converge after 10,000 generations, only to find it continues to improve after 20,000 generations.

Another benefit of this method is its relative simplicity. To implement it, all you have to do is keep track of the current generation. Open lib/genetic.ex and alter the evolve function to track a generation parameter, like this:

```elixir
def run(problem, opts \\ []) do
  population = initialize(&problem.genotype/0, opts)
  first_generation = 0

  population
  |> evolve(problem, first_generation, opts)
end
def evolve(population, problem, generation, opts \\ []) do
  # ...
  if problem.terminate?(population, generation) do
    # ...
  else
    generation = generation + 1
    ...
    |> evolve(problem, generation opts)
  end
end
```

Next, you'll need to slightly modify the Problem behaviour, so the terminate? function expects two parameters rather than one. Open the lib/problem.ex file and change the terminate? callback to this:

```elixir
@callback terminate?(Enum.t(), integer()) :: boolean()
```

Now, all you'll need to do is specify a generation stopping point in one of your genetic algorithms. Try it with lib/one_max.exs, like this:

```elixir
def terminate?(population, generation), do: generation == 100
```

Generation Tracking

 For the remainder of this book, this is what your terminate? callback should look like. You'll see another termination method next, but you'll only ever use generation-based or fitness-based termination.

When you run this script on the cargo problem, notice how sometimes the algorithm converges on an optimal solution and sometimes it doesn't:

```
$ mix run scripts/cargo.exs
Current Best: 30
%Types.Chromosome{
  age: 1,
  fitness: 30,
  genes: [0, 1, 0, 1, 1, 1, 1, 0, 0, 0],
  size: 10
}

Weight is: 39
```

```
$ mix run scripts/cargo.exs
Current Best: 35
%Types.Chromosome{
  age: 1,
  fitness: 35,
  genes: [0, 1, 1, 1, 0, 1, 0, 0, 0, 1],
  size: 10
}

Weight is: 38
```

This is the tradeoff with this approach—sometimes you get lucky and sometimes you don't. You could experiment with different generation thresholds, but that can be time consuming. After awhile, you'll find your algorithms will continue to converge to the same value after a certain number of generations.

Stopping Evolution with No Improvements

A more sophisticated technique for determining when to stop is by tracking how long it's been since your algorithm has improved and stopping when progress has stalled. Implementing the tracking necessary for this can be a little tricky; however, it can pay off because it automatically determines when the algorithm has converged.

The simplest way to stop based on changes in fitness is by using a *temperature*. Temperature tells you how hot or cold an algorithm is. Algorithms that are hot are making significant improvements between generations. Algorithms that are cold haven't made improvements in a long time.

Temperature

 You might recognize the term temperature from another optimization technique known as *simulated annealing*. Typically, temperature is a parameter that controls some of the movement in that algorithm; however, it's also useful in genetic algorithms for measuring when to stop. You may not want to refer to the measure of progress in the algorithm as temperature—you can also call it momentum or something else that makes sense to you.

To measure the temperature of your algorithm, you'll need to alter run/2 to track changes in fitness between generations. To accomplish this, open lib/genetic.ex and add the following changes:

```
def run(problem, opts \\ []) do
  population = initialize(&problem.genotype/0, opts)
  population
  |> evolve(problem, 0, 0, 0, opts)
end
```

```
def evolve(problem, generation, last_max_fitness, temperature, opts) do
    ...
    best = Enum.max_by(population, &problem.fitness_function/1)
    best_fitness = best.fitness
➤   temperature = 0.8 * (temperature + (best_fitness - last_max_fitness))
➤   if terminate?(population, generation, temperature) do
        ...
    else
        ...
➤       |> evolve(problem, generation, best_fitness, temperature, opts)
    end
end
```

As with tracking generations, you'll need to change the terminate? callback in the Problem behaviour to reflect the additional parameter.

One thing you'll see here is that the temperature is calculated by multiplying the sum of the old temperature and the change in maximum fitness by a factor of 0.8. You don't have to use 0.8. In fact, you may want to take an additional parameter, known as a *cooling rate*, which determines how fast the temperature lowers. Your formula would then look like this: (1 - cooling_rate) * (temperature + (best - last_max_fitness)). A higher cooling rate means your algorithms will terminate faster.

To see the temperature strategy in action, open lib/one_max.exs and adjust the termination criteria like this:

```
def terminate?(population, generation, temperature), do: temperature < 25
```

This example stops when the temperature is less than 25. This technique is useful because it allows you to determine when an algorithm has converged automatically. The temperature will automatically decrease when there's no progress being made. You can play around with different cooling rates and temperature thresholds to see which works best for you.

Applying Termination Criteria to Shipping

With three possible means of determining when to stop, you need to decide which one works best for your cargo problem. The simplest is to stop after a certain number of generations. Of course, you could use a temperature mechanism; however, it's too complicated for the task at hand.

Ensure the terminate? callback in the Problem module is set up to accept a generation argument. Additionally, ensure run and evolve are configured to track generations:

```
# problem.ex
@callback terminate?(Enum.t(), integer()) :: boolean()

# genetic.ex
def run(problem, opts \\ [])
  population = initialize(&problem.genotype/0, opts)
  population
  |> evolve(problem, 0, opts)
end

def evolve(population, problem, generation, opts \\ []) do
  ...
  if terminate?(population, generation) do
  ...
  |> mutation(opts)
  |> evolve(problem, generation+1, opts)
end
```

Now, implement your termination criteria like this:

```
def terminate?(_population, generation), do: generation == 1000
```

Now, run your algorithm:

```
$ mix run scripts/cargo.exs
Current Best: 35
[0, 1, 1, 1, 0, 1, 0, 0, 0, 1]
Weight is: 38
```

While your profit definitely went down, your cargo configuration stayed under the weight limit. You may find if you run this algorithm multiple times, your configuration will vary slightly. Remember, genetic algorithms are subject to randomness, so your solutions will vary. Try to run it mulitple times to see what the best configuration is.

As you can see, how you evaluate solutions significantly impacts the outcome of your algorithms. In this problem, you examined one specific way to evaluate one specific type of problem. Unfortunately, there are countless classes of problems out there. In the next section, you'll gain a better understanding of fitness and fitness functions, and you'll learn about some other types of optimization problems and how they're evaluated.

Crafting Fitness Functions

In the previous few sections, you explored the importance of evaluation through the context of a modified knapsack problem. While the problem shows the importance of crafting a good fitness function, you learned only one way to evaluate a specific type of problem. Countless problems exist, each requiring unique evaluation tools. Unfortunately, you can't generalize one fitness function to all problems. You need to fully understand what fitness functions aim to accomplish.

Understanding Fitness

Recall from Chapter 1, Writing Your First Genetic Algorithm, on page 1, the problem of being lost in the woods. Some of the trees are marked indicating how close you are to escaping the woods. The markings on the trees show the value of your current position—they tell you how to navigate the woods and where to go next. Without this information, it's likely you'd never escape.

Fitness is, in essence, the same as the markings on the trees. Specifically, fitness is the value assigned to a particular chromosome based on the criteria defined in the fitness function. Consider this: you're lost in the woods again, only this time, the trees aren't marked. Instead, you have a guide who tells you how close to civilization you are after every step. In this example, the guide acts as your fitness function, providing you with information based on your current position. This information is the fitness of your current position and tells you how close you are to making it back to civilization.

Understanding Schemas

Theoretically, fitness is supposed to be tied to a chromosome's viability for reproduction. Viability for reproduction means that the chromosome is likely to produce strong offspring—something about the chromosome makes it fundamentally better than others for creating children.

That "something" that makes some chromosomes better than others are the schemas that comprise the chromosome. In Chapter 1, Writing Your First Genetic Algorithm, on page 1, we briefly introduced the idea of schemas. Schemas are templates of genes that make up the genes of a chromosome. A schema is represented by a set of valid genes and wildcards represented by *. For example, the following are example schemas for a binary genotype.

- 11*01*
- 0*10*1
- 011*00

Schemas propagate from generation to generation as parents pass their schemas down to their children. Over time, as chromosomes exchange fit schemas, the presence of fit schemas in the population grows exponentially. Of course, with more fit schemas in the population, the fitness of the population inevitably grows as well. The theory behind schemas and how they improve populations is called the *schema theorem* or *fundamental theorem of genetic algorithms.*

The schema theorem is important because it tells you *why* genetic algorithms work. So, how does this relate to fitness functions? Ideally, you want to craft fitness functions that map meaningful schemas in your encoding of a problem to meaningful solutions in the real world. For example, if you tasked a genetic algorithm with designing a chair, you'd want a fitness function that was able to extract valuable schemas from certain designs, such as the presence of a flat surface to sit on or a support mechanism to hold weight.

In practice, you can't tell a fitness function exactly what to look for because you don't always know exactly what it should look for. Instead, you give it an estimate.

Fitness Functions Are Heuristics

A fitness function is a *heuristic.* In other words, it's an approximation or estimate based on limited information. For example, you can't tell your fitness function to look for seats or support in chair designs, but you can measure how much weight it will support or how comfortable the chair would be.

As another example, imagine you're writing a program that optimizes a portfolio of stocks. Your goal is to maximize your return on investment (ROI). Unfortunately, you can't perfectly predict what stocks will have the highest ROI. Instead, you have to make estimates based on the information available to you, such as the price-to-earnings ratio (P/E ratio). Picking stocks based on some metric like the P/E ratio won't guarantee you perfectly maximize ROI, but it will give you a much better approximation than random stock-picking.

In the portfolio example, the P/E ratio is a heuristic used to measure the potential of a stock to provide the greatest ROI. If you were writing a genetic algorithm to accomplish portfolio optimization, evaluating a chromosome—or in this case, a portfolio—based on the P/E ratio is an example of a good fitness function because it provides a somewhat accurate estimate of how good a portfolio is.

Heuristics, like all things, are imperfect. A good heuristic will be right most of the time, but occasionally, it can be wrong. For example, Amazon is a stock with a very high ROI over the last five years that would be completely ignored when using the P/E ratio as a heuristic. A fitness function will never perfectly assess every solution; it just needs to capture the essential characteristics of your problem.

Fitness Landscapes

One thing you'll see mentioned often with genetic algorithms is the concept of a *fitness landscape*. At a high level, the fitness landscape is a representation of all of the fitnesses of every possible solution in your search space. For example, in portfolio optimization, the fitness landscape would graphically depict every possible portfolio and its corresponding fitness. Fitness landscapes are an abstract concept, and you don't need to understand them to apply genetic algorithms effectively.

Exploring Different Types of Optimization

So far, the problems you've implemented in this book have focused on optimizing a single objective using a simple fitness function. In the real world, some of the problems you'll encounter will be much more complex.

In this section, you'll briefly explore two classes of optimization that require more advanced approaches to evaluation: multi-objective optimization and interactive optimization.

Optimizing Multiple Objectives

The real world is full of competing interests that need to be optimized. For example, you might find yourself trying to balance work, relationships, health, fun, and sleep every day—a classic example of a *multi-objective optimization problem*. A multi-objective optimization problem is one in which you have multiple parameters or objective functions that need to be optimized. Oftentimes, but not always, the objective functions are in competition with one another—when you increase the value of one, the value of the other goes down.

Multi-objective optimization problems are some of the most common problems that appear in the real world. They also can be the most difficult to solve because they require a means of balancing your objectives. It's important to note that there isn't a single global solution to a multi-objective optimization problem. Instead, the best solutions exist on a line representing a set of optimal solutions. You can intuitively think of this in the context of people balancing work, relationships, health, and so on. In this context, no single balance works for everybody—instead, people determine what works best for them. There are multiple solutions.

The simplest way to solve a multi-objective optimization problem is to transform it into a single objective. This makes the problem simple enough because you can use the same means you used to solve optimization problems with a single objective.

To better understand this concept, consider a trivial portfolio optimization problem. Start by creating a new file scripts/portfolio.exs. In this file, you'll write a genetic algorithm for solving a trivial portfolio optimization problem. In the original portfolio example, your goal was to maximize ROI. In this example, you're still trying to maximize ROI, but this time you also have to minimize risk.

To simplify the problem, assume you have a function which provides a predicted ROI and risk score for every stock in your portfolio. A solution in this situation is a collection of stocks. Stocks are represented as tuples of the form (ROI, Risk). Note that in a practical example, you'd need some way of differentiating between stocks using a Ticker or some other identifier. That's excluded to simplify the example.

Open scripts/portfolio.exs and implement genotype/0 and terminate?/1 like this:

```
defmodule Portfolio do
  @behaviour Problem
  alias Types.Chromosome

  @target_fitness 180

  @impl true
  def genotype do
    genes =
      for _ <- 1..10, do:
        {:rand.uniform(10), :rand.uniform(10)}
    %Chromosome{genes: genes, size: 10}
  end

  @impl true
  def fitness_function(chromosome) do
    # TODO
  end

  @impl true
  def terminate?(population, _generation) do
    max_value = Enum.max_by(population, &Portfolio.fitness_function/1)
    max_value > @target_fitness
  end
end
```

The genotype generates portfolios of 10 stocks each with ROI and risk scores between 0 and 10. The algorithm is set to terminate when the max fitness of the population is greater than @target_fitness, which is defined as 180.

Your goal, then, is to implement a fitness function that effectively optimizes both ROI and risk. The simplest way to do this is to turn it into a single objective. You can achieve this using a *weighted sum*. A weighted sum is when you assign weights to each parameter and sum them to produce a single fitness. A weighted sum for this problem would look something like this:

```
def fitness_function(chromosome) do
  chromosome
  |> Enum.map(fn {roi, risk} -> 2 * roi - risk end)
  |> Enum.sum()
end
```

Notice how the formula in this case weights ROI as two times more important than risk. With this fitness function, you've effectively turned your multi-objective optimization problem into a single-objective optimization problem. You can now run your algorithm using the same means as a simple optimization problem.

Real-Value Genotypes

If you tried running this novel genetic algorithm, you'd struggle to find any improvements in fitness. That's because you haven't yet been equipped with tools for driving real-value genotypes forward. You need special crossover and mutation operators to work with them. You'll learn some in Chapter 6, Generating New Solutions, on page 87 and Chapter 7, Preventing Premature Convergence, on page 107.

Weighted sums are easy to implement and they greatly simplify your problem, but it's difficult to determine how to weight some objectives versus others. This is once again where domain expertise comes into play. You can play around with multiple weights and determine which weights give you the best solutions.

Interactive Optimization

All of the techniques introduced in this chapter rely on numerical data that can be assessed explicitly using mathematical formulas. In every example, you were able to transform a chromosome according to a formula or set of rules; however, this isn't always the case.

Some optimization problems are impossible to encode numerically but could still benefit from the application of a genetic algorithm. One example of this is web design optimization. A website is written as a series of rules and styles. While it's possible to encode and interpret a website using a numerical representation, it is complex and would be difficult to change using a genetic algorithm. Additionally, it's impossible to mathematically assess one web design as being better than the other.

To handle and assess *perceptual data*, you can write interactive fitness functions. Perceptual data is information based off of sensory inputs. An interactive fitness function is useful when the solutions you're working with are impossible to assess mathematically. Instead, you present the user with a solution and ask them to assess its fitness. For example, in the case of web design, you'd show a user several different designs with slight alterations and ask them to rate the designs on a numerical scale. The values a user assigns to different solutions represents the fitness of the solution.

Another unique example of interactive optimization is generating suspect sketches from eyewitness responses. A sketch artist creates an initial sketch from an eyewitness description, and then the eyewitness is presented with variations of the sketch—rating each one based on how closely it resembles a suspect. Over time, the sketches evolve to closely match the eyewitness description, all thanks to a genetic algorithm.

Implementing interactive fitness functions is as simple as displaying a solution and asking for feedback from the user using Elixir's IO module. To demonstrate this concept, create and open a new file in the scripts directory named one_max_interactive.exs.

Next, copy the code from scripts/one_max.exs into the body of scripts/one_max_interactive.exs. Now, change the fitness function to look like this:

```
def fitness_function(chromosome) do
  IO.inspect(chromosome)
  fit = IO.get("Rate from 1 to 10 ")
  String.to_integer(fit)
end
```

When you run this algorithm, you'll be prompted to assess the fitness of every chromosome in the population during every generation. If you want the algorithm to run to completion, you can limit the population size and the size of a chromosome.

It's useful to note that how you display solutions to the user is problem-dependent. In the case of web design optimization, you'll want to display the actual design and ask the user to rate it. Additionally, understand that interactive fitness functions take time and are subject to a user's bias. You'll likely have to work with much smaller population sizes and determine a solution over the course of fewer generations than in a traditional algorithm.

You'll also likely have to take input from multiple users to mitigate the bias from a single user assessing fitness.

One final consideration is handling user input. In this example, there's no sanity checking on the input. The program will break pretty quickly if the user doesn't input exactly what's expected. You'll want to consider how to mitigate the possibility of users breaking your algorithms if you choose to work with interactive fitness functions. Interactive fitness functions have some interesting applications; however, they require much more time and effort to utilize effectively.

Other Types of Optimization

Optimization is an incredibly broad field with a wide array of applications in science, engineering, and math. As in this chapter, in the rest of the book you'll focus on constraint satisfaction problems, combinatorial optimization problems, single- and multi-objective optimization problems, and interactive optimizaton problems. You might also find numerous other subfields of optimization interesting:

- No-objective optimization: also called *feasability problems*, seeks to find feasible solutions without worrying about any particular objective.

- Convex optimization: optimization on special types of functions called *convex functions* that is very useful in computational finance.

- Shape optimization: seeks to find the optimal shape of an object that minimizes some cost function—for example, finding the optimal shape of a cam.

Genetic algorithms are applicable to all of these fields with varying degree. If you're ever faced with any optimization problem, genetic algorithms are always a good place to start.

What You Learned

In this chapter, you explored the importance of evaluation. You saw how bad fitness functions can yield incorrect solutions through the lens of a knapsack problem. You also explored the different ways of terminating your algorithm.

After you solved your shipping problem, you dove deeper into fitness and fitness functions and were introduced to the schema theorem, or the fundamental theorem of genetic algorithms. You saw how the schema theorem relates to fitness functions, and you explored the concepts of heuristics.

Finally, you were briefly introduced to two unique types of optimization that require different evaluation techniques.

With your evaluation techniques in place, it's time to move on to the next stage in the genetic algorithm: selection.

## CHAPTER 5

Selecting the Best

In the last chapter, you learned how to evaluate solutions using fitness functions. Remember, fitness functions measure the viability of a solution. Fitness functions are an important aspect of your genetic algorithm, but they mean nothing if you don't do anything with them. With your population evaluated, and each chromosome assigned a fitness, it's time to perform selection.

If you've ever been on a team, you understand the importance of having the right people. Whether it be in sports, music, work, or any collaboration, choosing the right people to fill positions and complement other members is vital to the success of the organization. This idea of selecting the right people to fill the right roles directly correlates to selection in genetic algorithms.

Selection is the first genetic operator in an evolution. On the surface, selection is responsible for choosing chromosomes that will reproduce in the next step. At its core, selection is responsible for ensuring the next generation of chromosomes is even stronger than the last.

Charles Darwin's theory of evolution suggests that strong traits that are key to survival become more common in successive generations. Whether you believe in evolution or not, the idea of *natural selection* is a key aspect of genetic algorithms.

In the context of genetic algorithms, the process of selection is better described as *artificial selection*. It's important to note the distinction between natural and artificial selection. In the case of genetic algorithms, you have the ability to define your selection and fitness criteria whereas in nature, selection is nondeterministic, and fitness is an emergent property of selection. That is to say the process of selection comes before the determination of fitness. In a genetic algorithm, you have the power to select which traits of a solution correlate to it's fitness and the power to select based on this fitness criteria, thus you have the power to determine which traits persist between generations. Note the process differs between natural selection because, in nature, fitness cannot be determined until *after* selection takes place.

Artificial selection gives you the power to choose which traits are important to your problem. To think about this more concretely, imagine you're coaching a team of sprinters. You have three sprinters, but you need to pick a fourth to have a full team for the 4x100m relay. You get to choose between two sprinters: one with a 100-meter time of 25 seconds and another with a time below 11 seconds. In this situation, you have the power to choose which sprinter you believe gives you a better chance of success and you have the power to define your notion of success.

The goal of selection is to build the best team of parents based on your predefined fitness criteria to increase your chances of success in later generations. In this chapter, you'll further explore how selection can impact the performance of your algorithms. You'll be introduced to selection rates and will learn about different selection techniques and how to choose the right one.

Exploring Selection

Selection is vital to the performance of a genetic algorithm because it contributes to the creation of good solutions for the next generation. The idea is that parents have characteristics that make them strong based on your fitness criteria and will pass these characteristics on to the next generation of solutions.

Consider this: in medieval and early modern Europe, monarchs would carefully select partners to maintain their status as royalty. The idea was based on the assumption that royal blood was stronger and the genes of a commoner would ruin the purity of the bloodline.

Monarchs practiced a loose derivative of selection. They would choose partners based on territory, power, money, and other factors, which essentially amounted to the "fitness" of a potential partner. They hoped that marrying other royals would lead to a strong bloodline and continued success for the royal family.

Unfortunately, the lack of royals to marry outside of preexisting royal families meant that later monarchs often had to "keep it in the family." A lot of monarchs were forced to marry cousins. While this initially didn't seem like an issue—both cousins would be royalty and thus strong, after all—as the practice of intermarriage increased, so did the severity of birth defects within the royal family. But, how could the purity and strength of the royal bloodline suffer from often crippling birth defects? The problem was a lack of *genetic diversity.*

The selection strategy of early monarchs focused too much on perceived fitness of partners and not enough on maintaining genetic diversity. The plight of the monarchs can teach lessons about the importance of selection in your genetic algorithms.

Selection is about balancing genetic diversity and fitness. Genetic diversity is the variety in your population. This doesn't mean variety in fitness—you can have equally strong individuals that are very different. Consider the two potential solutions to the One-Max problem in the image on page 73.

1	1	1	1	0	0	0	0

0	0	0	0	1	1	1	1

Both individuals have the same fitness, but they're very different. These two chromosomes would be a perfect match because their diverse characteristics would be combined to form a strong child during crossover. You can see an example of this here:

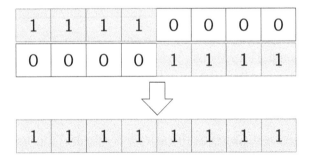

If you can't maintain the genetic diversity of your population, then your algorithm will likely converge without finding the best solution. While there are other strategies, such as mutation, for maintaining the genetic diversity of a population, selection is the first step and can make a significant difference in performance.

Selection Is Biased Sampling

If you're familiar with statistics, you understand that selection is a biased form of *sampling.* Sampling is the practice of choosing a smaller subset of the population to represent the entire population. Sampling is especially important in surveys and quality assurance because it's used to estimate the beliefs or characteristics of the population on the whole.

Sampling is done because it's almost always impossible to survey an entire population. Instead, statisticians aim to get a sample that is representative of the population. The goal is diversity. Selection, on the other hand, is done to improve the population over the next generation. This means that most selection strategies will favor certain individuals over others because they have a better chance of improving the population.

Just as sampling only chooses part of the population, it's common for selection strategies to only select part of the population as well. The idea is that not every chromosome is fit to be a parent, which would hopefully eliminate the weaker characteristics of a population while keeping the stronger ones.

The number of parents selected for crossover is known as the *selection rate*. The selection rate is a number between 0 and 1 that dictates the percentage of the population to select for crossover. For example, a selection rate of 0.8 with a population of 100 would mean 80 parents would be selected for crossover.

Varying the selection rate will affect the speed of your algorithms as well as how quickly they converge. Having a selection rate of 1 isn't a problem. Selection rates are typically high—somewhere in the 0.75–1 range.

Importance of Selection Pressure

You can measure how well a selection strategy balances genetic diversity and fitness by determining its *selection pressure*. Selection pressure is a mathematical measure of the likelihood of a chromosome getting selected to be a parent. It's defined as the ratio between the probability of the fittest individual getting picked versus the probability of an individual of average fitness getting picked.

Selection pressure is dictated by the selection rate and the selection strategy. In a truly random selection, the selection pressure is exactly 1 because every individual is equally likely to get picked. Higher selection pressures mean that a selection strategy more heavily favors fitter individuals. It's a measure of how biased a selection strategy is.

You can use selection pressure to quantify how well your selection strategy fits into the context of your problem. If you have a problem that requires more genetic diversity, you'll want a selection strategy with a lower selection pressure. If you want your problem to converge quickly, you'll want a selection strategy with high selection pressure.

Types of Selection

The two main types of selection are *fitness-based selection* and *rewards-based selection*.

Fitness-based selection is selection based strictly on fitness criteria. Fitness-based selection strategies are the most common selection strategies. The goal of selection is to increase fitness; therefore, these strategies assume that fitness is the best indication of future potential fitness.

Reward-based selection is selection based on the cumulative reward obtained by an individual. The idea is that parents with high rewards create the best children. The reward can be calculated by a number of different reward functions. Reward-based selection can be useful in multi-objective optimization; however, it's not all that common.

In this book, you'll only work with fitness-based selection strategies because they're the most common and the simplest to implement.

Customizing Selection in Your Framework

In Chapter 2, Breaking Down Genetic Algorithms, on page 15, you briefly learned about hyperparameters and how to pass configuration options to your framework. At the time, the only hyperparameter you could change was population size.

Selection introduces two more hyperparameters: selection strategy and selection rate. In this section, you'll tweak your framework to allow for changes in both.

Creating a Selection Toolbox

Before you begin, you'll want a place to store some common selection strategies that you may need to solve some of the problems you encounter. Create a new folder called toolbox. toolbox is your toolbox of genetic operators. You'll implement modules for selection, crossover, and mutation in the toolbox so you always have them available when you need them.

For now, create selection.ex and add the following module definition:

```
defmodule Toolbox.Selection do
  # ...strategies here
end
```

Whenever you implement a new selection strategy, add it to your toolbox so you never have to implement it again.

Changing Selection Strategies

Open up genetic.ex and examine select. It looks like this:

```
def select(population, opts \\ []) do
  population
  |> Enum.chunk_every(2)
  |> Enum.map(&List.to_tuple(&1))
end
```

Right now, your algorithm implements elitism selection in which you always select the most fit chromosomes for crossover. You'll want to adjust it so it can accept many different kinds of selection. To do that, add the following:

```
def select(population, opts \\ []) do
  select_fn =
    Keyword.get(opts, :selection_type, Toolbox.Selection.elite/2)
  parents =
    select_fn
    |> apply([population])
  # rest goes here
end
```

Keyword.get/3 takes the option list and searches for the key :selection_type. If nothing is there, it defaults to Toolbox.Selection.elite/2. You haven't implemented this yet, but you will later.

apply/2 takes a reference to a function and a list of arguments and applies the function. All of your selection strategies will take a population as input, so that's the only parameter you pass for now. In the next section, you'll pass the additional parameter that's required.

Adjusting the Selection Rate

In your first few genetic algorithms, you selected 100% of the population for reproduction. The purpose of this was to simplify your algorithms. Now, you'll need to account for different selection rates.

First, change select so it looks like this:

```
def select(population, opts \\ []) do
  select_fn =
    Keyword.get(opts, :selection_type, &Toolbox.Selection.elite/2)
  select_rate = Keyword.get(opts, :selection_rate, 0.8)

  n = round(length(population) * select_rate)
  n = if rem(n, 2) == 0, do: n, else: n+1

  parents =
    select_fn
    |> apply([population, n])
```

```
  leftover =
    population
    |> MapSet.new()
    |> MapSet.difference(MapSet.new(parents))

  parents =
    parents
    |> Enum.chunk_every(2)
    |> Enum.map(& List.to_tuple(&1))

  {parents, MapSet.to_list(leftover)}
end
```

A few things are going on here. First, you extract the selection rate from opts. Next, you calculate n, which represents the number of parents to select. The math and if statement simply ensure you have enough parents to make even pairs.

Next, you extract the parents using apply/2 and your selection strategy. You then determine who wasn't selected using Elixir's MapSet. Finally, you turn the parents into tuples for crossover and you return a tuple containing the parents and the leftover.

Now, you'll need to slightly modify evolve to reflect the changes you've made here. Change run to look like this:

```
def evolve(population, problem, generation, opts \\ []) do
  population = evaluate(population, &problem.fitness_function/1, opts)
  best = hd(population)
  IO.write("\rCurrent best: #{best.fitness}")
  if problem.terminate?(population, generation) do
    best
  else
    {parents, leftover} = select(population, opts)
    children = crossover(parents, opts)
    children ++ leftover
    |> mutation(opts)
    |> evolve(problem, generation+1, opts)
  end
end
```

Here you adjust run to account for select returning a tuple of parents and left-over chromosomes. Then you obtain the children by passing parents into crossover. Finally, you recombine children with leftover and mutate them before running an evolution again.

The practice of replacing parents with children in a genetic algorithm is fairly common. You'll learn more about reinsertion strategies in Chapter 8, Replacing and Transitioning, on page 125. For now, this naive approach works fine.

Now you can customize your algorithms with any selection strategy you implement by passing in a reference to your selection function.

Implementing Common Selection Strategies

Balancing genetic diversity with strong solutions can be difficult to achieve without a smart selection strategy. Fortunately, there are common selection strategies that are battle-tested and proven to work well for many different problem sets.

The strategies you'll learn about in this section are:

- Elitism selection
- Random selection
- Tournament selection
- Roulette selection

You'll see how these strategies work, what each of their drawbacks are, and how to implement them in Elixir so you can add them to your toolbox.

Elitism Selection

Elitism selection is the simplest and most common selection strategy. The idea is simple: choose the best n chromosomes to reproduce. Elitism selection gives preference to the most elite chromosomes.

The problem with elitism selection is that it doesn't factor genetic diversity into the mix at all. It's common with elitism selection that your algorithms will converge onto a strong solution quickly but fail to improve from that point on because your population is too similar. Fortunately, you can counteract the lack of diversity with mutation, large populations, and even large chromosomes.

The algorithm behind elitism selection is straightforward. Given a population of sorted chromosomes, select the n best. The image shown on page 79 should help you visualize elitism selection.

In Elixir, elitism selection is easy to implement using Enum.take/2. Open lib/genetic/toolbox/selection.ex and add the following function:

```
def elite(population, n) do
  population
  |> Enum.take(n)
end
```

That's all there is to it. Because you took the time to sort your population in the evaluation step of your algorithm, you don't need to worry about handling it here. Sorting guarantees that the first n chromosomes in the population

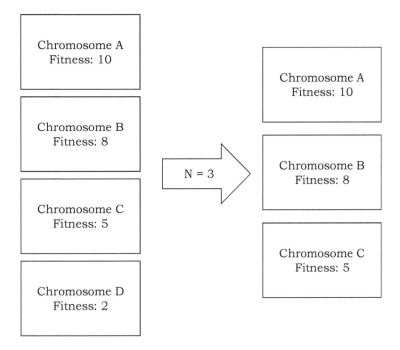

are the best n chromosomes. That means you can simply call Enum.take/2 which returns the first n elements of an enumerable.

Elitism selection is fast and simple, but it can lend itself to premature convergence.

Random Selection

Random selection, when compared to elitism selection, lies on the opposite end of balancing genetic diversity and fitness. Random selection pays no mind to a chromosome's fitness and instead selects a completely random sample of chromosomes from the population.

Random selection can be useful if your problem absolutely requires genetic diversity. This is an uncommon requirement, but it can pop up in certain cases. For example, *novelty search* is the search for new, different solutions. Rather than rewarding solutions for being strong, novelty search rewards solutions for being different.

One unique application of novelty search is *scenario generation*. In scenario generation, you're trying to come up with different, valid scenarios from a set of starting scenarios. For example, you could use novelty search to generate different starting configurations for Sudoku or crossword puzzles.

In novelty search, you could also design a fitness function that evaluates chromosomes based on how different they are; however, this could also overcomplicate your problem. Perhaps you want fitness to reflect a different aspect of your problem, like the difficulty of the puzzle. You could then use random selection to ensure you're maintaining your population's genetic diversity.

Random selection, like elitism selection, is straightforward. You can think of random selection like picking cards out of a shuffled deck or choosing names out of a hat.

Elixir provides a convenient function named Enum.take_random/2 that makes the implementation of random selection almost identical to elitism selection. Add the following function to Genetic.Toolbox.Selection:

```elixir
def random(population, n) do
  population
  |> Enum.take_random(n)
end
```

Enum.take_random/2 selects n random chromosomes from the population. This function will select chromosomes without any consideration of fitness.

Random selection is uncommon, but it can be useful in special cases. If your goal is genetic diversity, random selection is the way to go.

Tournament Selection

Tournament selection is a strategy that pits chromosomes against one another in a tournament. While selections are still based on fitness, tournament selection introduces a strategy to choose parents that are both diverse and strong.

Tournament selection works like this:

1. Choose a pool of n chromosomes where n is the "tournament size."
2. Choose the fittest chromosome from the tournament.
3. Repeat.

The image on page 81 might help you visualize tournament selection a little better.

The beauty of tournament selection is that it's simple, yet it effectively balances genetic diversity and fitness. The strongest solutions will still get selected, but they'll be mixed in with weak solutions that might otherwise have not been picked.

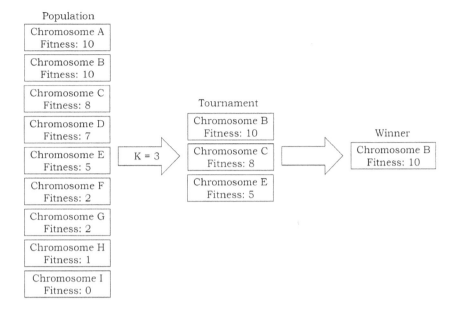

In tournament selection, tournaments can be any n-way: the tournament size can be any number from 1 to the size of the population. Notice, however, a 1-way tournament is equivalent to random selection, and a tournament the size of your population is equivalent to elitism selection.

Tournament selection works well in parallel and can effectively balance genetic diversity and fitness. One drawback of tournament selection is that it might not be appropriate for smaller populations.

You can implement tournament selection with two approaches: with duplicates and without duplicates. If you allow duplicate parents to be selected, you risk allowing your population to become less genetically diverse; however, you greatly simplify and speed up your algorithm. If you don't allow duplicates, your algorithm is slower, but genetic diversity will increase.

This is how you implement tournament selection with duplicates in Elixir:

```elixir
def tournament(population, n, tournsize) do
  0..(n-1)
  |> Enum.map(
    fn _ ->
      population
      |> Enum.take_random(tournsize)
      |> Enum.max_by(&(&1.fitness))
    end
  )
end
```

Allowing duplicates simplifies tournament selection. This implementation uses a range to create and then map over a list of size n. A tournament is conducted at every iteration where the strongest individual is selected from the tournament pool. The result is a list of selected chromosomes—some of which will be identical.

Alternatively, the following is how you implement tournament selection without duplicates in Elixir:

```
def tournament_no_duplicates(population, n, tournsize) do
  selected = MapSet.new()
  tournament_helper(population, n, tournsize, selected)
end

defp tournament_helper(population, n, tournsize, selected) do
  if MapSet.size(selected) == n do
    MapSet.to_list(selected)
  else
    chosen = population
      |> Enum.take_random(tournsize)
      |> Enum.max_by(&(&1.fitness))
    tournament_helper(population, n, tournsize, MapSet.put(selected, chosen))
  end
end
```

This implementation is slightly longer and uses a helper function, but the idea is the same. You use a MapSet to ensure no duplicate chromosomes are selected. Notice that this implementation uses the same code to implement a tournament at every iteration.

One thing you might notice is that the code can be optimized a little using *tail-recursive calls*. You can disregard this for now as it will be covered in Chapter 11, Optimizing Your Algorithms, on page 169.

Tournament selection is useful when you want to effectively balance genetic diversity with fitness. One thing you should remember is that tournament size will affect the balance in your selected parents. You can experiment with different tournament sizes to see what gives you the best results.

Roulette Selection

Roulette selection, also known as *fitness-proportionate selection*, chooses parents with a probability proportional to their fitness. Roulette selection puts every chromosome on a roulette wheel based on their fitness. Individuals with higher fitness occupy a larger space on the roulette wheel—meaning they have a higher chance of getting picked. You then spin the wheel to select parents. Like tournament selection, roulette selection can be implemented with or without duplicates.

Roulette selection attempts to balance genetic diversity and fitness based on probability. Individuals that are more fit have a higher chance of getting selected; however, it's still possible that individuals that are less fit will get selected as well. Think of it like this: in Wheel of Fortune, the more valuable spaces have a smaller area, meaning the probability of landing on them is lower. The relationship is the same in roulette selection, albeit in reverse.

The following image might help you visualize roulette selection:

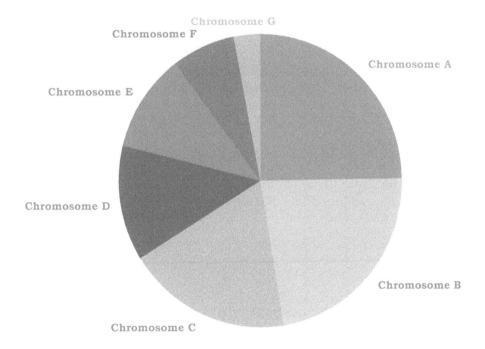

Roulette selection is by far the slowest and most difficult algorithm to implement; however, it does a great job of maintaining the fitness of a population while including some diverse parents.

This is how you can implement roulette selection with duplicates in Elixir:

```elixir
def roulette(chromosomes, n) do
  sum_fitness =
    chromosomes
    |> Enum.map(&(&1.fitness))
    |> Enum.sum()

  0..(n - 1)
  |> Enum.map(fn _ ->
```

```
  u = :rand.uniform() * sum_fitness
  chromosomes
  |> Enum.reduce_while(
    0,
    fn x, sum ->
      if x.fitness + sum > u do
        {:halt, x}
      else
        {:cont, x.fitness + sum}
      end
    end
  )
 end)
end
```

To get a better understanding of what's going on here, look at each section of code starting with the following section:

```
sum_fitness =
  chromosomes
  |> Enum.map(&(&1.fitness))
  |> Enum.sum()
```

This section calculates the total fitness of the population. This step is necessary to determine the proportion of the roulette wheel that each chromosome will occupy.

Now, examine the following section:

```
0..(n-1)
|> Enum.map(fn _ ->)
```

You should be familiar with this pattern by now. It's necessary to simulate a loop from 0 to n. In this case, you need to loop n times because you want to select n individuals.

```
u = :rand.uniform() * sum_fitness
chromosomes
|> Enum.reduce_while(
  0,
  fn x, sum ->
    if x.fitness + sum > u do
      {:halt, x}
    else
      {:cont, x.fitness + sum}
    end
  end
```

This is where the real magic happens. The first line calculates a random value u, which represents one spin of the wheel. You then use Enum.reduce_while/3 to loop over individuals in the population until you're within the selected area. Once you reach the selected area, you stop the reduction and return the selected individual.

Roulette selection is the slowest and most complex selection strategy presented here. You should try simpler strategies like tournament selection before experimenting with roulette selection.

Other Types of Selection

These selection strategies are by no means the only ones out there. You'll see numerous takes on selection and selection strategies. You can find descriptions of new and unique selection strategies in academic papers and in tutorials online. You might find it useful to research the following and try to implement them on your own.

- Boltzmann selection: selection according to a "temperature" function.
- Stochastic universal sampling: selection at evenly spaced intervals.
- Rank selection: selection based on "rank" in the population.

Remember, selection strategies are nothing more than algorithms for choosing samples from a population. Any statistical sampling strategy would work as a selection strategy. You could even implement your own unique selection strategy.

What You Learned

In this chapter, you learned about the importance of selection and how it correlates to picking the best team. You also learned about the importance of balancing genetic diversity with fitness and how selection pressure is an indication of how well a strategy balances those two characteristics.

You also learned about various selection strategies, how to implement them, and when they're useful. You should now have four different selection strategies in your toolbox to experiment with on various problems. Try messing around with each of these strategies to see what kind of results you get.

In the next chapter, you're going to utilize selected parents to create new solutions for your population.

## CHAPTER 6

Generating New Solutions

In the previous chapter, you learned about selection—the process of choosing parents for reproduction. Selection is important; however, you now need to decide what to do with your pairs of parents.

In Chapter 1, Writing Your First Genetic Algorithm, on page 1, you learned about the need to balance exploitation and exploration. Recall that exploitation is the process of using the information you have available, while exploration is the process of searching for new information. You exploit the environment to find your objective—like using the sun as a guide to navigate out of the woods. You explore the environment in search of better clues—like trying to find new roads or paths that lead you to your objective.

Crossover is how genetic algorithms exploit information. If you recall from Chapter 4, Evaluating Solutions and Populations, on page 51, different chromosomes have different schemas that make them better or worse than others. Crossover strategies attempt to combine schemas in an intelligent manner to create new, better solutions.

In this chapter, you'll see what crossover is and why it's important. You'll learn about different types of crossover and how to implement them. Finally, you'll see some problems crossover might cause and learn how to fix them. Before you begin, you'll start with an example of why you need different crossover strategies.

Introducing N-Queens

Imagine your friend challenges you to array eight queens on a standard chess board so that none of the queens conflict with another. This problem, known as N-queens, is a fundamental constraint satisfaction problem, similar to the knapsack problem introduced in Chapter 4, Evaluating Solutions and

Populations, on page 51. In N-queens, the objective is to configure N queens on a chess board so that no queen threatens another. In chess, a piece is "threatened" when another piece can move to the square it occupies to "capture" it. The queen is permitted to move horizontally, vertically, and diagonally any number of spaces on the board. Because queens can move in any direction horizontally or vertically, it's only possible to create a correct configuration of N queens on an NxN chess board.

The following image illustrates a correct solution to the N-queens problem with eight queens on an 8x8 chess board:

N-queens is a combinatorial optimization problem—which, as you already know, genetic algorithms are well-suited for. You'll attempt to solve N-queens to demonstrate the importance of using a good crossover strategy in your algorithms.

Start by creating a new file called n_queens.exs in your scripts folder. In this file, you'll write an encoding of the N-queens problem and run your algorithm to obtain a solution.

In n_queens.exs, define the module and specify the Problem behaviour, like this:

```
defmodule NQueens
  @behaviour Problem
  alias Types.Chromosome

  # Rest goes here
end
```

Implementing the Genotype

Remember, you need to define three functions to correctly implement the Problem behaviour. The first function is genotype/0, which returns the genotype your algorithm will use. At first, you might be tempted to encode solutions using a binary genotype where each index represents whether a queen is present or not. However, it's smarter to keep track of a permutation of size 8 representing the location of each queen on the board. For example, the solution [0, 2, 1, 3, 6, 4, 7, 5] represents the following configuration on the chess board:

To create a permutation genotype, add the following function to NQueens:

```
@impl true
def genotype do
  genes = Enum.shuffle(0..7)
  %Chromosome{genes: genes, size: 8}
end
```

Enum.shuffle/1 scrambles the given enumerable. In this function, you pass the range 0..7 to represent a permutation of size 8.

Next, you need to define a fitness function.

Implementing the Fitness Function

Remember, the objective is to configure a chess board so that there are no conflicts between any of the pieces on the board. Your objective is to minimize these conflicts; therefore, your fitness function should measure the number of conflicts in some way.

To do this, you need to check solutions across each row and diagonally. Your genotype restricts queens from being in the same column; however, they can still be in the same row.

Your fitness function should look like this:

```
@impl true
def fitness_function(chromosome) do
  diag_clashes =
    for i <- 0..7, j <- 0..7 do
      if i != j do
        dx = abs(i - j)
        dy =
          abs(
            chromosome.genes
            |> Enum.at(i)
            |> Kernel.-(Enum.at(chromosome.genes), j)
          )
        if dx == dy do
          1
        else
          0
        end
      else
        0
      end
    end
  length(Enum.uniq(chromosome.genes)) - Enum.sum(diag_clashes)
end
```

First, you calculate the number of diagonal clashes in the solution. Next, you filter out duplicate values in the chromosome because those represent row clashes. Finally, you return the difference. The fitness function will return the number of non-conflicts or the number of pieces that don't conflict with any others.

The final step is to define your termination criteria.

Defining Termination Criteria and Running

Because the fitness function returns the number of non-conflicts, your algorithm is complete when the maximum fitness of the population is 8. In other words, your algorithm is complete when there are no conflicts on the board.

Your termination criteria is:

```
@impl true
def terminate?(population, _generation), do:
  Enum.max_by(population, &NQueens.fitness_function/1).fitness == 8
```

To run your algorithm, add the following lines beneath your module definition:

```
soln = Genetic.run(NQueens)

IO.write("\n")
IO.inspect(soln)
```

Next, open a terminal and run mix run scripts/n_queens.exs:

```
$ mix run scripts/n_queens.exs
Current Best: 5
```

What's going on here? Your solution stagnates before ever reaching the maximum possible fitness.

The problem is your crossover function creates invalid chromosomes. Right now, your framework uses single-point crossover. Single-point crossover doesn't preserve the integrity of the permutation—you need to implement a crossover strategy that works for permutations.

Solving N-Queens with Order-One Crossover

To solve N-queens, you need to implement a crossover strategy that preserves the integrity of your permutation. While there are numerous approaches to doing this, one common strategy is known as *order-one crossover*.

Before you start, create a new file crossover.ex within the toolbox folder. Next, create a new module that looks like this:

```
defmodule Toolbox.Crossover do
  alias Types.Chromosome
  # ...
end
```

Just like selection.ex in toolbox contains useful selection strategies, you'll implement useful crossover strategies in Toolbox.Crossover.

Implementing Order-One Crossover

Order-one crossover, sometimes called "Davis order" crossover, is a crossover strategy on ordered lists or permutations. Order-one crossover is part of a unique set of crossover strategies that will preserve the integrity of a permutation solution.

Order-one crossover will maintain the integrity of the permutation without the need for chromosome repair. This is useful and eliminates some complexity in your algorithms.

Order-one crossover works like this:

1. Select a random slice of genes from Parent 1.
2. Remove the values from the slice of Parent 1 from Parent 2.
3. Insert the slice from Parent 1 into the same position in Parent 2.
4. Repeat with a random slice from Parent 2.

Order-one crossover will produce two new, valid children. The following image demonstrates the algorithm used to produce one child:

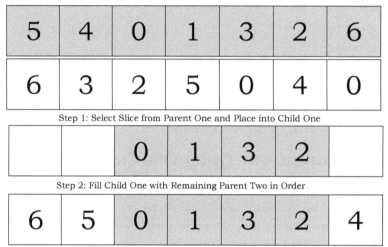

Step 1: Select Slice from Parent One and Place into Child One

Step 2: Fill Child One with Remaining Parent Two in Order

Step 3: Repeat with Parent Two for Child Two

Because of its complexity, order-one crossover is difficult to implement in Elixir. It requires the use of MapSet and is generally harder to understand than other crossover strategies. Add the following function to your Toolbox.Crossover module:

```elixir
def order_one_crossover(p1, p2) do
  lim = Enum.count(p1.genes) - 1
  # Get random range
  {i1, i2} =
    [:rand.uniform(lim), :rand.uniform(lim)]
    |> Enum.sort()
    |> List.to_tuple()

  # p2 contribution
  slice1 = Enum.slice(p1.genes, i1..i2)
  slice1_set = MapSet.new(slice1)
  p2_contrib = Enum.reject(p2.genes, &MapSet.member?(slice1_set, &1))
  {head1, tail1} = Enum.split(p2_contrib, i1)

  # p1 contribution
  slice2 = Enum.slice(p2.genes, i1..i2)
  slice2_set = MapSet.new(slice2)
  p1_contrib = Enum.reject(p1.genes, &MapSet.member?(slice2_set, &1))
  {head2, tail2} = Enum.split(p1_contrib, i1)

  # Make and return
  {c1, c2} = {head1 ++ slice1 ++ tail1, head2 ++ slice2 ++ tail2}

  {%Chromosome{
     genes: c1,
     size: p1.size
   },
```

```
%Chromosome{
  genes: c2,
  size: p2.size
}}
end
```

Start by examining the first code block under the first comment. The code creates a tuple that is a random range in ascending order within the length of your chromosome.

The next block creates a slice from p1 using the range you just created. It then determines which elements from p1 are present in p2 and eliminates them from p2's contribution to the child. Finally, it splits this contribution at the first index in the range, so the elements of p2's contribution are added in the correct place in the new chromosome.

The process is repeated with p2, and the chromosomes are combined to return two new child chromosomes.

Order-one crossover is one strategy for solving problems with permutation genotypes. One drawback of order-one crossover is that it's slow. With large solutions, order-one crossover will significantly slow down your algorithm. Fortunately, most problems that use permutation genotypes are small.

Adding Crossover Customization

Before you can finish solving N-queens, you need to tweak the crossover function in genetic.ex to support custom crossover functions. Recall from the previous chapter how you used opts to extract and apply a custom crossover function. You'll do the same thing here.

First, open genetic.ex and navigate to the crossover function. Right now, it should look like this:

```
def crossover(population, opts \\ []) do
  population
  |> Enum.reduce([],
      fn {p1, p2}, acc ->
        cx_point = :rand.uniform(length(p1))
        {{h1, t1}, {h2, t2}} =
          {Enum.split(p1, cx_point),
            Enum.split(p2, cx_point)}
        {c1, c2} = {h1 ++ t2, h2 ++ t1}
        [c1, c2 | acc]
      end
  )
end
```

Remember, this function takes a list of tuples representing pairs of parents. If you notice, the actual process of crossover takes place within the body of the anonymous function passed to Enum.reduce/3. That means you can replace this code with whatever crossover function you want.

First, extract a :crossover_type parameter from opts:

```
def crossover(population opts \\ []) do
  crossover_fn = Keyword.get(opts,
                            :crossover_type,
                            &Toolbox.Crossover.order_one/2)
end
```

For now, the default can remain Toolbox.Crossover.order_one/2 because that's the only one you've implemented thus far. Next, in the body of the anonymous function in reduce, replace the code with the following:

```
# ...
|> Enum.reduce([],
    fn {p1, p2}, acc ->
      {c1, c2} = apply(crossover_fn, [p1, p2])
      [c1, c2 | acc]
    end
  )
```

Remember from the last chapter that apply/2 simply applies the given function with the given arguments.

Now, you should be set to run N-queens. Add the following to nqueens.exs below your module:

```
soln = Genetic.run(NQueens)

IO.write("\n")
IO.inspect(soln)
```

A quick note: you don't need to specify any specific crossover type because order_one/2 is the current default. You can adjust the population size, selection type, or crossover rate if you'd like.

Next, open your terminal and run the script:

```
$ mix run scripts/nqueens.exs
Current best: 8
%Types.Chromosome{
  age: 1,
  fitness: 8,
  genes: [4, 6, 1, 5, 2, 0, 3, 7],
  size: 8
}
```

Exploring Crossover

With the N-queens problem, you saw how much choosing the correct crossover strategy can affect your algorithms. Now, you need to develop an understanding of what crossover is and how it works.

Crossover is analogous to reproduction—the process of combining the genes of two chromosomes to create new chromosomes. The idea is that solutions will combine to create even better solutions—like how evolution slowly optimizes organisms to adapt and become stronger in their environment.

While the parallels between biological reproduction and crossover are neither perfect nor sound, you can better understand crossover if you have a general understanding of biology. In biology, traits are passed down to children from parents. These traits, for example, include hair color, eye color, and muscle composition. If both parents possess the same traits, the child is more likely to inherit those traits from their parents.

Now, imagine two sets of parents. One set of parents consists of two world-class distance runners. The other set of parents consists of two world-class weightlifters. Which set of parents is more likely to produce a better distance runner? The set of distance runners, because they possess and are more likely to pass on traits that contribute to success in distance running.

The same idea applies to crossover in genetic algorithms. Your goal is to take the strongest traits present in two solutions and pass them on to child solutions. Over time, your strategy will produce a fitter population.

The crossover strategy you use can have a big impact on the performance of your algorithm. Strategies are very problem-dependent. Some strategies are designed with certain genotypes in mind. Other strategies are built for speed or simplicity. In the next section, you'll see how crossover can impact the performance of a genetic algorithm.

Implementing Other Common Crossover Strategies

The goal of crossover is to produce child solutions that are better than their parents. A good crossover strategy will produce, on average, better child solutions in the long run. Additionally, a good crossover strategy will respect the genotype of your chromosome. For example, if you're using a permutation genotype, a good crossover strategy will maintain the integrity of the permutation. You don't want to use a crossover strategy that will produce invalid solutions because, eventually, all of your solutions will become invalid and your algorithm will never produce the best solution.

In this section, you'll learn about several common crossover strategies that work on all of the genotypes you've learned about so far. With these crossover strategies in place, you'll be able to effectively solve problems that use binary, permutation, and real-value genotypes. The crossover strategies you'll implement are:

- Single-point crossover
- Uniform crossover
- Whole arithmetic recombination

Additionally, you'll be introduced to a variety of more advanced crossover strategies that you can research and implement on your own.

Single-Point Crossover

Single-point crossover is the most basic crossover strategy and the one you've been using since Chapter 1, Writing Your First Genetic Algorithm, on page 1. John Holland proposed it as the crossover strategy in the original genetic algorithm. Single-point crossover is common in solving basic problems because it's the easiest to implement.

The basic algorithm for single-point crossover is:

1. Choose a random number k between 0 and n-1 where n is the length of the parent chromosomes.

2. Split both parents at k to produce four slices of genes.

3. Swap the tails of each parent at k to produce two new children.

The following picture illustrates single-point crossover:

Crossover Point = 4

This is how you would implement single-point crossover in Elixir:

```
def single_point(p1, p2) do
  cx_point = :rand.uniform(p1.size)
  {p1_head, p1_tail} = Enum.split(p1.genes, cx_point)
  {p2_head, p2_tail} = Enum.split(p2.genes, cx_point)
  {c1, c2} = {p1_head ++ p2_tail, p2_head ++ p1_tail}
  {%Chromosome{genes: c1, size: length(c1)},
    %Chromosome{genes: c2, size: length(c2)}}
end
```

First, you select a random number. Remember, :rand.uniform/1 returns a uniform random number between 0 and n-1. Next, you split both chromosomes at cx_point. Enum.split/2 returns a tuple of slices. Finally, you swap the tails of each parent to produce new children. You then wrap these children in a Chromosome struct and return them as a tuple.

The advantages of single-point crossover lie in its simplicity. It's a simple algorithm that runs very fast on solutions of all sizes. Unfortunately, single-point crossover does a poor job producing stronger solutions. This fact is especially evident when you're dealing with large solutions. Additionally, single-point crossover won't maintain the integrity of a permutation, and it might not "blend" real-value solutions like you'd need. Single-point crossover works most effectively on binary genotypes where order matters.

Single-point crossover is only useful for basic problems; however, you can use it to prototype problems and as a benchmark against other crossover strategies.

Uniform Crossover

Uniform crossover is a slightly more advanced crossover strategy in which genes in the parent chromosome are treated separately. While single-point crossover only works on blocks of genes, uniform crossover works on individual genes.

Uniform crossover works by pairing corresponding genes in a chromosome and swapping them according to a rate. The rate is a number between 0 and 1 that represents the probability that two genes will be swapped. A rate of 0.5 indicates that genes have a 50% chance of swapping between parent chromosomes.

The image on page 98 demonstrates uniform crossover.

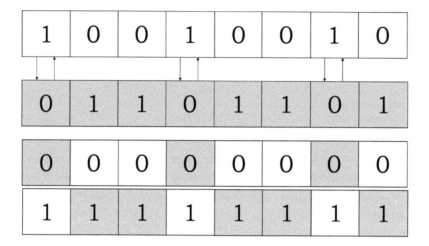

This is how you would implement uniform crossover in Elixir:

```elixir
def uniform(p1, p2, rate) do
  {c1, c2} =
    p1.genes
    |> Enum.zip(p2.genes)
    |> Enum.map(fn {x, y} ->
      if :rand.uniform() < rate do
        {x, y}
      else
        {y, x}
      end
    end)
    |> Enum.unzip()

  {%Chromosome{genes: c1, size: length(c1)},
    %Chromosome{genes: c2, size: length(c2)}}
end
```

First, you use Enum.zip/2 to pair corresponding genes from both parents. Enum.zip/2 returns a single enumerable from two enumerables with corresponding elements "zipped" in a tuple. Next, you iterate over each tuple with Enum.map/2 and swap genes according to the rate provided. Finally, you use Enum.unzip/1 to unpack the tuples back into two lists of new chromosomes.

Uniform crossover is more versatile in its ability to isolate and swap single genes that could significantly improve the fitness of child chromosomes. For example, imagine you have two parent solutions that look like the image on page 99.

| 1 | 1 | 1 | 1 | 0 | 1 | 1 | 0 |

| 1 | 1 | 1 | 1 | 1 | 0 | 0 | 1 |

If you were to try and use single-point crossover on those parent chromosomes, it would be difficult to produce solutions that effectively maximize the potential of each parent. Notice what happens when using single-point crossover at the following crossover point:

| 1 | 1 | 1 | 1 | 0 | 1 | 1 | 0 |

| 1 | 1 | 1 | 1 | 1 | 0 | 0 | 1 |

⇧ Crossover Point = 4

| 1 | 1 | 1 | 1 | 0 | 1 | 1 | 0 |

| 1 | 1 | 1 | 1 | 1 | 0 | 0 | 1 |

If you used uniform crossover, you could effectively isolate individual genes and potentially swap the correct genes to produce the best solution, like the image on page 100.

One thing to consider with uniform crossover is the impact the rate will have on its effectiveness. A higher uniform crossover rate means more genes will be swapped. A lower uniform crossover rate means fewer genes will be swapped. Think of it like this: a uniform crossover rate of 0.8 means that each child will be made up of 80% of one parent and 20% of the other. Typically, it's best to choose a rate of 0.5.

Uniform crossover doesn't work on permutations, nor will it produce desired results for most real-valued genotypes. Additionally, because uniform crossover needs to iterate over the entirety of both parent chromosomes, it can be slow

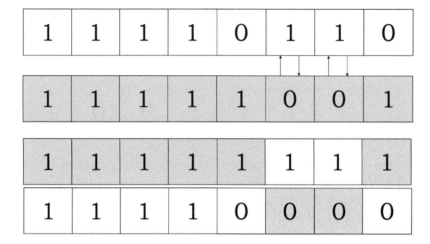

with extremely large chromosomes. Uniform crossover works best with binary genotypes. It's effective and relatively fast with small chromosomes.

Whole Arithmetic Recombination

Whole arithmetic recombination is a crossover strategy for real-value chromosomes that mathematically mixes each gene of the parents to produce children. Whole arithmetic recombination takes a percentage of each parent gene and adds them to produce new solutions. The percentage of each parent gene present in the child gene is determined by a parameter alpha.

Whole arithmetic recombination combines genes according to the formula:

$$z = x * \alpha + y * (1 - \alpha)$$

Where x and y are parent genes, and z is a resulting child gene.

That formula is applied on each corresponding gene in the parent chromosomes. One thing to note is that an alpha of 0.5 will produce identical child chromosomes.

The image on page 101 demonstrates whole arithmetic recombination.

This is how you would implement whole arithmetic recombination in Elixir:

```
def whole_arithmetic_crossover(p1, p2, alpha) do
  {c1, c2} =
    p1.genes
    |> Enum.zip(p2.genes)
    |> Enum.map(
```

| 0.9 | 0.6 | 0.8 | 0.5 | 0.2 | 0.3 | 0.1 |

| 0.5 | 0.2 | 0.4 | 0.7 | 0.6 | 0.1 | 0.9 |

Alpha = 0.5

| 0.7 | 0.4 | 0.6 | 0.6 | 0.4 | 0.2 | 0.5 |

| 0.7 | 0.4 | 0.6 | 0.6 | 0.4 | 0.2 | 0.5 |

```
    fn {x, y} ->
      {
        x*alpha + y*(1-alpha),
        x*(1-alpha) + y*alpha
      }
    end
  )
  |> Enum.unzip()
 {%Chromosome{genes: c1, size: length(c1)},
   %Chromosome{genes: c2, size: length(c2)}}
end
```

Because whole arithmetic recombination also works on corresponding genes in the parents, you use Enum.zip/2 to pair genes like in uniform crossover. Next, you use Enum.map/2 to iterate over each pair and combine them according to the formula mentioned earlier. Finally, you use Enum.unzip/2 to return two new sets of genes.

Whole arithmetic recombination is a basic strategy for combining real-value chromosomes. One issue it has is its tendency to converge quickly on poor solutions. Because there's no randomness involved, all chromosomes will inevitably become the same without other strategies to prevent premature convergence. You can defeat this by only combining a percentage of genes in the chromosome.

Whole arithmetic recombination, like uniform crossover, iterates over entire chromosomes. This means it will be slower on larger solutions. It can be useful with floating-point solutions—like in portfolio optimization and determining what percentage of your portfolio to allocate to each asset.

Other Crossover Strategies

Numerous algorithms for implementing crossover on various genotypes are available, such as:

- Messy single-point: messy crossover strategy doesn't preserve the length of chromosomes.

- Cycle: crossover on ordered list using cycles.

- Multi-point: crossover at multiple points.

You can find these algorithms online and attempt to implement them yourself.

Crossing Over More Than Two Parents

Some algorithms require you to select more than two parents for crossover. All of the algorithms presented above can be implemented on multiple parents.

Here's an example of single-point crossover on multiple parents:

```
def single_point_crossover([]), do:
  raise "You must have at least one parent!"
def single_point_crossover([p1 | []]), do: p1

def single_point_crossover(parents) do
    crossover_point = :rand.uniform(hd(parents).size)
    parents
    |> Enum.chunk_every(2, 1, [hd(parents)])
    |> Enum.map(&(List.to_tuple(&1)))
    |> Enum.reduce(
        [],
        fn {p1, p2}, chd ->
            {front, _} = Enum.split(p1.genes, crossover_point)
            {_, back} = Enum.split(p2.genes, crossover_point)
            c = %Chromosome{genes: front ++ back, size: length(p1)}
            [c | chd]
        end
    )
end
```

Start by examining the first two function definitions. Thanks to Elixir's rich set of pattern matching features, you can define functions on specific inputs. The first definition is to ensure that the function doesn't accept empty lists. The next definition simply returns the same chromosome if only one parent is provided.

The next function will work on a list of an arbitrary number of parents. The function starts by selecting a crossover point between 0 and the length of the first parent.

Now, examine this code block:

```
parents
|> Enum.chunk_every(2, 1, [hd(parents)])
|> Enum.map(&(List.to_tuple(&1)))
```

Enum.chunk_every/3 will pair every parent into groupings of two starting at index 1. The last argument, [hd(parents)], tells the function to group the leftover elements with the first element of parents. Then, each element is transformed into a tuple to make pattern matching easier.

Now, examine the final block:

```
|> Enum.reduce(
    [],
    fn {p1, p2}, chd ->
        {front, _} = Enum.split(p1.genes, crossover_point)
        {_, back} = Enum.split(p2.genes, crossover_point)
        c = %Chromosome{genes: front ++ back, size: length(p1)}
        [c | chd]
    end
```

Enum.reduce/3 takes an enumerable, an accumulator, and a function as input. The enumerable is the list of tuples that represent pairs of parents. The accumulator is an empty list. The function simply implements single-point crossover on each pairing of parents and returns the child at the front of the accumulator.

This same algorithm can be implemented for each crossover strategy, replacing the body of the anonymous function in Enum.reduce/3 with whatever strategy you want.

Crossing over more than two parents can add a lot of unnecessary complexity to your algorithms. It's best not to use this approach unless you absolutely have to.

Implementing Chromosome Repairment

Sometimes, you're limited in the crossover strategy you can use. In Chapter 4, Evaluating Solutions and Populations, on page 51, you explored a solution to the N-queens problem that wouldn't work because you used single-point crossover.

One approach that works around limitations in crossover strategies is the concept of *chromosome repairment*. Chromosome repairment is the process of ensuring solutions remain valid after crossover or mutation. In the case of N-queens, using single-point crossover ruins the integrity of the permutation. This means after crossover takes place, you have to go in and individually repair every chromosome.

Chromosome repairment isn't necessary if you choose a crossover strategy that maintains the integrity of your permutation; however, if you're restricted to using specific crossover strategies, then it will be necessary. To implement chromosome repairment into your genetic algorithm, add the following to crossover/1 in lib/genetic.ex:

```
def crossover(population, opts \\ []) do
  crossover_fn = Keyword.get(opts,
                             :crossover_type,
                             Toolbox.Crossover.single_point/2)
  population
  |> Enum.reduce([],
       fn {p1, p2}, acc ->
         {c1, c2} = apply(crossover_fn, [p1, p2])
         [c1, c2 | acc]
     )
  |> Enum.map(& repair_chromosome(&1))
end
```

The addition of Enum.map/2 will go through each chromosome in the population and call repair_chromosome/1, which is a function that will repair chromosomes. Now, implement the repair_chromosome/1 function like this:

```
def repair_chromosome(chromosome) do
  genes = MapSet.new(chromosome.genes)
  new_genes = repair_helper(chromosome, 8)
  %Chromosome{chromosome | genes: new_genes}
end
defp repair_helper(chromosome, k) do
  if MapSet.size(chromosome) >= k do
    MapSet.to_list(chromosome)
  else
    num = :rand.uniform(8)
    repair_helper(MapSet.put(chromosome, num), k)
  end
end
```

Here, you use a MapSet to get the unique elements of the provided chromosome. Next, you pass it into a recursive helper. The helper function will generate random numbers and attempt to put them into the MapSet until the chromosome is the appropriate length.

Now, if you change crossover/1 back to use single_point_crossover/2, you can run scripts/nqueens.exs and obtain a solution:

```
$ mix run scripts/nqueens.exs
Current Best: 8
[3, 6, 2, 7, 1, 4, 0, 5]
```

What You Learned

In this chapter, you learned about the importance of crossover and how crossover helps genetic algorithms exploit in search. You learned about N-queens and how choosing an appropriate crossover strategy affects the outcome of your algorithms.

You also learned four different types of crossover strategies that can be applied to different genotypes. Single-point crossover is the most basic and is only useful with binary genotypes. Uniform crossover is a slightly more useful crossover strategy, but it doesn't preserve order in permutations. Order-one crossover is a crossover strategy specifically for permutation genotypes. Whole arithmetic recombination is a basic strategy for real-value genotypes.

With these four strategies, you have the ability to solve a wide variety of problems with different genotypes. You also should have a basic understanding of what strategies will work with different genotypes.

Finally, you learned about other less common techniques for generating new solutions, including crossing over multiple parents and chromosome repairment.

In the next chapter, you'll explore how selection and crossover alone can lead to problems in your algorithm, and you'll see how mutation addresses these problems.

## CHAPTER 7

Preventing Premature Convergence

The previous two chapters were dedicated to the process of making better populations from an existing population. Chapter 5, Selecting the Best, on page 71, focused on choosing solutions for reproduction that give you the best opportunity to increase the overall fitness of your population. Chapter 6, Generating New Solutions, on page 87, focused specifically on the process of creating new solutions.

Correctly applying selection and crossover on populations is vital to the success of your genetic algorithms. Selection and crossover alone are sufficient for a complete genetic algorithm—you don't need any additional steps for varying your population if you don't want to. However, using selection and crossover alone can lead you into a common pitfall: *premature convergence.*

Premature convergence refers to the stalling of progress in your algorithms as a result of a lack of genetic diversity in your population. As you saw in Chapter 5, Selecting the Best, on page 71, over time, populations tend to drift toward a similar genetic pattern. To understand why this can be problematic, consider this small population of binary chromosomes as shown in the image on page 108.

Notice the first gene in every chromosome. If your objective was to maximize the number of 1s in each sequence, it would be impossible for you to reach an optimal solution with crossover alone. The first gene in every chromosome is a 0—there's no way to turn that gene into a 1. In practice, you would call this a *converged allele.*

Remember from Chapter 3, Encoding Problems and Solutions, on page 33, an allele is simply the value of a particular gene. A converged allele is one that is the same in a majority of the solutions of the population.

0	1	1	0	0
0	1	0	1	1
0	0	0	1	1
0	1	1	0	0
0	0	1	0	1

While it's not practical to have a population size of 5 with chromosomes of size 5, it doesn't mean this phenomenon isn't possible in practice. In the next section, you'll implement a genetic algorithm with and without mutation to see the very real impact of premature convergence.

Population Diversity and Premature Convergence

It's generally agreed upon that mutation works to prevent premature convergence because it helps maintain population diversity. It's understood that a decrease in population diversity has a direct correlation to premature convergence; however, there's no real formalized understanding or measures of population diversity. So, while you may intuitively understand your algorithm stopped improving because there's insufficient diversity in the population, there's no formal definition for when a population is considered converged.

Breaking Codes with Genetic Algorithms

Imagine that you've been tasked with protecting the integrity of your firm's data. One day, a hacker manages to get on your system and encrypts all of your data before demanding a ransom to decrypt it.

Luckily, the hacker decided to use a basic XOR cipher with what appears to be a 64-bit key. That means, if you're able to determine the key, you'll be able to easily apply the cipher in reverse to restore all of your data.

XOR ciphers are reversible ciphers that work by applying a bitwise XOR with a key on every character in a string. Unicode characters are represented with 16-bits. Given a key and a string, you can encrypt the string by applying an

XOR of every character with your key. The following image demonstrates this process:

Encrypted: "NMLK"	N 01001110	M 01001101	L 01001100	K 01001011

XOR $\oplus$

Key: 15	Key = 15 00001111	Key = 15 00001111	Key = 15 00001111	Key = 15 00001111

	01001110 $\oplus$ 00001111	01001101 $\oplus$ 00001111	01001100 $\oplus$ 00001111	01001011 $\oplus$ 00001111

Plain Text: "ABCD"	A 01000001	B 01000010	C 01000011	D 01000100

To decrypt an XOR cipher, you can apply the same process in reverse—if you know the key. XOR is the inverse of itself, so you can apply the cipher on encrypted text with the same key to obtain the decrypted version. The following image illustrates this:

Plain Text: "ABCD"	A 01000001	B 01000010	C 01000011	D 01000100

XOR $\oplus$

Key: 10	Key = 15 00001111	Key = 15 00001111	Key = 15 00001111	Key = 15 00001111

	01000001 $\oplus$ 00001111	01000010 $\oplus$ 00001111	01000011 $\oplus$ 00001111	01000100 $\oplus$ 00001111

Encrypted: "NMLK"	N 01001110	M 01001101	L 01001100	K 01001011

Because of the hacker's choice to use a basic XOR cipher, all you need to do is find the 64-bit key they used to encrypt your data. Unfortunately, it's not feasible to search through all 2^64 possible keys. Instead, it makes sense to use a genetic algorithm.

Representing the Problem

First, create a new file scripts/codebreaker.exs.

Next, create the shell of your Problem definition:

```
defmodule Codebreaker do
  @behaviour Problem
  alias Types.Chromosome
  use Bitwise

  def genotype, do: # genotype

  def fitness_function(chromosome), do: # fitness

  def terminate?(population, generation), do: # population
end
```

Notice the additional use Bitwise at the beginning of your module definition. You'll need this to implement the fitness function.

Now you need to implement your problem-specific functions.

You're trying to find the 64-bit key the hacker used to encrypt your information. Naturally, you'll want to represent your chromosome as a bitstring with 64-bits:

```
def genotype do
  genes = for _ <- 1..64, do: Enum.random(0..1)
  %Chromosome{genes: genes, size: 64}
end
```

Here, you generate random binary genotypes of size 64 and return a new Chromosome struct.

Evaluating and Stopping

Next, you need a way of evaluating how close you are to finding the correct key. Luckily, you remember one of the names of the files on your desktop: ILoveGeneticAlgorithms. It appears the name of this file has been changed to LIjs`B`k`qlfDibjwlqmhv. Given you have an encrypted string, and you know the decrypted version, you can guess a key and apply it on your encrypted string to see how close it gets you to the decrypted version.

Implement your fitness function like this:

```
def fitness_function(chromosome) do
  target = 'ILoveGeneticAlgorithms'
  encrypted = 'LIjs`B`k`qlfDibjwlqmhv'
  cipher = fn word, key -> Enum.map(word, rem(& &1 ^^^ key, 32768)) end
  key =
    chromosome.genes
    |> Enum.map(& Integer.to_string(&1))
    |> Enum.join("")
    |> String.to_integer(2)

  guess = List.to_string(cipher.(encrypted, key))
  String.jaro_distance(target, guess)
end
```

You start the function by declaring your target, which is the correctly decrypted version of one of your encrypted filenames, as a charlist. You also define encrypted in the same way. Next, you define a basic XOR cipher which iterates through each character in a provided word and applies an XOR before taking the remainder of the result of the XOR and 32768 to ensure your guessed cipher has codepoints within the usable character range for Elixir strings.

The next step generates an integer key from the provided chromosome. Your chromosomes are lists of 1s and 0s. To convert the list of 1s and 0s to a decimal integer, you need to convert the list to a string and then parse the string with a base 2, indicating the number is a binary representation of an integer.

After you've defined your key, you need to generate a guess from your key. The guess is just an attempt at decrypting encrypted with the key your chromosome represents. Finally, you compare your guess with the target using String.jaro_distance/2. String.jaro_distance/2 is a measure of the similarity between two strings. It returns a value between 0 and 1, with 1 meaning the compared strings are identical.

Because your fitness function returns 1 only when the strings are identical, you can safely assume that you've identified the correct key when the fitness of a chromosome is 1. Therefore, your termination criteria is this:

```
def terminate?(population, _generation), do:
  Enum.max_by(population, &Codebreaker.fitness_function/1).fitness == 1
```

Running the Algorithm

Now, add the following below your module definition:

```
soln = Genetic.run(Codebreaker,
                  crossover_type: &Toolbox.Crossover.single_point/2)
```

```
{key, ""} =
  soln.genes
  |> Enum.map(& Integer.to_string(&1))
  |> Enum.join("")
  |> Integer.parse(2)

IO.write "\nThe Key is #{key}\n"
```

With your algorithm complete, you're ready to run. First, go to lib/genetic.ex and edit the evolve/3 function to run generations without mutation by commenting out the mutation line, like this:

```
def evolve(population, problem, generation, opts \\ []) do
  population = evaluate(population, &problem.fitness_function/1, opts)
  best = hd(population)
  IO.write("\rCurrent best: #{best.fitness}\tGeneration: #{generation}")
  if problem.terminate?(population, generation) do
    best
  else
    {parents, leftover} = select(population, opts)
    children = crossover(parents, opts)
    children ++ leftover
    # |> mutation(opts)
    |> evolve(problem, generation+1, opts)
  end
end
```

Now, run your algorithm like this:

```
$ mix run examples/codebreaker.exs
Current Best: 0.273
```

After awhile, you might get tired of your algorithm running and not making any progress. More than likely, your algorithm is suffering from premature convergence. Uncomment the mutation/1 function in run/2 and try running your algorithm again:

```
$ mix run examples/codebreaker.exs
Current Best: 1.000
Key is 2491717835680677893
```

To see that this key is, in fact, the correct key, open up iex and use it to uncipher your encrypted string, like this:

```
$ iex
iex(1)> use Bitwise
Bitwise
iex(2)> key = 2491717835680677893
2491717835680677893
iex(3)> cipher = fn word, key -> Enum.map(word, & rem(&1 ^^^ key, 32768)) end
```

```
#Function<13.126501267/2 in :erl_eval.expr/5>
iex(4)> List.to_string(cipher.('LIjs`B`k`qlfDibjwlqmhv', key))
"ILoveGeneticAlgorithms"
```

Congratulations, you've cracked the code.

Understanding Mutation

As with most of the other aspects of a genetic algorithm, mutation has a loose analogy to a real biological process. In biology, mutation is a random change in an individual's DNA sequence that often manifests itself in physical traits. For example, if you have blue eyes, you can thank genetic mutation.

Mutation in genetic algorithms works in much the same way. It's a random change to some or all of the genes in a chromosome. The purpose of mutation is to introduce genetic diversity into the population.

If you recall from Chapter 1, Writing Your First Genetic Algorithm, on page 1, the algorithm you wrote to solve the One-Max problem struggled to find the best solution until you added mutation. When dealing with binary geno-types, premature convergence is more common because genes can only take on one of two values. The possibility of premature convergence increases when dealing with small population sizes relative to your search space.

Stimulating Change

Mutation works by stimulating change—it prevents your algorithm from becoming complacent. Imagine you roll a ball down a small hill. Halfway down the hill there's a slight rise in elevation, but afterwards, the hill declines again very sharply. You roll the ball down the hill, but it doesn't have enough momentum to make it over the bump. What do you do? You give it a little push. You can visualize this in the following image:

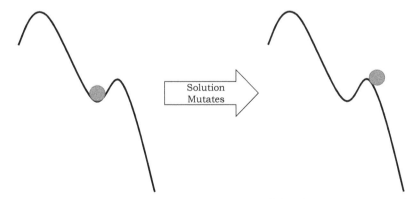

Solution Cannot Improve in Either Direction   Solution Can Improve Downwards

The purpose of mutation is to give your algorithms a little push in a different, possibly better direction. Mutations drive change when selection and crossover are otherwise not enough. The goal of mutation is to introduce new solutions that may improve upon or be better than old ones.

One thing that's important to note is that premature convergence doesn't necessarily mean your algorithm has reached a global or even local optimum. That is to say, premature convergence doesn't mean your algorithm has found good solutions. Premature convergence simply means you're no longer able to produce different solutions due to a lack of population diversity.

A final consideration is that while the intent of mutation is to stimulate change, it can be difficult to quantify whether or not it actually works. Genetic algorithms are sensitive to the random nature of their operators. Mutation is random, and sometimes it doesn't improve your algorithms at all. For example, perhaps your first solution to the codebreaking problem converged faster than your second. It's hard to predict or even prove that mutation will offer you any benefits at all. Sometimes you just have to try it.

Balancing Diversity and Fitness

The key struggle with mutation is finding a balance between population diversity and overall fitness.

Remember from Chapter 1, Writing Your First Genetic Algorithm, on page 1, the struggle between exploration and exploitation. Mutation is a means of exploration. If you mutate too much, your algorithm works essentially the same as random search, and you have no way of exploiting the environment around you.

Mutation rate is the rate at which you mutate chromosomes. Some genetic algorithms call for the mutation of every child, some call for the mutation of only a few children, and some call for the mutation of only surviving chromosomes. The choice of *who* to mutate isn't necessarily as important to your algorithm as the choice of *how many* you mutate.

A mutation rate of 5% essentially means that you mutate about 5% of your population every generation. It's common to have a mutation rate at or around 5%, because it's low enough that it still allows your algorithm to progress but high enough that it maintains the genetic diversity of your population. You may want to experiment with different mutation rates to see how they affect your algorithms.

One uncommon technique is to use a changing mutation rate. For example, you might want your mutation rate to decay over time—indicating that your algorithm should stop exploring at later generations. This technique is common with learning rates in other machine learning algorithms, but it's not as effective with genetic algorithms.

Mutation Aggressiveness

An additional parameter that's not often mentioned with mutation is the notion of *mutation aggressiveness*. The aggressiveness of a mutation dictates how much it changes a chromosome. For example, you can choose to change all of the genes in a chromosome with new genes, or you can choose to replace only some.

Most of the algorithms you find online will opt to mutate the entire chromosome, but sometimes you might find it useful to further control your mutations. In a later section, you'll see exactly how you can introduce additional parameters to control how aggressive your mutations are.

Customizing Mutation in Your Framework

Just like in Chapter 5, Selecting the Best, on page 71, and Chapter 6, Generating New Solutions, on page 87, you'll need to slightly modify your framework to allow you to customize mutation hyperparameters. These hyperparameters are mutation strategy and mutation rate.

In this section, you'll create a mutation toolbox and modify your framework to allow you to easily customize mutation in your algorithms.

Creating the Toolbox

First, you need to create a mutation toolbox, just like you created a selection and crossover toolbox. Create a new file in toolbox called mutation.ex.

Next, create the Toolbox.Mutation module, like this:

```
defmodule Toolbox.Mutation do
  alias Types.Chromosome

  # ...
end
```

You'll be working a lot with the Chromosome struct in this module, so you'll want to create an alias. Now, whenever you implement a new mutation strategy, you'll add it to your mutation toolbox.

Changing Mutation Strategy

Open up genetic.ex and navigate to the mutation/2 function. It looks like this:

```
def mutation(population, opts \\ []) do
  population
  |> Enum.map(
      fn chromosome ->
        if :rand.uniform() < 0.05 do
          %Chromosome{genes: Enum.shuffle(chromosome.genes)}
        else
          chromosome
        end
      end
    )
end
```

Remember, opts is a Keyword representing the options you can pass to your algorithm when you call Genetic.run/2. First, you need to extract a mutation strategy from opts, like this:

```
mutate_fn = Keyword.get(opts, :mutation_type, &Toolbox.Mutation.flip/1)
```

Right now, the default is called flip mutation, which is a mutation strategy you'll implement in the next section. You can change this default to another method if you prefer.

Next, you need to apply your mutation strategy to chromosomes in the population. Change the body of Enum.map/2 to look like this:

```
|> Enum.map(
    fn chromosome ->
      if :rand.uniform() < 0.05 do
        apply(mutate_fn, [chromosome])
      else
        chromosome
      end
    )
```

Here you use apply/2 to apply your extracted mutation strategy to chromosome. The mutation strategies you'll implement in this chapter accept a chromosome and return the mutated chromosome, so apply/2 returns a mutated version of chromosome.

Adjusting Mutation Rate

You also need a way to control the mutation rate of your algorithm. Start by extracting :mutation_rate from opts:

```
mutate_fn = Keyword.get(opts, :mutation_type, &Toolbox.Mutation.flip/1)
rate = Keyword.get(opts, :mutation_rate, 0.05)
```

0.05 represents a mutation rate of 5%, which is a good default.

Next, you need to change Enum.map/2 to only mutate chromosomes according to rate. To do this, change the if-condition to look like this:

```
|> Enum.map(
    fn chromosome ->
      if :rand.uniform() < rate do
        apply(mutate_fn, [chromosome])
      else
        chromosome
      end
    )
```

Your new mutation/2 function should look like this:

```
def mutation(population, opts \\ []) do
  mutate_fn = Keyword.get(opts, :mutation_type, &Toolbox.Mutation.scramble/1)
  rate = Keyword.get(opts, :mutation_rate, 0.05)
  population
  |> Enum.map(
      fn chromosome ->
        if :rand.uniform() < rate do
          apply(mutate_fn, [chromosome])
        else
          chromosome
        end
      end
    )
end
```

Implementing Common Mutation Strategies

You'll likely only ever need to work with a few mutation strategies depending on the genotype of your solutions. The mutation strategy you use has less of an impact on your algorithm than, say, crossover strategy or selection strategy. The presence of mutation matters more—so long as the mutation strategy you choose maintains the validity of your solutions.

In this section, you'll learn how to implement three different types of mutation that you can use for binary, permutation, and real-value genotypes. At the end of this section, you'll find a list of other common mutation strategies to research and implement on your own.

Flip Mutation

Flip mutation, also known as bit flip mutation, is the type of mutation proposed in the Holland's original genetic algorithm. It's simple and effective on binary genotypes. Flip mutation "flips" some or all of the bits in the chromosome. So, if a gene is a 1, it's flipped to a 0. If a gene is a 0, it's flipped to a 1.

The following image depicts flip mutation:

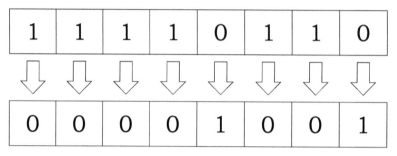

Flip mutation can be implemented in a few lines of code using Elixir's Enum library. First, at the top of your Toolbox.Mutation module, add the following line:

```
use Bitwise
```

Bitwise is a module in the Elixir standard library for working with bitwise operations. Bitwise is applicable here because flip mutation is essentially just a bitwise XOR between 1 and the value of a gene. XOR with 1 produces the desired flip because 1 XOR 1 is 0 and 0 XOR 1 is 1.

To implement flip mutation in Elixir, add the following code to your Toolbox.Mutation module:

```
def flip(chromosome) do
  genes =
    chromosome.genes
    |> Enum.map(& &1 ^^^ 1)

  %Chromosomes{genes: genes, size: chromosome.size}
end
```

This function maps over every gene in chromosome and performs a bitwise XOR with the value at the gene and 1. Of course, this function changes *every* gene in the chromosome. Sometimes, you want to implement something less aggressive. The following function performs flip mutation with a given probability:

```
def flip(chromosome, p) do
  genes =
    chromosome.genes
    |> Enum.map(
        fn g ->
```

```
      if :rand.uniform() < p do
        g ^^^ 1
      else
        g
      end
    end
  )

  %Chromosome{genes: genes, size: chromosome.size}
end
```

This function simply adds a "coin-flip" to determine which genes to flip. The probability of a gene being flipped is equal to the provided parameter p. You can modify this p to adjust the aggressiveness of the flip mutation. In practice, a probability of around 50%, or 50% of the genes in a chromosome being flipped, is usually suitable.

Flip mutation is simple and effective. One drawback, however, is that it only applies to binary genotypes.

Scramble Mutation

Scramble mutation is the type of mutation you implemented in Chapter 1, Writing Your First Genetic Algorithm, on page 1. You simply shuffled all of the genes in a given chromosome to create a new chromosome. While shuffling the bits had no impact on the fitness of a chromosome, it served to ensure some percentage of your population remained different from the rest.

Scramble mutation is versatile in that it can apply to almost all genotypes. You saw it in practice with binary genotypes, but it also can apply to permutation genotypes and some real-value genotypes.

Scramble mutation is like shuffling a deck of cards. The following image demonstrates scramble mutation on a permutation genotype:

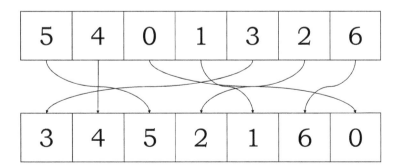

You can implement scramble mutation in Elixir using the Enum.shuffle/1 method. The following function demonstrates scramble mutation:

```elixir
def scramble(chromosome) do
  genes =
    chromosome.genes
    |> Enum.shuffle()

  %Chromosome{genes: genes, size: chromosome.size}
end
```

This function uses Enum.shuffle/1 to scramble or randomize all of the genes in the chromosome to create a new chromosome. You can also implement scramble mutation on a random slice of size n, like this:

```elixir
def scramble(chromosome, n) do
  start = :rand.uniform(n-1)
  {lo, hi} =
    if start + n >= chromosome.size do
      {start - n, start}
    else
      {start, start + n}
    end
  head = Enum.slice(chromosome.genes, 0, lo)
  mid = Enum.slice(chromosome.genes, lo, hi)
  tail = Enum.slice(chromosome.genes, hi, chromosome.size)
  %Chromosome{genes: head ++ Enum.shuffle(mid) ++ tail, size: chromosome.size}
end
```

In this function, you pick a start point for your random slice. You then choose whether to slice forward or backward, based on the start point. Once you determine lo and hi, you divide your chromosome into three slices: head, mid, and tail. You recombine the slices, but shuffle mid.

Scramble mutation is versatile and effective. It does a good job of ensuring chromosomes change sufficiently to avoid premature convergence.

Gaussian Mutation

Gaussian mutation is a mutation operator meant specifically for real-value representations of chromosomes. It generates *Gaussian random numbers* based on the provided chromosome. A Gaussian random number is just a random number from a *normal distribution*.

The normal distribution is perhaps the most common distribution in statistics. If you know what a bell curve is, then you know what the normal distribution is. It's a bell curve centered around 0 that slopes off in both directions as shown in the image on page 121.

Standard Normal Curve

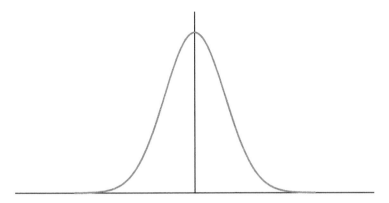

In Gaussian mutation, you calculate the mean and standard deviation of the genes in the chromosome, and then use them to generate numbers in the distribution.

The idea behind Gaussian mutation is that you are able to slightly adjust a chromosome without changing it too much. The random numbers that replace the genes in your chromosome belong to the same distribution as the existing genes in your chromosome. It's like picking new CEOs and managers from inside a company, rather than introducing new personnel to the mix.

To implement Gaussian mutation in Elixir, you first need to calculate the mean and standard deviation, and then you generate new numbers at every gene with :rand.normal/2. :rand.normal/2 pulls random numbers from a Gaussian or normal distribution. This code implements Gaussian mutation:

```elixir
def gaussian(chromosome) do
  mu = Enum.sum(chromosome.genes) / length(chromosome.genes)

  sigma =
    chromosome.genes
    |> Enum.map(fn x -> (mu - x) * (mu - x) end)
    |> Enum.sum()
    |> Kernel./(length(chromosome.genes))

  genes =
    chromosome.genes
    |> Enum.map(fn _ ->
      :rand.normal(mu, sigma)
    end)

  %Chromosome{genes: genes, size: chromosome.size}
end
```

The variable mu represents the mean of the genes in the chromosome which is calculated by the sum of the genes divided by the length of the genes. sigma represents the standard deviation which is calculated by the sum of the distance squared between every gene in the chromosome and the mean divided by the length. You can think of standard deviation as a measure of how far something is from the mean.

After you calculate mu and sigma, you map through every gene in the chromosome and replace it with a number using :rand.normal/2.

Gaussian mutation is useful for real-value genotypes. It's perhaps one of the most effective types of mutation for real-value genotypes because it introduces diversity to the population with small, incremental changes. Over time, Gaussian mutation does a great job of balancing diversity and fitness.

Other Mutation Strategies

Numerous mutation strategies aim to maintain the diversity of your population while also increasing the overall fitness of your population. Some are specific to specific genotypes and others are generalized for all genotypes. Below is a list of just a few. See if you can implement them:

- Swap: swap random pairs of genes.
- Uniform: replace genes with uniform random numbers.
- Invert: invert the order of the chromosome.

Other Methods to Combat Convergence

Mutation is the most common method for preventing premature convergence in the real world. This is largely because it's so effective.

While mutation is the most common method of preventing premature convergence, other methods exist. In Chapter 5, Selecting the Best, on page 71, you saw how important it was to select sufficiently different chromosomes for crossover. A proper selection strategy can go a long way in preventing premature convergence.

Choosing an effective crossover strategy is another means of preventing premature convergence. For example, if you use uniform crossover instead of single-point crossover, your algorithms are less susceptible to premature convergence.

Yet another means is by replacing similar individuals with new children—this is something you'll explore further in Chapter 8, Replacing and Transitioning, on page 125.

A ton of research is dedicated to methods of preventing genetic algorithms from converging. You might find it interesting to research and implement some theoretical strategies on your own.

In practice, you'll likely never need more than a good mutation strategy to keep your algorithms from converging too soon.

What You Learned

In this chapter, you learned about premature convergence and some of the conditions that lead to premature convergence. You saw how mutation can help prevent premature convergence and learned about what mutation is and how it works.

You also implemented flip mutation, scramble mutation, and Gaussian mutation that you can use for binary, permutation, and real-value genotypes, respectively. You saw how to add additional parameters to adjust the aggressiveness of these mutations, and you learned which ones are the best to implement for different problems.

Finally, you briefly learned about other strategies for preventing premature convergence and how mutation is the most common and often all you need.

In the next chapter, you'll learn how to move on from old populations and how to combine the parents, children, and mutants that you've been producing in the previous chapters.

## CHAPTER 8

Replacing and Transitioning

In the previous three chapters, your primary focus was on transforming the existing population of chromosomes into a better population using selection, crossover, and mutation.

In Chapter 5, Selecting the Best, on page 71, you isolated a collection of chromosomes to be used as parents. You learned that it's important that your parents are both fit and genetically diverse—so you can avoid premature convergence. In Chapter 6, Generating New Solutions, on page 87, you learned how to take chosen parents and use them to create new solutions. In Chapter 7, Preventing Premature Convergence, on page 107, you learned about mutation and how you can use it to stop your algorithms from converging too early.

Each of these steps—selection, crossover, and mutation—accepted a collection of chromosomes and transformed the collection in some way to produce a new collection of chromosomes. At this point, you can divide your population into three categories: parents, children, and leftovers.

You have three groups of chromosomes from which to choose, and you need to combine them in such a way that your new population retains the strengths of old chromosomes while integrating the strengths of new chromosomes. Ideally, good selection, crossover, and mutation strategies would effectively capture the strongest traits of older generations and combine them to make stronger generations; however, the process of combining the products of all of these steps is crucial to the success of an evolution.

The process of combining the byproducts of selection, crossover, and mutation into a new population is known as *reinsertion* or *replacement*. Both of these terms mean essentially the same thing; however, you'll learn about some of the minute differences later on in this chapter.

For the remainder of this chapter, you'll explore several approaches to reinsertion and replacement by applying different approaches to a realistic problem: creating the best class schedule for your next college semester.

Creating a Class Schedule

Imagine you're trying to decide what classes you should sign up for for the fall semester. You can choose from the following classes: Algorithms, Artificial Intelligence, Calculus, Chemistry, Data Structures, Discrete Math, History, Literature, Physics, and Volleyball. You can only take eighteen credits. Additionally, you weigh each of these classes based on their difficulty, usefulness to you, and your own interest in them. You've rated each class in each of these categories from 1 to 10. To keep things simple, you weigh each of these criteria evenly.

Your goal is to make the best possible schedule according to these criteria that also meets your credit-hour limitation. You've already assigned weights to each class according to the following table:

Class	Credit Hours	Difficulty	Usefulness	Interest
Algorithms	3.0	8.0	8.0	8.0
Artificial Intelligence	3.0	9.0	9.0	8.0
Calculus	3.0	4.0	6.0	5.0
Chemistry	4.5	3.0	2.0	9.0
Data Structures	3.0	5.0	8.0	7.0
Discrete Math	3.0	2.0	9.0	2.0
History	3.0	4.0	1.0	8.0
Literature	3.0	2.0	2.0	2.0
Physics	4.5	6.0	5.0	7.0
Volleyball	1.5	1.0	1.0	10.0

This is a constrained optimization problem with multiple objectives—meaning, it's perfect to address using a genetic algorithm.

Start by creating a new file schedule.exs in scripts. Next, in schedule.exs outline a basic Problem implementation, like this:

```
defmodule Schedule do
  @behaviour Problem
  alias Types.Chromosome

  @impl true
  def genotype, do: # ...
```

```
@impl true
def fitness_function(chromosome), do: # ...

@impl true
def terminate?(population, generation), do: # ...
end
```

Now all you have to do is implement each of these functions and run your algorithm.

Representing Schedules

The easiest way to represent a schedule is with a binary genotype. A binary genotype ensures the size of your chromosome remains fixed, even with a varying number of classes in your schedule.

In this case, each index represents a specific class. The value at that index, 1 or 0, represents whether or not you're taking that class. The schedule [1, 1, 0, 0, 0, 1, 0, 0, 1, 1] means you're taking Algorithms, Artificial Intelligence, Discrete Math, Physics, and Volleyball.

Implement genotype/0 like this:

```
def genotype do
  genes = for _ <- 1..10, do: Enum.random(0..1)
  %Chromosome{genes: genes, size: 10}
end
```

You've seen this before in problems like the One-Max problem, introduced in Chapter 1, Writing Your First Genetic Algorithm, on page 1. You create a binary genotype of size 10 with a for-comprehension.

Evaluating Schedules

Evaluating a schedule is a bit tricky. First, you need to equally weigh all of your criteria: difficulty, usefulness, and interest. Second, you obviously want to maximize interest and usefulness while minimizing difficulty. Third, you need to consider the constraint of eighteen credit hours when constructing schedules.

You've decided to weigh each criteria evenly, so difficulty, usefulness, and interest are all worth 33% of a class's final rating. You can use each of these weights to calculate the fitness of each schedule as a sum of each weighted criteria. Additionally, you'll have to introduce a penalty for schedules that don't meet your credit-hour obligation. Because it's possible for a schedule to be rated negatively, you'll want your penalty to be a really large negative value, like -99999.

Implement fitness_function/1 like this:

```elixir
def fitness_function(chromosome) do
  schedule = chromosome.genes
  fitness =
    [schedule, difficulties(), usefulness(), interest()]
    |> Enum.zip()
    |> Enum.map(
        fn {class, diff, use, int} ->
          class * (0.3*use + 0.3*int - 0.3*diff)
        end
      )
    |> Enum.sum()
  credit =
    schedule
    |> Enum.zip(credit_hours())
    |> Enum.map(fn {class, credits} -> class * credits end)
    |> Enum.sum()

  if credit > 18.0, do: -99999, else: fitness
end

defp credit_hours, do: [3.0, 3.0, 3.0, 4.5, 3.0, 3.0, 3.0, 3.0, 4.5, 1.5]
defp difficulties, do: [8.0, 9.0, 4.0, 3.0, 5.0, 2.0, 4.0, 2.0, 6.0, 1.0]
defp usefulness, do: [8.0, 9.0, 6.0, 2.0, 8.0, 9.0, 1.0, 2.0, 5.0, 1.0]
defp interest, do: [8.0, 8.0, 5.0, 9.0, 7.0, 2.0, 8.0, 2.0, 7.0, 10.0]
```

Quite a bit is going on here. First, you define each of the associated criteria values outside of the function for clarity. Next, you use Enum.zip/1 to combine all of these values into a tuple. Then you use Enum.map/2 to determine the score for each class based on criteria and whether or not it's present in the schedule. Finally, you calculate the number of credit hours in a schedule, and if it exceeds the limit, return -99999; otherwise, you return fitness.

All that's left to do is define some termination criteria and run the algorithm.

Terminating and Running

Because you don't know the exact fitness of the optimal schedule, you'll terminate based on the generation. 1000 generations is sufficient, but you can experiment with evolving for more or less generations. Implement terminate?/2 like this:

```elixir
def terminate?(_population, generation), do: generation == 1000
```

Next, you need to run your algorithm. Add the following below Schedule:

```elixir
soln = Genetic.run(Schedule)

IO.write("\n")
IO.inspect(soln.genes)
```

Now, run the algorithm:

```
$ mix run scripts/schedule.exs
Current best: 14.7000 Generation: 1000
%Types.Chromosome{
  age: 1,
  fitness: 14.7,
  genes: [0, 1, 1, 0, 1, 1, 1, 0, 0, 1],
  size: 10
}
```

According to this evolution, the best schedule is [0, 1, 1, 0, 1, 1, 1, 0, 0, 1], which represents Artificial Intelligence, Calculus, Data Structures, Discrete Math, History, and Volleyball.

Now, you'll experiment with different reinsertion strategies to see how they affect your evolutions, if at all.

Understanding Reinsertion

Reinsertion is the process of taking chromosomes produced from selection, crossover, and mutation and inserting them back into a population to move on to the next generation.

Look at evolve/4 in genetic.ex. It looks like this:

```
def evolve(population, problem, generation, opts \\ []) do
  population = evaluate(population, &problem.fitness_function/1, opts)
  best = hd(population)
  IO.write("\rCurrent best: #{best.fitness}\tGeneration: #{generation}")
  if problem.terminate?(population, generation) do
    best
  else
    {parents, leftover} = select(population, opts)
    children = crossover(parents, opts)
    children ++ leftover
    |> mutation(opts)
    |> evolve(problem, generation+1, opts)
  end
end
```

If you recall from Chapter 5, Selecting the Best, on page 71, you combined children and leftover and mutated the result to form a new population. This was a naive approach, but it ensured your population size remained fixed and worked well enough at the time.

Your goal with reinsertion is to utilize all of the chromosomes at your disposal to create a new population that has a good amount of genetic diversity and has a better fitness than your previous one. Your previous reinsertion strategy was to replace your parents with their children. This approach works well enough, but you'll want to be able to experiment with different reinsertion strategies and take smarter approaches to creating new populations.

Now, you will see how you can implement a few common reinsertion strategies and integrate them in your framework. First, edit evolve/4 so that it matches this:

```
def evolve(population, problem, generation, opts \\ []) do
  population = evaluate(population, &problem.fitness_function/1, opts)
  best = hd(population)
  fit_str =
    best.fitness
    |> :erlang.float_to_binary(decimals: 4)
  IO.write("\rCurrent best: #{fit_str}\tGeneration: #{generation}")
  if problem.terminate?(population, generation) do
    best
  else
    {parents, leftover} = select(population, opts)
    children = crossover(parents, opts)
    mutants = mutation(population, opts)
    offspring = children ++ mutants
    new_population = reinsertion(parents, offspring, leftover, opts)
    evolve(new_population, problem, generation+1, opts)
  end
end
```

Here, you've broken your population down into four parts: parents, leftover, mutants, and children. mutants and children are combined to form offspring—this is the most traditional approach; however, you could just as easily choose to mutate your children or mutate your new combined population.

Next, you call reinsertion/4 to create a new_population. reinsertion/4 will use one of a number of reinsertion strategies to create a new population for you. Finally, you call evolve/4 on the new population.

You can create reinsertion/4 like this:

```
def reinsertion(parents, offspring, leftover, opts \\ []) do
  strategy = Keyword.get(opts,
                      :reinsertion_strategy,
                      &Toolbox.Reinsertion.pure/3)
  apply(strategy, [parents, offspring, leftover])
end
```

In this function, you use apply to apply the specified reinsertion strategy. To customize a reinsertion strategy, you'd pass a function to the :reinsertion_strategy argument.

Next, you'll want to edit the mutation function so that it only returns the chromosomes it's mutated:

```elixir
def mutation(population, opts \\ []) do
  mutate_fn = Keyword.get(opts, :mutation_type, &Toolbox.Mutation.scramble/1)
  rate = Keyword.get(opts, :mutation_rate, 0.05)
  n = floor(length(population) * rate)
  population
  |> Enum.take_random(n)
  |> Enum.map(& apply(mutate_fn, [&1]))
end
```

Next, you need to create your reinsertion toolbox. Create a file reinsertion.ex in toolbox. Inside the file, define a module Toolbox.Reinsertion. This module will contain all of your reinsertion strategies.

You now need to define a few reinsertion strategies in your toolbox.

Pure Reinsertion and Generational Replacement

Pure reinsertion is the type of reinsertion you used in the first few chapters of this book. Every chromosome in the old population is replaced with an offspring of the new population. With pure reinsertion, you can either treat mutants as offspring—which is fairly common—and ensure your selection rate and your mutation rate add to 1. Another option is to simply have a selection rate of 1 and mutate children.

Pure reinsertion is a type of *generational replacement*. Generational replacement refers to the process of creating an entirely new population so that there's no overlap between populations. Technically, in a generational replacement strategy, offspring directly replace parents.

You're likely to encounter two derivatives of generational replacement when working with genetic algorithms. They are $\mu+\lambda$, read "mu plus lambda" and μ,λ, read "mu comma lambda." In $\mu+\lambda$ replacement, a child competes with its parent for survival—the winner being the one with the larger fitness. In μ,λ replacement, more children than the required population size are created and the best children survive. You might also see μ,λ replacement referred to as fitness-based insertion.

Given parents, offspring, and leftovers, you can implement pure reinsertion like this:

```elixir
def pure(_parents, offspring, _leftovers), do: offspring
```

Notice only offspring is returned to the next generation.

Pure reinsertion maintains none of the strengths of the old population and instead relies on the ability of selection, crossover, and mutation to form a

stronger population. Pure reinsertion is fast, but you could potentially eliminate some of your stronger characteristics in a population as a result.

Elitist Reinsertion

Elitist reinsertion or *elitist replacement* is a type of reinsertion strategy in which
you keep a top-portion of your old population to survive to the next generation.
With this strategy, you introduce the notion of a *survival rate*. The survival
rate dictates the percentage of parent chromosomes that survive to the next
generation. With a population of 100 and a survival rate of 20% or 0.2, you'd
keep the top 20% of your parents.

One thing to consider with elitist reinsertion is how survival rate affects your
population size. Later in this chapter, you'll see how your population grows
based on different survival rates.

Given parents, offspring, leftovers, and a survival_rate, this is how you would implement elitist reinsertion:

```
def elitist(parents, offspring, leftovers, survival_rate) do
  old = parents ++ leftovers
  n = floor(length(old) * survival_rate)
  survivors =
    old
    |> Enum.sort_by(& &1.fitness, &>=/2)
    |> Enum.take(n)
  offspring ++ survivors
end
```

In this function, you combine parents and leftovers to represent your old population. You ensure the old population is sorted by each chromosome's fitness
in descending order. You then select the first n where n is calculated from the
population size and the survival rate. Next, you combine offspring with the top
n chromosomes from your old population.

Elitist reinsertion is probably the most common reinsertion strategy. It's
reasonably fast with small populations, and it works well because it preserves
the strengths of your old population. The purest form of elitist reinsertion
maintains only the strongest individual from the previous population. You
can do this by specifying a selection rate that selects only one chromosome
from the old population to move on to the next generation.

Uniform Reinsertion

Uniform reinsertion or *random replacement* is a reinsertion strategy that
selects random chromosomes from the old population to survive to the next

generation. The purpose of uniform reinsertion is to maintain as much genetic diversity as possible in the new population. Uniform reinsertion isn't very common, but it's worth trying to see what happens.

Just as with elitist reinsertion, you need to consider how your survival rate will impact your population size when using uniform reinsertion. With uniform reinsertion, you select n random chromosomes from the old population to survive to the next generation.

Given parents, offspring, leftover, and a survival_rate, you can implement uniform reinsertion like this:

```
def uniform(parents, offspring, leftover, survival_rate) do
  old = parents ++ leftover
  n = floor(length(old) * survival_rate)
  survivors =
    old
    |> Enum.take_random(n)
  offspring ++ survivors
end
```

This implementation of uniform reinsertion is very similar to elitist reinsertion with a few key differences. First, there's no need to sort the old population based on fitness because you don't care about the fitness when selecting survivors. Second, you use take_random/2 rather than take/2 to sample random chromosomes from the old population.

You'll likely never want to use uniform reinsertion, but it can be good in maintaining the genetic diversity of your population.

Experimenting with Reinsertion

To see the impact of each of these reinsertion strategies in action, you can apply them to the scheduling problem you implemented earlier in this chapter to see how your outcomes differ.

Pure reinsertion is the default reinsertion strategy, so you should try that one first because you don't have to change anything in your original problem:

```
$ mix run scripts/schedule.exs
Current best: 15.9000 Generation: 1000
%Types.Chromosome{
  age: 1,
  fitness: 15.899999999999999,
  genes: [1, 1, 0, 1, 1, 1, 0, 0, 0, 1],
  size: 10
}
```

Next, try elitist reinsertion with a survival rate of 10%. To use elitist reinsertion, you have to use a partial application of the elitist/4 function, like this:

```
soln = Genetic.run(Schedule,
                reinserton_strategy:
                  &Toolbox.Reinsertion.elitist(&1, &2, &3, 0.1),
                selection_rate: 0.8,
                mutation_rate: 0.1)

IO.write("\n")
IO.inspect(soln)
```

You use & to create a partial application of elitist/4 and then specify a survival rate of 0.1. Additionally, you ensure that selection_rate, mutation_rate, and the specified survival rate all add up to 1.0. You'll see why that's important in the next section.

Run your algorithm with elitist reinsertion:

```
$ mix run scripts/schedule.exs
Current best: 15.9000 Generation: 1000
%Types.Chromosome{
  age: 1,
  fitness: 15.899999999999999,
  genes: [1, 1, 0, 1, 1, 1, 0, 0, 0, 1],
  size: 10
}
```

Finally, test your problem with uniform reinsertion. To do this, take the same approach you took with elitist reinsertion:

```
soln = Genetic.run(Schedule,
                reinserton_strategy:
                  &Toolbox.Reinsertion.elitist(&1, &2, &3, 0.1),
                selection_rate: 0.8,
                mutation_rate: 0.1)

IO.write("\n")
IO.inspect(soln)
```

Now run your algorithm with uniform reinsertion:

```
$ mix run scripts/schedule.exs
Current best: 15.3000 Generation: 1000
%Types.Chromosome{
  age: 1,
  fitness: 15.299999999999999,
  genes: [1, 1, 1, 1, 1, 0, 0, 0, 0, 1],
  size: 10
}
```

You can see that each reinsertion strategy performed similarly. They all converged on similar results, albeit likely with different levels of efficiency. Uniform reinsertion performed slightly worse than both elitist and pure reinsertion—which is to be expected, considering it doesn't account for fitness at all. It's also likely that pure reinsertion and elitist reinsertion converged before uniform reinsertion. The results of this experiment are sensitive to the random nature of genetic algorithms.

What you should take away from this is that in practice, if you need your algorithms to converge quickly and efficiently, use elitist or pure reinsertion. Ultimately, elitist reinsertion is usually the better choice, although it's difficult to determine without concrete statistics. In Chapter 9, Tracking Genetic Algorithms, on page 139, you'll learn more about comparing different genetic algorithms.

Growing and Shrinking Populations

Genetic algorithms can operate on either fixed or variable population sizes. All of the genetic algorithms you've implemented so far have had fixed size populations. The distinction between replacement and reinsertion lies in how the population size is affected. Replacement strategies focus specifically on maintaining a fixed population size—they replace old chromosomes with new ones. Reinsertion strategies focus mainly on inserting new chromosomes into a population—they integrate new chromosomes with old ones. Although you'll often see the terms used interchangeably, their meanings are slightly different.

If you opt for populations of variable size, you need to consider how fast the size of the population changes. For example, if you have a selection rate of 80% and choose to keep the top 30% of chromosomes every generation, your population will grow by 10% every generation. If you start with a population of 100 chromosomes, your population will have 1.37 *million* chromosomes by the hundredth generation. You'd notice your algorithm quickly stalls and crashes as it consumes all of the memory on the machine.

Alternatively, if you choose to have a selection rate of 80%, but only keep the top 10% of your chromosomes, your population will shrink by 10% every generation. If you start with a population of 100 chromosomes, your population will only have 1 chromosome by the fortieth generation. You'd stop making progress at that point, and more than likely won't have converged on a good solution.

Your population size is subject to *exponential growth* or *exponential decay* if you choose to grow or shrink them according to selection and survival rates. The following graph illustrates how population sizes grow or shrink according to exponential growth or decay:

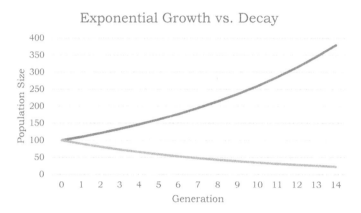

As you can see, it's infeasible to maintain a constant rate of growth or decay and maintain progress in your genetic algorithm. Fortunately, there are a few solutions.

One solution is to constrain the growth rate of your population based on the size of your population. If you don't want your population to get any larger than 1000 chromosomes, you can ensure that both selection and survival rates coincide with a 0% growth rate once your population hits 1000 chromosomes.

Another solution is to alternate growing and shrinking of the population. With odd generations your population grows, and with even populations your population shrinks. This ensures your population size always falls in some reasonable size window.

One final solution is to subject your population to constant growth or decay rather than exponential growth or decay. Rather than grow by 10% each generation, you can choose to explicitly grow by ten chromosomes every generation.

Of course, you can always come up with your own unique solution to addressing exponential growth or decay in population sizes. Most of the populations you work with will function fine with fixed population sizes. In the event you need to vary the size of your population, you'll need to consider these factors.

Local Versus Global Reinsertion

One concept you may come across when working with genetic algorithms is the concept of *local populations*. Local populations are populations that consist of *neighborhoods* of chromosomes. A neighborhood is a collection of adjacent chromosomes in a population. Neighborhoods are of different types with various structures. The following image illustrates a basic linear neighborhood:

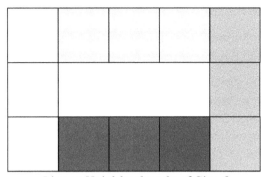
Linear Neighborhoods of Size 3

Local populations constrain interactions between chromosomes. A chromosome can only interact with chromosomes inside its neighborhood. Additionally, in some local populations, chromosomes can migrate between neighborhoods. Some genetic algorithms employ special techniques like assigning neighborhood leaders.

Genetic algorithms that employ local populations are often called *multi-population genetic algorithms*. Strategies for implementing multi-population genetic algorithms fall out of the scope of this book; however, it's useful to understand what they are and how they differ from the genetic algorithms you've implemented.

Because chromosomes are constrained to only interact with other chromosomes in their neighborhood, multi-population genetic algorithms require special selection and reinsertion strategies for ensuring neighborhoods maintain their local integrity. This is where the notion of global versus local reinsertion comes into play. Local reinsertion operates on neighborhoods; global reinsertion operates on entire populations.

Multi-population genetic algorithms are often used to help parallelize a genetic algorithm because evolution can take place independently in each neighborhood. Multi-population genetic algorithms are also used to simulate competition over resources in different environments.

What You Learned

In this chapter, you learned about reinsertion and different types of reinsertion strategies. You learned how to implement different reinsertion strategies, and you analyzed the impacts of different reinsertion strategies on a scheduling problem.

You also learned how you can grow and shrink your population—and do so without falling into the traps of exponential decay and growth.

Finally, you learned about local reinsertion and local populations and how they differ from global reinsertion strategies and global genetic algorithms.

In the next chapter, you'll step away from the internals of a genetic algorithm and instead focus on how you can track how fitness, age, and other metrics change during evolutions. Rather than focus on improving your algorithms and learning new techniques, you'll learn how to compare performance between algorithms and better track the progress of an algorithm.

## CHAPTER 9

Tracking Genetic Algorithms

Up to this chapter, you've spent all your time learning about the details and intricacies that drive genetic algorithms. You learned how to represent solutions, how to evaluate solutions, and how to alter populations using selection, crossover, mutation, and reinsertion.

The goal of all of the problems you've solved has been to optimize an objective. In all of the algorithms you've written, you define the problem, configure the algorithm, and run the algorithm until you obtain a solution. While, for the most part, the process of obtaining the solution is the most important thing, sometimes you need a way to track the progress of an evolution over time.

Imagine if you wanted to analyze how your population's collective fitness grew over time. Or perhaps you want to visualize how the distribution of fitness changed between generations. Or even still, perhaps you want to trace the genealogy of your best solution when the algorithm returns.

Metrics are important because they offer insights that can help you make decisions about how to reconfigure or adjust your algorithm. It's difficult to make decisions and identify bottlenecks in your algorithm without detailed metrics to analyze.

In this chapter, you'll learn how to integrate utilities that allow you to track various metrics in your framework. You'll build these utilities around a unique application of genetic algorithms.

Using Genetic Algorithms to Simulate Evolution

One of the more interesting applications of genetic algorithms that you have yet to discover is their ability to model real evolutionary processes. Genetic algorithms are inspired by evolution, and while the internal processes that guide genetic algorithms such as selection, crossover, and mutation are only loosely based on science, they can still be used to offer valuable insights into the evolutionary process.

Say you've been tasked by a biologist to write a simulation of how tigers evolve under different environmental conditions. Obviously, the traits required to survive in a desert versus an arctic tundra differ drastically. Your goal is to write a simulation that models the basic evolution of the tiger in two different environments, tropical and tundra, over the course of 1000 generations. Additionally, your simulation needs to keep track of valuable statistics such as average fitness, average age, genealogy, and the most fit chromosome from every generation.

Using a genetic algorithm and a bit of knowledge about tigers, you can accomplish this task in no time.

Start by creating a new file in scripts named tiger_simulation.exs. Next, create a shell for a Problem in tiger_simulation.exs, like so:

```
defmodule TigerSimulation do
  @behaviour Problem
  alias Types.Chromosome

  @impl true
  def genotype, do: # ...

  @impl true
  def fitness_function(c), do: # ...

  @impl true
  def terminate?(population, generation), do: # ...
end
```

By now, all of this code should be familiar. Now you need to figure out how to fit your simulation into the Problem behaviour.

Representing Tigers as Chromosomes

The first thing you need to do is determine how to represent tigers as chromosomes.

While there's no right or wrong answer, the easiest way is to use a binary genotype that represents various traits present in a single tiger. Each of these traits contributes in one way or another to the tiger's ability to survive in different environments.

You'll monitor eight traits as shown in the table on page 141.

Because you're monitoring eight traits, your chromosome will consist of eight binary genes. Implement the genotype like this:

	0	1
Size	smaller	larger
Swimming Ability	low	high
Fat Stores	less	more
Activity Period	diurnal	nocturnal
Hunting Range	smaller	larger
Fur Thickness	less thick	more thick
Tail Length	smaller	larger

```
def genotype do
  genes = for _ <- 1..8, do: Enum.random(0..1)
  %Chromosome{genes: genes, size: 8}
end
```

As you've seen before, this is a basic binary genotype of size 8. The initial population will contain tigers of varying combinations of traits.

The next thing you need to do is determine how to evaluate each tiger based on its traits in both a tropical and tundra environment.

Evaluating Fitness in Different Environments

Remember, your goal is to determine how tigers evolve in each environment. Because the importance of each trait differs between environments, you need to evaluate chromosomes differently depending on the environment.

The easiest way to do this is to assign weights or scores to each trait, indicating whether or not a trait is positive or negative to survival. The magnitude of a weight or score indicates the relative importance of that trait in a given environment.

The table on page 142 shows the scores you'll assign to each trait in both environments.

Determining Scores

The scores chosen for each trait in this example are arbitrary. In a practical simulation, you'd want to determine scores with research and data, and hopefully be able to provide a justification for each one. These scores were chosen based on intuition. They don't mean anything nor are they scientifically correct. You can always adjust them and see how it affects your evolutions.

Trait	Tropical	Tundra
Size	0.0	1.0
Swimming Ability	3.0	3.0
Fur Color	2.0	-2.0
Fat Stores	-1.0	1.0
Activity Period	0.5	0.5
Hunting Ground	1.0	2.0
Fur Thickness	-1.0	1.0
Tail Length	0.0	0.0

Notice that some scores are negative, indicating that they have a negative impact on survival; some scores are zero, indicating they have no impact on survival; and some are positive, indicating they have a positive impact on survival.

Now, to translate these scores into a fitness function, add the following code to tiger_simulation.exs:

```
def fitness_function(chromosome) do
  tropic_scores = [0.0, 3.0, 2.0, 1.0, 0.5, 1.0, -1.0, 0.0]
  tundra_scores = [1.0, 3.0, -2.0, -1.0, 0.5, 2.0, 1.0, 0.0]
  traits = chromosome.genes

  traits
  |> Enum.zip(tropic_scores)
  |> Enum.map(fn {t, s} -> t*s end)
  |> Enum.sum()
end
```

The fitness function pairs traits with their corresponding score, multiplies them together, and returns the sum to represent a tiger's ability to survive in the given environment. For simplicity, you can just change tropic_scores with tundra_scores in Enum.map/2 when running trials on different environments. In practice, you'd want a way to change this dynamically and run experiments side by side.

Finishing and Running the Simulation

All that's left for you to do is define some termination criteria. You'll want to stop the evolution after 1000 generations. Implement your termination criteria like this:

```
def terminate?(_population, generation), do: generation == 1000
```

Next, add the following below the TigerSimulation module:

```
tiger = Genetic.run(TigerSimulation,
                    population_size: 20,
                    selection_rate: 0.9,
                    mutation_rate: 0.1)

IO.write("\n")
IO.inspect(tiger)
```

You pass your TigerSimulation into Genetic.run/2 as well as specify a population size of 20, selection rate of 0.9 and a mutation rate of 0.9.

Remember, Genetic.run/2 returns the best chromosome in the population after the termination criteria has been met. That means that tiger will be the current best chromosome in the population after 1000 generations.

Now, run your genetic algorithm in a tropic environment (with tropic_scores):

```
$ mix run scripts/tiger_simulation.exs
Current best: 7.5000  Generation: 1000
%Types.Chromosome{
  age: 1,
  fitness: 7.5,
  genes: [0, 1, 1, 1, 1, 1, 0, 1],
  size: 8
}
```

And again in a tundra environment (with tundra_scores):

```
$ mix run scripts/tiger_simulation.exs
Current best: 7.5000  Generation: 1000
%Types.Chromosome{
  age: 1,
  fitness: 7.5,
  genes: [1, 1, 0, 0, 1, 1, 1, 0],
  size: 8
}
```

You've successfully analyzed and produced the fittest tiger in each environment. You can see that in tropical environments, the best tiger is smaller, a strong swimmer, and has dark fur and a generally smaller hunting territory. The tundra tiger is larger, a strong swimmer, and has lighter fur and larger fat stores.

You might be thinking that achieving this result isn't that impressive. You could have derived them yourself intuitively or through a simple brute-force search. However, the most important aspect of this experiment isn't the final result but what happens before that. You need a way to peek inside.

Logging Statistics Using ETS

During an evolution, you may want to track statistics about fitness, age, or variation in your population over the course of the evolution. For example, perhaps you want to determine the distribution of a particular gene at different generations during the evolution.

In this section, you'll create a statistics server using a GenServer and an ETS table. Remember, a GenServer is an abstraction around state that models client-server behavior. It allows you to spin up a long-running process and alter its state through message passing. ETS stands for Erlang Term Storage and offers a built-in storage API through Erlang interpolation. The GenServer will allow you to supervise the ETS table. The ETS table will allow you to quickly and easily insert and look up statistics across generations. Additionally, it'll be easy for you to expand this approach to all kinds of statistics and metrics.

Creating the Statistics Server

Start by creating a new utilities directory inside lib, and inside that new directory, add a new file named statistics.ex. This file will contain the implementation for your statistics server. Start by defining a bare-bones GenServer implementation:

```
defmodule Utilities.Statistics do
  use GenServer

  def init(_opts) do
    :ok
  end

  def start_link(opts) do
    GenServer.start_link(__MODULE__, opts, name: __MODULE__)
  end
end
```

Your GenServer is a wrapper around the ETS table to ensure it's created when your application is started. You only need to implement callbacks for init/1 and start_link/1.

You'll also want to add the Statistics module to your supervision tree. You'll need to create a new file application.ex that implements a supervision tree. The file should look like this:

```
defmodule Genetic.Application do
  use Application
```

```
  def start(_type, _args) do
    children = [
      {Utilities.Statistics, []},
    ]

    opts = [strategy: :one_for_one, name: Genetic.Supervisor]
    Supervisor.start_link(children, opts)
  end
end
```

You also need to update application in mix.exs to look like this:

```
def application do
  [
    extra_applications: [:logger],
    mod: {Genetic.Application, []}
  ]
end
```

This code ensures your GenServer starts on application start.

Now you'll need functionality for accessing the statistics for a generation and for inserting the statistics of a generation. ETS allows you to store any Elixir term in a key-value pair. That means you can use generations as keys and maps of statistics as values. Each field in the map will represent a different statistic you want to track, such as minimum fitness, maximum fitness, average fitness, and so on.

GenServers typically use a client-server paradigm, but for this example, you just need the GenServer to encapsulate your ETS table and initialize it on Application startup. The only GenServer function you need to implement is init/1, like this:

```
def init(opts) do
  :ets.new(:statistics, [:set, :public, :named_table])
  {:ok, opts}
end
```

This function will run when your application is started and ensures you have a new ETS table that you can access with the name :statistics.

You now need to implement insert and lookup functions. insert takes a generation and a map of statistics. You can implement it like this:

```
def insert(generation, statistics) do
  :ets.insert(:statistics, {generation, statistics})
end
```

ETS lookup works much the same way as insertion. You can implement lookup like this:

```
def lookup(generation) do
  hd(:ets.lookup(:statistics, generation))
end
```

:ets.lookup/2 returns a list, so you return the head of the list to extract the statistics entry. There should only be one entry for every generation, so this implementation is fine.

In these functions, you use the ETS API to implement basic insertion and lookup functionality. Your statistics will be logged as a map of statistics every generation. For example, if you wanted to track mean fitness and mean age for an evolution of 1000 generations, your ETS table would contain 1000 entries each with a map containing mean_fitness and mean_age entries.

With your Statistics server set up, you just need to ensure your algorithm tracks statistics during your evolution.

Tracking Statistics in Your Framework

Before you can access the different statistics of an evolution, you need to ensure your algorithm tracks them after every generation. To do this, you'll implement a new function statistics that runs immediately after your population is evaluated and updates the statistics server appropriately.

Start by updating evolve/4 to call statistics/2, like this:

```
def evolve(population, problem, generation, opts \\ []) do
  population = evaluate(population, &problem.fitness_function/1, opts)
  statistics(population, generation, opts)
  best = hd(population)
  # ...
end
```

Next, you need to implement statistics/3. To customize the statistics you take between generations, you can accept a :statistics option in opts, which is a keyword list of functions that implement different calculations on your population. You'll want to define a default suite of statistics so you don't have to define these every time. Implement statistics/3 like this:

```
def statistics(population, generation, opts \\ []) do
  default_stats = [
    min_fitness: &Enum.min_by(&1, fn c -> c.fitness end).fitness,
    max_fitness: &Enum.max_by(&1, fn c -> c.fitness end).fitness,
    mean_fitness: &Enum.sum(Enum.map(&1, fn c -> c.fitness end))
  ]
  stats = Keyword.get(opts, :statistics, default_stats)
  stats_map =
    stats
    |> Enum.reduce(%{},
```

```
        fn {key, func}, acc ->
          Map.put(acc, key, func.(population))
        end
      )
  Utilities.Statistics.insert(generation, stats_map)
end
```

First, you define a suite of default statistics, in this case min and max fitness. You then use Keyword.get/3 to obtain the statistics passed to opts. Next, you create a statistics map that applies every function in stats to your population. Finally, you insert this map into your statistics table.

Accessing the Statistics

To access the statistics of an evolution, you can either use the basic API you implemented previously or you can access the :statistics table using ETS. For example, if you wanted to look up the minimum fitness during the third generation of your simulation, you'd do this:

```
# After Algorithm runs

{_, third_gen_stats} = Utilities.Statistics.lookup(3)
IO.write("Min fitness after 3rd Generation: #{third_gen_stats.min_fitness}")
```

The ETS entry is a tuple of {generation, map}. In this example you use pattern matching to extract just the map of statistics.

You can use the basic statistics you've implemented to see how the population tends toward the best fitness over time. Try taking a look at the mean fitness of the 0th, 500th, and 1000th generations:

```
{_, zero_gen_stats} = Utilities.Statistics.lookup(0)
{_, fivehundred_gen_stats} = Utilities.Statistics.lookup(500)
{_, onethousand_gen_stats} = Utilities.Statistics.lookup(1000)

IO.write("""
0th: #{zero_gen_stats.mean_fitness}
500th: #{fivehundred_gen_stats.mean_fitness}
1000th: #{onethousand_gen_stats.mean_fitness}
""")
```

When you run your algorithm, you'll see:

```
$ mix run scripts/tiger_simulation.exs
...
0th: 2.43
500th: 7.09
1000th: 7.0
```

Notice your mean fitness doesn't change much at all between the 500th and 1000th generation. It actually goes slightly down. Your population probably converges well before your algorithm terminates. In Chapter 10, Visualizing the Results, on page 157, you'll see how you can turn these statistics into graphs and identify about when your algorithm begins to converge.

That's all it takes. You can extend the statistics utility using libraries like elixir-statistics or your own custom statistics functions.

Finding the Average Tiger

Now that you have extensible statistics tracking in place, you can use it to monitor more insightful statistics for your evolution—such as the average tiger for each climate.

You've already identified the fittest tiger for each climate; however, what matters more is how the entire population changes in a given climate. To identify this, you can implement an average_tiger statistic that tells you the average tiger for any given generation.

Start by creating the following average_tiger/1 function in your TigerSimulation module:

```
def average_tiger(population) do
  genes = Enum.map(population, & &1.genes)
  fitnesses = Enum.map(population, & &1.fitness)
  ages = Enum.map(population, & &1.age)
  num_tigers = length(population)

  avg_fitness = Enum.sum(fitnesses) / num_tigers
  avg_age = Enum.sum(ages) / num_tigers
  avg_genes =
    genes
    |> Enum.zip()
    |> Enum.map(& Enum.sum(&1) / num_tigers)

  %Chromosome{genes: avg_genes, age: avg_age, fitness: avg_fitness}
end
```

If you recall from how you implemented statistics/3, each statistic reflects a measure of some value over the entire population. Your average_tiger/1 function takes in the entire population and calculates averages for age, fitness, and genes. Average genes are the average value of each trait.

Now you need to adjust your run to account for this statistic on every generation:

```
tiger = Genetic.run(TigerSimulation,
                    population_size: 20,
                    selection_rate: 0.9,
                    mutation_rate: 0.1,
                    statistics:
                      %{average_tiger: &TigerSimulation.average_tiger/1})
```

Next, rather than inspecting the mean fitness at the 0th, 500th, and 1000th generation, inspect the average tiger:

```
{_, zero_gen_stats} = Utilities.Statistics.lookup(0)
{_, fivehundred_gen_stats} = Utilities.Statistics.lookup(500)
{_, onethousand_gen_stats} = Utilities.Statistics.lookup(1000)

IO.inspect(zero_gen_stats.average_tiger)
IO.inspect(fivehundred_gen_stats.average_tiger)
IO.inspect(onethousand_gen_stats.average_tiger)
```

When you run the simulation in a tropic climate, this is what you should see:

```
%Types.Chromosome{
  age: 1.0,
  fitness: 3.19,
  genes: [0.46, 0.51, 0.38, 0.55, 0.48, 0.6, 0.49, 0.54],
}
%Types.Chromosome{
  age: 1.0,
  fitness: 7.245,
  genes: [0.58, 0.98, 0.99, 0.97, 0.99, 0.96, 0.1, 0.66],
}
%Types.Chromosome{
  age: 1.0,
  fitness: 7.165,
  genes: [0.6, 0.98, 0.94, 0.96, 0.99, 0.97, 0.08, 0.67],
}
```

And you'll see this in a tundra climate:

```
%Types.Chromosome{
  age: 1.0,
  fitness: 2.3,
  genes: [0.49, 0.51, 0.58, 0.39, 0.6, 0.49, 0.55, 0.49],
}
%Types.Chromosome{
  age: 1.0,
  fitness: 6.98,
  genes: [0.96, 0.98, 0.1, 0.09, 0.94, 0.98, 0.94, 0.64],
}
%Types.Chromosome{
  age: 1.0,
  fitness: 7.055,
  genes: [0.98, 0.96, 0.06, 0.08, 0.97, 0.97, 0.97, 0.66],
}
```

You can notice some distinct differences here. In a tropical climate, fat stores and fur thickness are detrimental to a tiger's ability to survive, so over time tigers with those traits become less prevalent. Similiarly, in a tundra climate, these traits are important, so tigers with these traits become more prevalent.

You can also notice the traits that didn't have any meaning in a climate, such as tail length, tend to be present in around 50%–60% of tigers. The evolution doesn't place much emphasis on shorter or longer tails in either environment, so there isn't much of a trend in either direction.

If you're wondering what type of tigers are developed in each environment, it's the Bengal tiger and Siberian tiger.

Tracking Genealogy in a Genealogy Tree

Sometimes, especially in evolutionary simulations, it's useful to track the *genealogy* of the evolution. Genealogy is the study of families and family histories. In the context of genetic algorithms, genealogy is the history of a chromosome's lineage. It allows you to trace the ancestry of a specific chromosome—all the way back to the initial population.

To track genealogy, you'll take advantage of the libgraph[1] package. libgraph is an Elixir package for creating graph structures. libgraph offers a ton of convenient features for creating, manipulating, and querying graphs. If you want to learn more about the beauty of graphs in Elixir, check out *Elixir for Graphs [Ham20]*.

You'll use libgraph to implement a *genealogy tree*. A genealogy tree is a *directed graph* that points from parent chromosome to child chromosome and shows the transition of the evolution from the first population to the last population. A directed graph is a graph whose edges have a direction—edges start on one node (the parent) and point to another (the child).

You can use the genealogy tree to trace the origins of your strongest chromosome or to see how traits evolved over time. You can even export your genealogy tree and visualize the genealogy of your evolution with third-party tools. First, you'll need to implement it.

Before you begin, start by adding libgraph to your dependencies:

```
defp deps do
  {:libgraph, "~> 0.13"}
end
```

Then, run mix deps.get.

One important thing you need to do before you begin tracking genealogy is to ensure that each chromosome has a unique id associated with it. libgraph will overwrite existing entries in a genealogy tree if the attributes of a chromosome

---

1. https://github.com/bitwalker/libgraph

match one that's already in the genealogy tree. To prevent this, alter your Types.Chromosome struct to look like this:

```
defmodule Types.Chromosome do
  @enforce_keys :genes
  defstruct [:genes,
             id: Base.encode16(:crypto.strong_rand_bytes(64)),
             size: 0,
             fitness: 0,
             age: 0]
end
```

This code will generate a unique ID every time a chromosome is created. This will allow you to more easily query your graph for unique chromosomes.

Creating the Genealogy GenServer

Just like with statistics, you'll use a GenServer to store your genealogy tree. Start by creating a new file genealogy.ex in utilities. In genealogy.ex, create a module, like this:

```
defmodule Utilities.Genealogy do
  use GenServer
end
```

Now, go to application.ex and ensure Utilities.Genealogy is started with your application:

```
defmodule Genetic.Application do
  use Application

  def start(_type, _args) do
    children = [
      {Utilities.Statistics, []}
      {Utilities.Genealogy, []}
    ]

    opts = [strategy: :one_for_one, name: Genetic.Supervisor]
    Supervisor.start_link(children, opts)
  end
end
```

Now, you need to implement the client-server behaviour of the GenServer. You'll need to be able to do the following:

- Add chromosomes.
- Add child chromosome with parent(s).
- Access libgraph graph.

To keep things simple, you'll only use the GenServer to add chromosomes to the genealogy tree and to obtain the current tree. If you need to explore the tree, you can obtain the graph from the GenServer and use any of libgraph's functions.

You'll start by implementing the server. First, you need to define what happens when the GenServer starts via the init function. This function should just initialize a new libgraph graph. libgraph's API is exposed via the Graph module. Creating a new graph is as easy as calling Graph.new. Implement init, like so:

```elixir
def init(_opts) do
  {:ok, Graph.new()}
end
```

Graph.new automatically creates a new directed graph. Once your GenServer starts, it'll be initialized with an empty directed graph.

Next, you'll need a function that inserts multiple chromosomes at once. You'll need this function to store the initial population of chromosomes in the graph. Because you're updating the state of the genealogy tree, this functionality will be invoked via cast messages, so you'll handle it using handle_cast/2. The message should come with a list of chromosomes to add and should be invoked using :add_chromosomes:

```elixir
def handle_cast({:add_chromosomes, chromosomes}, genealogy) do
  {:noreply, Graph.add_vertices(genealogy, chromosomes)}
end
```

libgraph has a convenient function, Graph.add_vertices/2, that handles adding multiple vertices to your graph.

Now you need to implement functionality for adding a chromosome with either one parent, in the event a chromosome is the result of mutation, or two parents, in the event a chromosome is the result of crossover. This functionality will be invoked via cast messages using the :add_chromosome message with either two or three chromosomes. Add the following to Utilities.Genealogy:

```elixir
# Child is mutant of Parent
def handle_cast({:add_chromosome, parent, child}, genealogy) do
  new_genealogy =
    genealogy
    |> Graph.add_edge(parent, child)
  {:noreply, new_genealogy}
end

# Child is crossover of Parents
def handle_cast({:add_chromosome, parent_a, parent_b, child}, genealogy) do
  new_genealogy =
```

```
    genealogy
    |> Graph.add_edge(parent_a, child)
    |> Graph.add_edge(parent_b, child)
  {:noreply, new_genealogy}
end
```

Graph.add_edge/3 adds an edge between two vertices. In this example, Graph.add_edge/3 will add an edge from parent to child. You don't need to add child to the graph because Graph.add_edge/3 will automatically add it to the graph for you.

Finally, you need a way to obtain the current genealogy tree from the GenServer. This functionality will be invoked via call messages, so you'll handle them with handle_call/3. Implement this functionality like this:

```
def handle_call(:get_tree, _, genealogy) do
  {:reply, genealogy, genealogy}
end
```

This function is invoked with the message :get_tree and returns the current state of the genealogy tree.

With the server implemented, you need to implement accompanying client functions. The client functions should be friendly interfaces that invoke server methods. You'll implement one client method for each server method you implemented: add_chromosomes/1, add_chromosome/2, add_chromosome/3, and get_tree/0. Additionally, you need to implement start_link, which initializes the GenServer. You can implement the client like this:

```
def start_link(_opts) do
  GenServer.start_link(__MODULE__, _opts, name: __MODULE__)
end

def add_chromosomes(chromosomes) do
  GenServer.cast(__MODULE__, {:add_chromosomes, chromosomes})
end

def add_chromosome(parent, child) do
  GenServer.cast(__MODULE__, {:add_chromosome, parent, child})
end

def add_chromosome(parent_a, parent_b, child) do
  GenServer.cast(__MODULE__, {:add_chromosome, parent_a, parent_b, child})
end

def get_tree do
  GenServer.call(__MODULE__, :get_tree)
end
```

Now that you've successfully implemented the functionality of a genealogy tree, you'll need to update the genealogy tree using the GenServer in your framework.

Tracking Genealogy in Your Framework

The genealogy tree should be updated every time you add a new chromosome into the population. That means you should update the genealogy tree after population initialization, after any crossover takes place, and after any mutation takes place.

Start with population initialization. After you create your population in initialize/2, you'll want to immediately add those chromosomes to your genealogy tree, like this:

```
def initialize(genotype, opts \\ []) do
  population_size = Keyword.get(opts, :population_size, 100)
  population = for _ <- 1..population_size, do: genotype.()
  Utilities.Genealogy.add_chromosomes(population)
  population
end
```

In this function, rather than immediately returning a new population, you initialize the population to a variable and add the list of chromosomes to the genealogy tree using the Utilities.Genealogy client. You then return the population.

Next, you'll need to update your genealogy tree when children are created from crossover. Update your crossover/2 function to look like this:

```
def crossover(population, opts \\ []) do
  crossover_fn = Keyword.get(opts,
                       :crossover_type,
                       &Toolbox.Crossover.single_point/2)
  population
  |> Enum.reduce([],
      fn {p1, p2}, acc ->
        {c1, c2} = apply(crossover_fn, [p1, p2])
        Utilities.Genealogy.add_chromosome(p1, p2, c1)
        Utilities.Genealogy.add_chromosome(p1, p2, c2)
        [c1, c2 | acc]
      end
    )
end
```

This function is pretty much the same as it originally was; however, you add both c1 and c2 to your genealogy tree with p1 and p2 as parents.

Finally, you need to update the mutation/2 function. Change it so it looks like this:

```
def mutation(population, opts \\ []) do
  mutate_fn = Keyword.get(opts, :mutation_type, &Toolbox.Mutation.scramble/1)
  rate = Keyword.get(opts, :mutation_rate, 0.05)
  n = floor(length(population) * rate)
  population
  |> Enum.take(n)
  |> Enum.map(
      fn c ->
        mutant = apply(mutate_fn, [c])
        Utilities.Genealogy.add_chromosome(c, mutant)
        mutant
      end
    )
end
```

Again, the only change here is adding the mutant to the genealogy tree with the original chromosome as its parent. At this point, you're all set to track your genealogy during every genetic algorithm.

Exploring Genealogy of a Simulation

You can use any of the functions in the libgraph API to explore your genealogy tree. For example, if you wanted to see every chromosome that ever existed over the course of an evolution, you can access the vertices of the genealogy tree, like this:

```
tiger = Genetic.run(TigerSimulation,
                    population_size: 20,
                    selection_rate: 0.9,
                    mutation_rate: 0.1,
                    statistics:
                        %{average_tiger: &TigerSimulation.average_tiger/1})

genealogy = Utilities.Genealogy.get_tree()

IO.inspect(Graph.vertices(genealogy))
```

If you run this, you'll see a very long list of chromosomes. In the next chapter, you'll learn how to export a visualization of the genealogy tree to better see how your evolution progresses over time.

What You Learned

In this chapter, you learned about a unique application of genetic algorithms in simulating evolution. You saw how this worked through a basic tiger evolution simulation. Through this simulation, you learned that tracking what happens between generations is just as important as the final result.

You also learned how to track statistics during an evolution. You implemented a basic statistics server and saw how you could use it to track any statistics you want over the course of an evolution.

Finally, you were introduced to the concept of a genealogy tree, and you saw how to implement a genealogy tree using libgraph and a GenServer.

In the next chapter, you'll use some of your work in this chapter to visualize the results of your algorithm using Phoenix LiveView.

## CHAPTER 10

Visualizing the Results

In the previous chapter, you worked to add some tracking mechanisms to your genetic algorithm. The purpose of tracking things like statistics, genealogy, and other metrics is not only to improve the performance of your algorithms but also to demonstrate the overall effectiveness of your algorithm at solving a particular problem. For example, a biologist simulating the evolution of tigers would use the metrics implemented in the previous chapter to theorize about how evolution in the wild takes place.

Of course, good biologists wouldn't present the data collected in its raw form. Instead, they would do some analysis, transform the data in some way, and then create graphs, charts, and other visualizations that best depict evidence supporting their theories. These visualizations are often the best way to present results. You might also benefit from analyzing certain visualizations to determine how to tweak your algorithm in certain ways.

Additionally, depending on the problem you're trying to solve, you want to be able to see what's going on in real time. For example, if you were trying to create a Tetris-playing AI, you'd want to watch it play Tetris in real time.

In this chapter, you're going to learn how to create visualizations for both of these purposes—visualizing metrics and visualizing evolutions in real time. You'll start by visualizing the genealogy of the tiger evolution you created earlier. Then you'll export some basic statistics to a graph and visually analyze the statistics before moving on to a different problem—playing Tetris with a genetic algorithm.

Visualizing the Genealogy of the Tiger Evolution

In the previous chapter, you fully integrated some basic tracking mechanisms into your genetic algorithm framework. These mechanisms allowed you to track statistics on age, fitness, and pretty much any other aspect of your genetic algorithm. You also created a mechanism for tracking the genealogy of your evolution. Remember, genealogy is a family tree of the entire evolution.

In this section, you'll learn how to export the genealogy tree and visualize it using a third-party tool.

Start by opening tiger_simulation.exs. At the moment, it looks like this:

```elixir
defmodule TigerSimulation do
  @behaviour Problem
  alias Types.Chromosome

  @impl true
  def genotype do
    genes = for _ <- 1..8, do: Enum.random(0..1)
    %Chromosome{genes: genes, size: 8}
  end

  @impl true
  def fitness_function(chromosome) do
    tropic_scores = [0.0, 3.0, 2.0, 1.0, 0.5, 1.0, -1.0, 0.0]
    tundra_scores = [1.0, 3.0, -2.0, -1.0, 0.5, 2.0, 1.0, 0.0]
    traits = chromosome.genes

    traits
    |> Enum.zip(tundra_scores)
    |> Enum.map(fn {t, s} -> t*s end)
    |> Enum.sum()
  end

  @impl true
  def terminate?(_population, generation), do: generation == 1000

  def average_tiger(population) do
    genes = Enum.map(population, & &1.genes)
    fitnesses = Enum.map(population, & &1.fitness)
    ages = Enum.map(population, & &1.age)
    num_tigers = length(population)

    avg_fitness = Enum.sum(fitnesses) / num_tigers
    avg_age = Enum.sum(ages) / num_tigers
    avg_genes =
      genes
      |> Enum.zip()
      |> Enum.map(& Enum.sum(Tuple.to_list(&1)) / num_tigers)

    %Chromosome{genes: avg_genes, age: avg_age, fitness: avg_fitness}
  end
end

tiger = Genetic.run(TigerSimulation,
                    population_size: 20,
                    selection_rate: 0.9,
```

```
    mutation_rate: 0.1,
    statistics:
      %{average_tiger: &TigerSimulation.average_tiger/1})

IO.write("\n")
IO.inspect(tiger)
genealogy = Utilities.Genealogy.get_tree()

IO.inspect(Graph.vertices(genealogy))
```

You'll need to start by adjusting the termination criteria. Currently, the algorithm is set to terminate after 1000 generations. For the purposes of this chapter, you'll decrease this number significantly to make it easier to visualize the genealogy. In this example, you'll decrease the number of generations to 1 and the population size to 5:

```
defmodule TigerSimulation do
  # ...
  def terminate?(_population, generation), do: generation == 0
  # ...
end

tiger = Genetic.run(TigerSimulation,
                    population_size: 2,
                    selection_rate: 1.0,
                    mutation_rate: 0.0,
                    statistics:
                      %{average_tiger: &TigerSimulation.average_tiger/1})
```

Next, you need to export your genealogy tree to a DOT file, like this:

```
genealogy = Utilities.Genealogy.get_tree()

{:ok, dot} = Graph.Serializers.DOT.serialize(genealogy)
{:ok, dotfile} = File.open("tiger_simulation.dot", [:write])
:ok = IO.binwrite(dotfile, dot)
:ok = File.close(dotfile)
```

In this snippet, you serialize the genealogy tree to a DOT binary using the libgraph API. DOT is a standard serialized graph format. You then create a new file and write the serialized graph to it.

When you run your algorithm, you'll see tiger_simulation.dot in your main directory. Now, to visualize, you can download Graphviz[1] or navigate to Webgraphviz[2] and copy the contents of tiger_simulation.dot into the text field. Your genealogy tree will end up looking something like the image on page 160.

---

1. http://www.graphviz.org
2. http://www.webgraphviz.com/

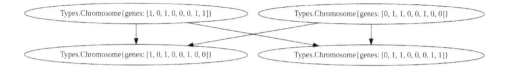

Notice the genealogy is essentially a tree starting from 2 chromosomes in the first generation and spanning out from there. This type of visualization is excellent in showing how the fittest chromosome transformed over time.

Visualizing Basic Statistics

In the previous chapter, one of the issues you encountered during your evolution was continuing your algorithm after it had already converged. When you analyzed the mean fitness at different generations, you saw that there was basically no change between the 500th and 1000th generation. This is because the algorithm had already converged.

The easiest way to recognize roughly when your algorithm converges is by creating a graph of mean fitness versus generation. When you do this, you'll notice a dramatic plateau.

To create a basic graph, you'll use gnuplot-elixir.[3] gnuplot-elixir is a port of the Gnuplot library. Gnuplot is a library for generating simple plots using the command line. You first need to ensure you have Gnuplot installed. Go to the Gnuplot home page[4] to learn how to install it for your specific operating system. In Ubuntu, you install Gnuplot like this:

```
$ sudo apt-get install gnuplot
```

Once it's installed, you need to add gnuplot-elixir to your dependencies in mix.exs:

```
defp deps do
  # ...
  {:gnuplut, "~> 1.19"}
end
```

Next, adjust your algorithm to only run with the default statistics:

```
tiger = Genetic.run(TigerSimulation,
                    population_size: 5,
                    selection_rate: 0.9,
                    mutation_rate: 0.1)
```

---

3.   https://github.com/devstopfix/gnuplot-elixir
4.   http://www.gnuplot.info/

Finally, you need to export these statistics to a format that is compatible with gnuplot-elixir:

```
stats =
  :ets.tab2list(:statistics)
  |> Enum.map(fn {gen, stats} -> [gen, stats.mean_fitness] end)
```

The tab2list/1 function converts an ETS table to a list of tuples. You need to adjust this list of tuples to be a list of lists where each list contains a generation and the mean fitness of each generation. Now you can generate a plot using the Gnuplot library:

```
{:ok, cmd} =
  Gnuplot.plot([
    [:set, :title, "mean fitness versus generation"],
    [:plot, "-", :with, :points]
  ], [stats])
```

When you run your script, you'll see a window appear that looks like this:

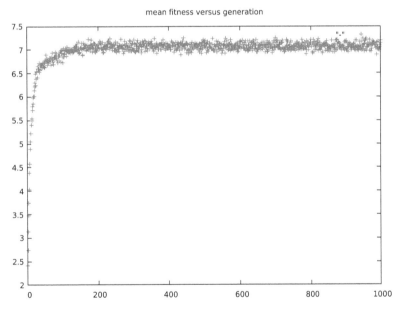

Notice how almost immediately the mean fitness climbs up to around 7 before it plateaus. If you move your cursor around the plot, you'll notice that after around 150 generations the evolution plateaus. Try adjusting your termination criteria to 150 generations. Your graph should now look something like the image on page 162.

Your graph looks similar to the last one; however, you should notice a slight increase in mean fitness versus generation up to the 150th generation.

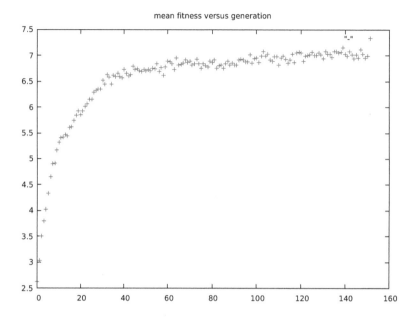

Gnuplot is a useful tool for providing insights into some of the statistics you gather during your evolutions. This section introduced only one way of visualizing one statistic. The possibilities are literally endless.

Now, you can finally wrap up your work on the tiger evolution and move into a different problem requiring visualizations: playing Tetris.

Playing Tetris with Genetic Algorithms

The Arcade Learning Environment (ALE) is a framework designed to allow programmers to easily develop AI agents for Atari 2600 games. The ALE was originally written in C++ with interfaces to Python, Java, and other languages. The ALE supports numerous Atari ROMs, including popular titles like Tetris, Space Invaders, and Pac-Man.

ALEx stands for Arcade Learning Environment in Elixir. ALEx uses NIFs to create an Elixir wrapper around the ALE to allow Elixir programmers to develop agents for the ALE. ALEx offers all of the same functionality as the ALE, conveniently packaged in an Elixir library.

In this section, you'll use ALEx to evolve agents to play Tetris. The agents you design in this chapter will be naive—the purpose is simply to see how genetic algorithms can integrate with visual tools to produce real results.

Installing and Compiling ALEx

The ALE, and subsequently ALEx, requires libsdl1.2[5] and cmake.[6] If you don't have either, you can install them like this:

```
$ sudo apt-get install libsdl1.2-dev libsdl-gfx1.2-dev \
    libsdl-image1.2-dev cmake
```

The easiest way to build ALEx on Windows is by installing the Windows Subsystem for Linux (WSL) and running your project in the WSL.

Next, you need to add ALEx to your dependencies in mix.exs:

```
defp deps do
  ...
  {:alex, "~> 0.3.2"}
  ...
end
```

Now, run mix deps.get. After your dependencies are downloaded, run mix deps.compile. You should see something like this:

```
$ mix deps.compile
Compiling ALE. This will take some time.
```

As the output says, the ALE compilation will take a very long time to complete. If your compilation fails, it's likely because ALEx can't find erl_nif.h. This usually happens if you don't have erlang-dev installed. You can fix this by running the following:

```
$ sudo apt-get install erlang-dev
```

And then run this:

```
$ mix deps.clean
$ mix deps.get
$ mix deps.compile
```

After awhile, here's what you should see:

```
$ mix deps.compile
Compiling ALE. This will take some time.
Successfully compiled ALE.
```

Once that's done, you're ready to go. Fortunately, you won't have to recompile the ALE every time you recompile your program.

---

5. https://www.libsdl.org/
6. https://cmake.org/

Interacting with ALEx

ALEx offers functionality through the Alex module. You'll likely only ever need to work with the functions in the Alex module; however, ALEx also offers a number of modules for interacting with things like game state, RAM, Atari ROMs, and the screen. The Alex.Interface module offers functions that directly interact with the ALE interface.

Future versions of ALEx will offer interactions with the ALE interface through a GenServer. For now, to interact with ALEx inside your genetic algorithm, you'll need to create a basic wrapper around the ALE interface. To keep things simple, you'll create a simple game Agent that holds a reference to the ALE interface.

First, create a new file tetris.exs in scripts. In tetris.exs, define a new TetrisInterface module, like this:

```
defmodule TetrisInterface do
  use Agent

  def start_link(path_to_tetris_rom) do
  end

end
```

You'll only need to implement start_link/1 to spin up a new Agent around an ALEx interface. Implement start_link/1 like this:

```
def start_link(path_to_tetris_rom) do
  int = Alex.new()

  game =
    int
    |> Alex.set_option(:display_screen, true)
    |> Alex.set_option(:sound, true)
    |> Alex.set_option(:random_seed, 123)
    |> Alex.load(path_to_tetris_rom)

  Agent.start_link(fn -> game end, name: __MODULE__)
end
```

This function spins up a new Agent that's a wrapper around an ALEx interface. It takes a path to a ROM file—which you'll learn about in the next section—and initializes a new ALEx interface with some options. :display_screen ensures you can see the gameplay that's happening, :sound ensures you can hear the sound, and :random_seed is the seed the game starts with. Setting the seed ensures every single iteration of game play is exactly the same. This is important for comparing between solutions.

Creating a Tetris Agent

Before you can get started evolving Tetris agents, you need to download a copy of an Atari 2600 Tetris ROM. Fortunately, the ALE repo offers the official Tetris ROM.[7] Atari 2600 ROMs are also available from a number of websites. If you're worried about the contents of a ROM, you can see the checksums of supported ROMs here.[8]

Once you download tetris.bin, create a new folder named priv and place tetris.bin into it. Next, in tetris.exs, create a new problem:

```
defmodule Tetris do
  @behaviour Problem
  alias Types.Chromosome

  @impl true
  def genotype, do: # ...

  @impl true
  def fitness_function(chromosome), do: # ...

  @impl true
  def terminate?(population, generation), do: # ...
end
```

Now you need to get started encoding your problem.

Your Tetris AI will need to perform a series of actions that change the game state. If you recall, Tetris is a game where tiles fall into the playing field until they stack on another tile or hit the bottom. If the tiles are stacked such that they create a horizontal line filling the entire playing field, all of the blocks on the horizontal line disappear, and the player is awarded points.

In Tetris, you can choose to move left or right or rotate a tile. You can also choose to speed up or slow down the falling of the tile. In ALEx, actions are encoded as positive integers and stored in the legal_actions field of an ALEx interface. You want your agent to make a series of actions that maximize the score of the game. If your goal is to find the best series of actions, you can encode solutions as a list of integer actions, like this:

```
def genotype do
  game = Agent.get(TetrisInterface, & &1) # Get the ALE
  genes = for _ <- 1..1000, do: Enum.random(game.legal_actions)
  %Chromosome{genes: genes, size: 1000}
end
```

7. https://github.com/mgbellemare/Arcade-Learning-Environment/blob/master/ale_py/tests/fixtures/tetris.bin
8. https://hexdocs.pm/alex/supported-roms.html#content

First, you grab the running game from the TetrisGame Agent. The game gives you access to legal_actions, which is the set of legal actions you can perform in Tetris. Next, you use Enum.random/1 to select 100 random actions to perform in a series. Note, 1000 actions is probably not long enough to complete a full game of Tetris. Additionally, implementing agents in this way is a bit naive—typically you'd want to make decisions based off of the game state, but doing this is outside of the scope of this book.

Next, you need to define a fitness function. Remember, your goal is to maximize the reward of a series of 100 actions. To do this, you need to run a series of 100 actions and get the final score. You can accomplish that like this:

```
def fitness_function(chromosome) do
  game = Agent.get(TetrisInterface, & &1) # Get the ALE
  actions = chromosome.genes

  game =
    actions
    |> Enum.reduce(game, fn act, game -> Alex.step(game, act) end)

  reward = game.reward
  Alex.reset(game) # Reset the game after a run
  reward
end
```

In this function, you start by getting the ALEx interface. Next, you get the actions specified by the current solution. After that you run each action, updating the game state every time with Enum.reduce/3. Alex.step/2 represents a single step through the game, given an action. After you complete all of the actions, you extract the current reward from the game and then reset the game.

The fitness function corresponds to a single *episode* of 100 steps. An episode is a static run through a game. After each episode, you need to reset the game to evaluate the next episode.

Now you need to define your termination criteria. You don't know exactly what the best score possible is, so it's best to terminate based on generation:

```
def terminate?(_population, generation), do: generation == 5
```

Each episode will take a long time to run, so you'll want to keep the number of generations low. You can always run the algorithm longer if you want to.

Now, you're ready to run.

Running the Tetris Agent

With your algorithm implemented, you're ready to roll. First, you need to start the TetrisGame agent so your algorithm can interact with the game, like this:

```
TetrisInterface.start_link("priv/tetris.bin")
```

Next, add the following:

```
soln = Genetic.run(Tetris, population_size: 10)
IO.write("\n")
IO.write("Best is #{soln}\n")
```

Because it takes so long to run a solution, you'll want to keep your population size small as well. Now, you can run your algorithm:

```
$ mix run scripts/tetris.exs
```

While your algorithm is running, you should see something like this:

ALEx will display a small Tetris window that runs through each solution in your population and tests it. It will reset each solution once the run is complete. All you need to do is wait.

If you don't wish to watch the evolution in real time, you can always set :display_screen to false and instead take screenshots at the end of every episode using Alex.screenshot/1.

After the algorithm runs for awhile, you'll get some output like this:

```
$ mix run scripts/tetris.exs
%Types.Chromosome{
  age: 1,
  fitness: 0,
  genes: [0, 1, 1, 2, 3..., 1, 0],
  size: 1000
}
```

Your algorithm didn't learn how to play Tetris very well. That's OK—you can improve upon it in plenty of ways. See if you can build off of your work here and create a better Tetris agent. Additionally, you can implement agents for a ton of different Atari 2600 games, so be sure to check them out.

ALEx is just one tool—a sandbox for creating algorithms that interact with actual environments. OpenAI has lots of other environments for a wide variety of different games and scenarios. Hopefully, you saw how these tools can help you understand how solutions translate to actions in an environment.

What You Learned

In this chapter, you learned a few different ways to add visualizations to your algorithms.

In the first section, you learned how to create visualizations from the genealogy tree generated over the course of an evolution. You learned how to export the tree to a DOT file and use a third-party tool like Graphviz to view the result.

After that, you learned how to use Gnuplot to generate plots of basic statistics like mean fitness over the course of an evolution. You learned how to use the graph to adjust your termination criteria.

Finally, you learned how to visualize specific solutions to specific problems using a tool like ALEx.

You now have a fully-featured genetic algorithm library with the following features:

- Basic problem definitions
- Customizable hyperparameters
- Customizable selection, crossover, mutation, and reinsertion strategies
- Customizable statistics
- Genealogy tracking

You can customize this library to accomplish any task imaginable. In the next chapter, rather than add new features, you'll improve your library by learning how to optimize your existing code base.

## CHAPTER 11

Optimizing Your Algorithms

Thus far, you haven't needed to worry too much about the performance of the algorithms you've implemented. The solutions have been small, and you've been working with relatively small populations. Because of this, you haven't needed to be concerned with efficiency. In the real world, you'll often need to deal with significantly larger solutions and populations when applying genetic algorithms to practical problems.

As it turns out, Elixir is a language that wasn't designed to be extremely efficient at computationally expensive tasks. Things like floating-point math and matrix multiplication are slow in Elixir. Elixir runs on the BEAM, which was designed for telecommunication systems. This doesn't mean you can't write performant genetic algorithms in Elixir; it means you need to be deliberate in optimizing those algorithms.

The BEAM is the Erlang virtual machine. It's the core of Erlang/OTP. Every Elixir file compiles to BEAM bytecode. The best way to understand the performance of your applications is to understand what happens when your application compiles and runs the BEAM bytecode. This chapter will briefly cover some aspects of the BEAM; however, the material isn't comprehensive by any means. For a fantastic explanation of the internals of the BEAM, check out The BEAM Book.[1]

In this chapter, you'll learn how to benchmark and profile your algorithms, and you'll briefly learn about where performance really matters. Additionally, you'll learn different ways to optimize your algorithms. We'll walk through a series of optimizations, in the following order:

1. Creating benchmarks and profiling your algorithms.
2. Optimizing the performance of Elixir code.

---

1. https://github.com/happi/theBeamBook

3. Parallelizing your algorithms.
4. Writing NIFS.

When working through optimizations, this is generally the order of optimizations you should make—only progressing to the next step when absolutely necessary.

Benchmarking and Profiling Genetic Algorithms

The first step in any optimization process is doing some investigative work by establishing baselines and determining where your code is slow. *Benchmarking* is the process of evaluating your code from a performance point of view. Benchmarking is usually done to assess the performance of units of code in the context of space (memory usage) or time (execution time). *Profiling* is the process of evaluating specific aspects of a program in space or time to aid in performance optimization. Profiling helps you identify specific bottlenecks in your code.

The difference between benchmarking and profiling is subtle. The purpose of benchmarking is to establish performance metrics for an entire operation to compare between operations. This could mean comparing operations performed with different settings or comparing operations on different hardware.

The purpose of profiling is to understand the behavior of a program. For example, a profiler might tell you where a program spends most of its time or what functions a program invokes the most. Profiling offers detailed insights into where you should try to optimize your code the most.

You can use a number of tools to benchmark and profile your code. In this section, you'll use Benchee to benchmark your algorithms and ExProf to profile them. But before you begin optimizing, you need to decide if it's even worth it.

Deciding When to Optimize

Oftentimes, programmers make the decision to optimize code prematurely and unnecessarily. Optimization isn't a bad thing; however, choosing to optimize at the wrong time—or for the wrong reasons—hinders the development process.

Practical genetic algorithms are computationally expensive—real-world problems will often require you to work with significant amounts of data. Fortunately, modern hardware alleviates a lot of the pressure on software to be optimized. Often, the available computing power far exceeds computational requirements. In a lot of situations, optimization isn't necessary.

Of course, when you're dealing with a lot of data, optimization can be necessary to prevent algorithms from crashing. On a moderately powerful machine, your genetic algorithms will become noticeably slower when the population size, and the size of each chromosome, multiplies to around 1,000,000. In most other circumstances, you'll see no noticeable performance dips and optimization is unnecessary.

You can reference the Erlang documentation[2] for explicit information on the limits of the BEAM and memory usage of different data types. This might help you in determining if you need to devote time to optimization.

Using Benchee to Analyze Performance

If you decide that optimization is necessary, the first thing you need to do is establish a baseline. Benchmarking your algorithm allows you to determine if the optimizations you're making are having any impact on the overall performance of your algorithm. Benchmarking is a necessary first step to determine if your optimizations are meaningful.

Benchee[3] is an Elixir benchmarking package that's easy to use and provides a lot of information out of the box. You'll use Benchee to benchmark the different aspects of your genetic algorithms.

Start by adding Benchee to your dependencies in mix.exs:

```
defp deps do
  # ... other deps
  {:benchee, ~> "1.0.1"}
end
```

Next, create a new file benchmark.exs in a new directory bench. You'll declare basic benchmarks of each of your core functions in this file.

Benchmarks are typically done on large parts of programs. In this example, you'll benchmark each of the core functions in your genetic algorithm framework, and you'll also benchmark a single evolution. To do this, you need to declare a DummyProblem that serves as a baseline problem for your genetic algorithm to work on. The problem you declare won't solve anything useful, but it will serve as a means to benchmark the different functions in your algorithm. In benchmark.exs, declare your DummyProblem, like this:

```
defmodule DummyProblem do
  @behaviour Problem
  alias Types.Chromosome
```

---

2. http://erlang.org/documentation/doc-5.8.4/doc/efficiency_guide/advanced.html
3. https://github.com/bencheeorg/benchee

```
@impl true
def genotype do
  genes = for _ <- 1..100, do: Enum.random(0..1)
  %Chromosome{genes: genes, size: 100}
end

@impl true
def fitness_function(chromosome), do: Enum.sum(chromosome.genes)

@impl true
def terminate?(_population, generation), do: generation == 1
end
```

initialize requires a genotype that returns a new chromosome. Here, you declare a genotype that's identical to one you've used in other problems. You can change this to whatever you like, but the idea is to use a typical genotype so that you understand how initialize performs in an average scenario.

evaluate requires a fitness_function. In the same spirit as the genotype you declared for initialize, you'll use a fitness function that's identical to other ones you've used before. Once again, you can change the fitness function, but the function you defined here will represent a typical fitness function for any problem.

terminate? is a dummy termination function. It terminates after a single generation to ensure you can get one full iteration of the evolve function. You could create a dummy evolve function and see negligible differences in performance; however, this methodology ensures you get a true picture of the performance of your functions.

Next, you need to declare dummy populations to pass to your other functions. You can use initialize and the genotype you declared, like this:

```
dummy_population = Genetic.initialize(&DummyProblem.genotype/0,
                                      population_size: 100)
{dummy_selected_population, _} = Genetic.select(dummy_population,
                                                selection_rate: 1.0)
```

You need two different populations for the functions in your algorithm. dummy_population is a standard population that can be passed to select, evaluate, and mutation. dummy_selected_population represents a population of parents for use in crossover. If you recall from Chapter 2, Breaking Down Genetic Algorithms, on page 15, crossover requires a list of tuples. Calling select on the dummy_population takes care of this for you. Additionally, you declare a :selection_rate of 1.0. You can change this, but understand that the performance of crossover changes with respect to the selection rate because the selection rate determines how many parents are in the selected population.

The final step is to declare your benchmarks for each function. At the bottom of benchmark.exs, add the following:

```
Benchee.run(
  %{
    "initialize" => fn -> Genetic.initialize(&DummyProblem.genotype/0) end,
    "evaluate" =>
      fn ->
        Genetic.evaluate(dummy_population, &DummyProblem.fitness_function/1)
      end,
    "select" => fn -> Genetic.select(dummy_population) end,
    "crossover" => fn -> Genetic.crossover(dummy_selected_population) end,
    "mutation" => fn -> Genetic.mutation(dummy_population) end,
    "evolve" => fn -> Genetic.evolve(dummy_population, DummyProblem, 0) end
  },
  memory_time: 2
)
```

Here, you declare the functions you're trying to benchmark. Benchee will run each of these functions and report the performance of each. The :memory_time option tells Benchee how long memory tests should be performed for. The default is 0, so to turn it on, you need to declare a positive number.

Next, run your benchmarks, like this:

```
$ mix run bench/benchmark.exs
...

Comparison:
evaluate          8.94 K
select            7.84 K - 1.14x slower +15.72 µs
mutation          5.59 K - 1.60x slower +67.12 µs
crossover         2.30 K - 3.88x slower +322.20 µs
evolve            0.88 K - 10.17x slower +1025.02 µs
initialize        0.26 K - 34.72x slower +3770.38 µs

...

Comparison:
evaluate           24.29 KB
select             31.66 KB - 1.30x memory usage +7.37 KB
mutation          117.23 KB - 4.83x memory usage +92.94 KB
crossover         264.77 KB - 10.90x memory usage +240.48 KB
evolve            412.39 KB - 16.98x memory usage +388.10 KB
initialize       2201.65 KB - 90.64x memory usage +2177.36 KB
```

After some system information, you'll see the results of the benchmarks. Your results might differ slightly from what you see here. You should see some statistics related to each benchmark. That information has been left out here.

You can also see the baseline performance of each of your functions in both memory usage and overall performance. You might notice that initialize/2 is the slowest function. Your immediate reaction here might be to aggressively optimize initialize/2; however, that wouldn't make much sense because initialize/2 only runs once. You wouldn't get much benefit out of optimizing it.

In the next section, you'll learn how to use a profiler to determine where you should optimize.

Identifying Bottlenecks with ExProf

ExProf[4] is an Elixir profiling tool that wraps around Erlang's :eprof. A profiler tells you about the behavior of your code and helps you determine where to optimize.

To start using ExProf, first add it as a dependency:

```
defp deps do
  ...
  {:exprof, "~> 0.2.0"}
  ...
end
```

Next, create a new file profile.exs in bench. In the newly created file, add a DummyProblem module identical to the one you declared in the last section, like this:

```
defmodule DummyProblem do
  @behaviour Problem
  alias Types.Chromosome

  @impl true
  def genotype do
    genes = for _ <- 1..100, do: Enum.random(0..1)
    %Chromosome{genes: genes, size: 100}
  end

  @impl true
  def fitness_function(chromosome), do: Enum.sum(chromosome.genes)

  @impl true
  def terminate?(_population, generation), do: generation == 1
end
```

You'll use this problem to benchmark the performance of your algorithm. Next, create a Profiler module like this:

```
defmodule Profiler do
  import ExProf.Macro
```

---

4. https://github.com/parroty/exprof

```
  def do_analyze do
    profile do
      Genetic.run(DummyProblem)
    end
  end

  def run do
    {records, _block_result} = do_analyze
    total_percent = Enum.reduce(records, 0.0, &(&1.percent + &2))
    IO.inspect "total = #{total_percent}"
  end
end
```

This code uses the profile macro from ExProf to profile the performance of your genetic algorithm. You wrap whatever functions you want to profile inside of the profile macro. The rest of the code is required to run the overall profile.

Next, you need to run the profiler in the script:

```
Profiler.run()
```

Now, run the profiler:

```
$ mix run scripts/profile.exs
...
```

You should see a long list of results indicating where your genetic algorithm spends most of its time. Overall, you'll notice that most of the work in the algorithm happens in list functions and random number generation. So how do you best address these? You can speed up list functions by writing algorithmically efficient code and by parallelizing the code. You'll learn about both of those concepts in the next two sections. You can speed up RNG by rolling simpler, custom RNGs with NIFs. You'll learn about that in Improving Performance with NIFs, on page 183.

Writing Fast Elixir

One of the first rules of thumb for optimizing code states: "you can't optimize a bad algorithm." The most significant performance gains in your code will often come from better algorithms. Efficient algorithms can make up for limitations in computing power.

A comprehensive introduction to data structure and algorithm design is outside of the scope of this book. If you want to learn about writing efficient algorithms and improving your code's performance, check out *A Common-Sense Guide to Data Structures and Algorithms [Wen20]*.

Instead, this section will cover some basic tips to increase the performance of your Elixir code—this is simply an overview and is not meant to be a comprehensive guide for writing fast Elixir. You can reference Fast Elixir[5] for a more in-depth look at the performance of different functions.

Reduce or Map?

A basic optimization you can make when you don't need to preserve the order of your lists is to replace Enum.map/2 with Enum.reduce/3. The reason this works is because all of Elixir's Enum functions are implemented using a reduce function. For example, in crossover, you could just as easily use Enum.map/2 to apply crossover to every pair of parents in the population, like this:

```
def crossover(population, opts \\ []) do
  crossover_fn = Keyword.get(opts,
                            :crossover_type,
                            &Toolbox.Crossover.single_point/2)
  population
  |> Enum.map(fn {p1, p2} -> apply(crossover_fn, [p1, p2]) end)
end
```

This function is much more concise than your original implementation:

```
def crossover(population, opts \\ []) do
  crossover_fn =
    opts
    |> Keyword.get(:crossover_type, &Toolbox.Crossover.single_point/2)
  population
  |> Enum.reduce([],
      fn {p1, p2}, acc ->
        {c1, c2} = apply(crossover_fn, [p1, p2])
        [c1, c2 | acc]
      end
    )
end
```

However, it's also slightly less performant. Note that Enum.reduce/3 will reverse the order of your list. If you need to preserve order, use Enum.map/2.

Take and Drop

When using Enum.take/2 and Enum.drop/2, you have the option to use negative numbers to indicate "taking" or "dropping" from the back of the list. Doing so will result in a significant performance drop.

---

5.   https://github.com/devonestes/fast-elixir

The reason lies in how these two functions are implemented in the Elixir standard library. If you find yourself using Enum.take/2 with a negative number, like this:

```
x = Enum.take(some_list, -50)
```

You can replace it with Enum.drop/2, like this:

```
x = Enum.drop(some_list, 50)
```

Performing this "optimization" on my machine resulted in an almost 2x increase in performance. It's also more correct to use drop in this instance.

Lazy Evaluation

Elixir offers the Stream module which allows you to use lazy evaluation over eager evaluation. Lazy evaluation ensures that you only execute functions when you need to. It eliminates unnecessary calculations. In general, the Stream module is slightly less performant than Enum for the same tasks; however, Stream offers some benefits that can increase performance.

For example, when creating new populations, you can use Stream.repeatedly/2 in initialize, like this:

```
def initialize(genotype, opts \\ []) do
  Stream.repeatedly(genotype)
end
```

You can then pass the Stream from function to function until you absolutely need the entire population. This saves some memory up until you need to produce the entire population for selection, crossover, and mutation. In general, you might not see performance increases from this approach; however, you can benefit from using streams when you need to cut out unnecessary calculations.

Improving Performance with Parallelization

One of the strengths of genetic algorithms is their ability to be parallelized. *Parallelism* is when processes execute simultaneously on multiple cores, systems, and the like. The tasks that make up an evolution can be performed in parallel to yield significant performance gains. The BEAM is optimized for orchestrating computations in parallel. You can take advantage of this fact to improve the performance of your genetic algorithms.

The benefit of writing genetic algorithms in Elixir is the availability of a rich set of parallelization features. Parallelizing algorithms in Elixir is straightforward thanks to modules like Task, Agent, and GenServer. You can parallelize your program in just a few lines of code, and let the Erlang Scheduler handle the orchestration of computation for you. The Erlang Scheduler is responsible for orchestrating the processes you spawn during the life cycle of your Elixir applications. You can think of a scheduler like a parent who forces siblings to share toys. Each sibling (process) gets some time (runtime) to play with the toy (computing power). To learn more about how the Erlang Scheduler works, check out The BEAM Book.[6]

You can achieve parallelization in your genetic algorithms on the BEAM in many ways. In this section, you'll explore two: using the Task module and using Agents. However, before you begin, it's important to understand the difference between concurrency and parallelism, and how parallelism in Elixir works.

Concurrency Versus Parallelism

The distinction between *concurrency* and parallelism is important when determining how best to speed up your genetic algorithms. Erlang is built to be a concurrent language. Processes are concurrent when they appear to be executing simultaneously but they're actually executing on the same thread. The scheduler achieves concurrency by alternating between processes until all processes are complete.

You can achieve true parallelism on the BEAM if you have a multi-core or distributed system. The BEAM will automatically parallelize your processes using *symmetric multiprocessing (SMP)*. You don't need to understand what SMP is or how it works. If your machine supports SMP and has multiple cores, the scheduler handles the parallelization for you.

To check if you have SMP enabled, open iex and type:

```
iex(1)> :erlang.system_info :smp_support
true
```

If it returns true, your system is capable of parallel execution. To see how many schedulers your system will use, type the following:

```
iex(2)> :erlang.system_info :schedulers_online
12
```

The number of schedulers indicates the number of processes that will run in parallel on your machine. Most modern machines will have at least four cores and thus four schedulers. Just because you have four cores, however, doesn't mean that the BEAM will bind one scheduler per core or thread. Instead, the

---

6. https://github.com/happi/theBeamBook

BEAM will leave it up to your operating system to decide how to allocate schedulers.

One thing to remember is that parallelism doesn't always lead to better performance. Some code just isn't parallelizable. Sometimes the overhead associated with parallelism is too expensive for simple tasks. You need to consider these things when determining which parts of your code will benefit the most from parallelism.

An additional consideration is that there's a point of diminishing returns when it comes to parallelism. In most languages, creating threads is expensive and has a certain amount of overhead. The overhead makes it such that creating too many threads will decrease performance rather than increase. Additionally, on small tasks, parallelism would be unnecessary because of the associated overhead.

On the BEAM, spawning processes is an inexpensive process; however, you still need to be conscious of how attempts at parallelism will impact the performance of your algorithms. If you're processing relatively small amounts of data, it doesn't usually make sense to parallelize because the associated overhead of parallelism will decrease your performance. You should turn to parallelism when dealing with larger amounts of data that takes a long time to process.

Using the Task Module

The easiest way to parallelize in Elixir is using the Task module. The Task module offers convenience functions for working with *tasks*. In Elixir, a task is a process meant to perform a single action throughout its lifetime. You can use the Task module to execute code concurrently or in parallel.

In genetic.ex, create a new function pmap/2 like this:

```
def pmap(collection, func) do
  collection
  |> Enum.map(&Task.async(func.(&1)))
  |> Enum.map(&Task.await(&1))
end
```

This function comes from *Programming Elixir [Tho14]*. It implements a parallel map function by attaching every element in a collection to a process. The processes will then all execute in parallel. Task.await/2 will return the result of every process.

You can use pmap/2 to replace the traditional Enum.map/2 calls in your code; however, it doesn't always make sense to do this. To understand why, you'll look at some basic examples.

Create a new file pmap.exs in scripts. At the top of the file, create two anonymous functions expensive and inexpensive, like this:

```
expensive =
  fn x ->
    x = x * x
    :timer.sleep(500)
    x
  end
inexpensive = fn x -> x * x end
```

expensive simulates a computationally expensive function using :timer.sleep/1. inexpensive is a computationally inexpensive function.

Next, create some dummy data with 100 elements, like this:

```
data = for x <- 1..100, do: x
```

Finally, benchmark pmap/2 and Enum.map/2 with both inexpensive and expensive functions:

```
Benchee.run(%{
  "pmap, expensive" => fn -> Genetic.pmap(data, &(expensive.(&1))) end,
  "pmap, inexpensive" => fn -> Genetic.pmap(data, &(inexpensive.(&1))) end,
  "map, expensive" => fn -> Enum.map(data, &(expensive.(&1))) end,
  "map, inexpensive" => fn -> Enum.map(data, &(inexpensive.(&1))) end
}, memory_time: 7)
```

You'll benchmark both performance and memory usage to get a clear picture of what's happening. Now, run pmap.exs:

```
$ mix run scripts/pmap.exs
...

Comparison:
map, inexpensive        423.09 K
pmap, inexpensive         3.13 K - 134.98x slower +316.68 µs
pmap, expensive         0.00200 K - 212074.08x slower +501245.72 µs
map, expensive          0.00002 K - 21196897.26x slower +50099963.86 µs

...

Comparison:
map, inexpensive          1.62 KB
pmap, inexpensive        51.78 KB - 32.02x memory usage +50.17 KB
pmap, expensive          52.46 KB - 32.44x memory usage +50.85 KB
map, expensive            1.62 KB - 1.00x memory usage +0 KB
```

What you'll notice here is that pmap/2 runs significantly faster on the computationally expensive function and significantly slower on the inexpensive function. Why is this? It's all about overhead.

Notice the memory usage of pmap/2 is much higher than map/2. That's because you create a new process for every element in your list. Every process on the BEAM comes with its own stack, heap, message area, and process control block. You don't need to know what each of these areas is for, but you should understand that process creation comes with some associated memory overhead.

With the inexpensive function, the creation of new processes is more expensive than the work being parallelized. Using pmap/2 on an inexpensive function is overkill. With the expensive function, pmap/2 is significantly faster because it can execute all of the expensive work in parallel.

In your genetic algorithm framework, it makes the most sense to replace Enum.map/2 in areas where computation is most expensive. For example, you'll probably see speedups using pmap/2 over Enum.map/2 in evaluate, crossover, and mutation if you're using expensive fitness functions and crossover or mutation strategies. If you aren't using expensive fitness functions or strategies, you'll likely end up hurting rather than helping performance.

Treating Chromosomes as Processes

The strongest aspect of the BEAM is its ability to create and work with processes. You saw how easy it was to spin up new processes using the Task module in the last section. In this section, you'll use the Agent module to accomplish parallelization in a different manner.

An Agent is an abstraction around state. Agents allow you to keep track of state between entities. In your original genetic algorithm framework, you perform transformations on Chromosome structs. Using an Agent, you can replace these transformations with interactions between processes. These processes will naturally run in parallel and your algorithms will achieve parallelism naturally.

Note that you probably won't see significant performance increases using this approach on normal machines. Using this approach in practice requires a massively parallel system to be viable. It also requires some additional complexities to implement correctly. In this section, you'll implement a basic agent and see how you can evaluate a population of agents.

Start by opening chromosome.ex in types. At the top of the file, add the following line:

```
use Agent
```

This line tells Elixir that you'll be implementing the Agent behaviour.

Next, you need to implement some functions for interacting with the Agent. Add the following to chromosome.ex:

```
def start_link(genes) do
  Agent.start_link(fn -> %Chromosome{genes: genes, size: Enum.count(genes)})
end

def get_fitness(pid) do
  Agent.get(pid, & &1.fitness)
end

def eval(pid, fitness) do
  c = Agent.get(pid, & &1)
  Agent.update(pid, fn -> %Chromosome{c | fitness: fitness.(c)})
end
```

Here, you implement three functions start_link/1, get_fitness/1, and eval/2. start_link/1 creates a new Chromosome given some genes. get_fitness/1 returns fitness for use in evaluate/1. eval/2 evaluates a Chromosome given a fitness function. You'll use this function to evaluate chromosomes in parallel.

Now you need to tweak how you implement initialize/1 and evaluate/2. In genetic.ex, change both functions to match this:

```
def initialize(genotype, opts \\ []) do
  population_size = Keyword.get(opts, :population_size, 100)
  for _ <- 1..100, do: Chromosome.start_link(genes: genotype.())
end

def evaluate(population, fitness_function, _opts \\ []) do
  population
  |> Enum.map(&Task.async(fn -> Chromosome.eval(&1, fitness_function)))
  |> Enum.sort_by(fn c -> Chromosome.get_fitness(c) end, &>=/2)
end
```

You'll notice a few changes here. First, in initialize/0 you replace the declaration of a new Chromosome struct with a call to start_link/1. Next, in evaluate/1 you use both eval/2 and get_fitness/1 to first evaluate every chromosome process and then sort them. Note, for simplicity, in this example evaluate doesn't update the age of a chromosome.

Now, when you run evaluate on an expensive fitness function, they'll execute in parallel as messages sent to each Agent process.

This approach follows similar approaches taken in evolutionary-based algorithms written in Erlang, but it's not necessary for the situations you will encounter.

Improving Performance with NIFs

Native Implemented Functions (NIFs) are a great way to inject speed into your Elixir/Erlang programs. NIFs are programs implemented in compiled languages like Rust or C/C++ that are then linked and loaded into your Elixir module at runtime.

NIFs were designed to be a simpler and more efficient way of interfacing with native code than *ports*. Ports interact with external programs and offer a mechanism of implementing program features in a different language.

NIFs are often used in places where Elixir/Erlang alone isn't enough to efficiently get the job done. For example, the Matrex[7] library uses NIFs to perform fast matrix operations because Elixir/Erlang isn't optimized to perform these operations alone.

One thing to consider with NIFs is that they have the potential to crash your program. NIFs take the fault-tolerance out of applications because the code loaded is from an external program. Additionally, NIFs have a strange way of interacting with Erlang's scheduler. The scheduler expects NIFs to return in a certain amount of time; however, if they don't, it can dramatically impact the performance of your programs.

You can use NIFs to boost performance on your crossover and mutation functions or to augment Elixir implementations of slower functions. For example, random number generation is a notoriously expensive task. You can augment random number generation with a simple and fast C/C++ implementation of a more basic RNG like an XOR-Shift RNG. This repository[8] implements a number of XOR-shift RNGs in C.

To get a better idea of how to implement NIFs, you'll implement a basic RNG NIF in C. Start by creating a new file genetic.c in a new directory src. In the file, add the following:

```
#include <erl_nif.h>
#include <inttypes.h>
#include <stdint.h>

static uint32_t x = 123456789, y = 362436069, z = 521288629;

static ERL_NIF_TERM xor96(ErlNifEnv* env, int argc, const ERL_NIF_TERM argv[])
{
  uint32_t t = (x^(x<<10));
  x = y;
```

---

7. https://github.com/versilov/matrex
8. https://github.com/WebDrake/xorshift/

```
  y = z;
  z = (z^(z>>26))^(t^(t>>5));

  return enif_make_int(env, z);
}
static ErlNifFunc nif_funcs[] =
{
  {"xor96", 0, xor96}
};

ERL_NIF_INIT(Elixir.Genetic, nif_funcs, NULL, NULL, NULL, NULL);
```

This code defines an XOR96 random number generator and returns it to the Erlang environment using the Erlang NIF C interfaces. Most of the code you see defined here is boilerplate code necessary to create NIFs in C.

Next, you need to define a new Mix compiler in mix.exs, like this:

```
defmodule Mix.Tasks.Compile.Genetic do
  use Mix.Task.Compiler

  def run(_args) do
    {result, _errcode} =
      System.cmd(
        "gcc",
        ["-fpic", "-shared", "-o", "genetic.so", "src/genetic.c"],
        stderr_to_stdout: true
      )
    IO.puts(result)
  end
end
```

This code uses the Mix.Compiler API to create a new Mix compiler that will compile your NIFs to a shared-object library using GCC. If you're using Windows, you'll have to either use MingW, Windows Subsystem for Linux (WSL), or integrate this workflow with Visual Studio. MingW is probably the most straightforward option. It's a port of the C compiler, GCC, to Windows.

Next, you add your compiler to your projects :compilers like this:

```
defmodule Genetic.Mixfile do
  use Mix.Project

  def project do
    [
      app: :genetic,
      ...
      compilers: [:genetic] ++ Mix.compilers,
    ]
  end
  ...
end
```

Now, whenever you compile your algorithms, Mix will run your custom compiler and compile your NIFs for you. To call xor96 from your code, add the following to the top of genetic.ex:

```elixir
defmodule Genetic do
  @on_load :load_nif

  def load_nif do
    :erlang.load_nif('./genetic', 0)
  end

  def xor96, do: raise "NIF xor96/0 not implemented."

  ...
end
```

This code defines a function to run once the module is loaded. The function load_nif/0 uses Erlang's load_nif/2 function to load your shared object library at runtime. You also define a fallback implementation of xor96 to run if Elixir can't find your C implementation.

xor96/0 will generate integers. You can use it to generate integers between 0 and some number, like this:

```elixir
iex(0)> rem(xor96(), 100)
42
```

In an example function like single_point_crossover/2, it would look like this:

```elixir
def single_point_crossover(p1, p2) do
  cx_point = rem(Genetic.xor96(), p1.size)
  {p1_head, p1_tail} = Enum.split(p1.genes, cx_point)
  {p2_head, p2_tail} = Enum.split(p2.genes, cx_point)
  {c1, c2} = {p1_head ++ p2_tail, p2_head ++ p1_tail}
  {%Chromosome{genes: c1, size: length(c1)},
    %Chromosome{genes: c2, size: length(c2)}}
end
```

One issue with this RNG is that it starts from the same state every time your application is run. So it will produce the same order of random numbers every time you run your genetic algorithm. You can find other, better ways to take advantage of NIFs. For example, you could implement entire crossover or mutation functions using NIFs and use your current implementations as fallbacks in case the NIFs don't load for some reason.

What You Learned

In this chapter, you learned some basic tips for optimizing your genetic algorithms. You also learned how to decide when to optimize and that it's often unnecessary to optimize on modern machines. You used benchmarking and profiling tools to establish baselines and determine where to optimize.

You then went through some basic optimization tips and the order in which to try them. You also learned some basic tips for writing faster Elixir and improving the performance of your algorithms.

Next, you learned how parallelization can be used to speed up the performance of your algorithms under certain conditions. You learned when it's best to try and parallelize your algorithms and when it's best to avoid it.

Finally, you learned about NIFs and where you can use NIFs to see performance gains.

Remember, the optimization tips you learned about in this chapter should generally be worked through in the order they were presented here. Start by determining if optimization is even necessary, and then go through some investigative work to establish baselines and determine where you need to optimize. Next, attempt to optimize your Elixir code. After that, you should see if your algorithms would benefit from parallelism in certain places. Finally, if you need to, you can see if NIFs would speed up the performance of some of your functions.

In the next chapter, you'll build up the resiliency of your genetic algorithm framework by learning how to test and analyze the correctness of the code you've written so far.

## CHAPTER 12

Writing Tests and Code Quality

In the last chapter, you learned how to optimize your framework in three different ways to get the most performance out of Elixir and the BEAM. So far, you've created a framework for writing genetic algorithms capable of solving a wide variety of problems. One thing you haven't done, however, is test and analyze this framework to ensure your code is correct and clean.

Testing is a crucial part of any development process. Typically, you'd want to write tests that mirror a specification or some behavior first, before writing any code. This process, called *test driven development*, calls for writing small *unit tests* first and then improving code to mirror a specification. Elixir emphasizes the importance of tests and makes the process of writing unit tests a breeze.

In addition to testing, another key aspect of the development process is ensuring your code is concise and understandable for yourself and any other developers that may be contributing to your project. Fortunately, Elixir has a few packages that make analyzing your code easy, such as credo[1] and dialyxir.[2]

In this chapter, you'll learn how to use ExUnit[3] and StreamData[4] to write property-based tests for your code. You'll also learn how to use credo and dialyxir to improve the code in your framework with some code analysis. Normally, you'd want to use these tools much earlier in the development process; however, I've omitted them until this point to place more emphasis on the core concepts of genetic algorithms. This chapter will get you on track with using these tools to improve upon your existing code base.

---

1. https://github.com/rrrene/credo
2. https://github.com/jeremyjh/dialyxir
3. https://hexdocs.pm/ex_unit/ExUnit.html
4. https://hexdocs.pm/stream_data/StreamData.html

Understanding Randomness

One challenge to writing tests for genetic algorithms is their *stochastic* nature. When something is stochastic, it's dictated by random processes—usually with some associated probability. For example, if you examine how you implemented flip mutation in Chapter 7, Preventing Premature Convergence, on page 107, it looks like this:

```
def flip(chromosome, p) do
  genes =
    chromosome.genes
    |> Enum.map(
      fn g ->
        if :rand.uniform() < p do
          g ^^^ 1
        else
          g
        end
      end
    )
  %Chromosome{genes: genes, size: chromosome.size}
end
```

Remember this function performs a bit-flip with probability p on the genes in a chromosome. Notice the highlighted if-condition. The condition :rand.uniform < p represents a coin-flip that is true with probability p and false with probability 1-p. If you were to test this function with a probability of 0.5, on average, 50% of the genes in your chromosome would be flipped. If you tried to test this, you'd quickly run into problems because the behavior of the function is stochastic. You could run this function on the same chromosome 100 times and get a different outcome every time.

Testing with randomness is difficult because testing often relies on you being able to dictate and understand the outcome of a function. Because most of the functions in your genetic algorithm rely on randomness, you're unable to predict exactly what the output of a function is, which in turn makes it difficult to write tests. Fortunately, there are ways to address the challenge of randomness to effectively test your functions.

In this chapter, you'll learn how to use *property-based testing* to test the functions in your framework. You'll learn more about property-based testing in the next section. For now, you'll learn about two alternative approaches to testing with randomness: *seeding* and *mocking*.

Seeding relies on the need for random number generators to be initialized with a *random seed* from which they generate new random numbers. The

:rand module you've been using implements *pseudo-random number generation (PRNG)* algorithms. This means that the algorithms aren't truly random but give the illusion of randomness. An algorithm is truly random if it can generate numbers infinitely many times without repeating itself. The PRNGs implemented in the :rand module have periods of around 2^64, which means they repeat themselves after 2^64 calls. Essentially, you'll never have to worry about your algorithms not being truly random.

You can provide a random seed to :rand before you generate numbers to control the behavior of the numbers generated. To see this in action, open iex and try the following:

```
iex(1)> :rand.seed(:exsss, 1)
...
iex(2)> :rand.uniform(100000000000000)
82609428762732
iex(3)> :rand.seed(:exsss, 2)
...
iex(4)> :rand.uniform(100000000000000)
4
iex(5)> :rand.seed(:exsss, 1)
...
iex(6)> :rand.uniform(100000000000000)
82609428762732
```

If you repeat that process forever, you'll continue to get the same numbers every time. You could use this same strategy to seed the PRNG before running your tests to guarantee the behavior of your random functions is the same every time. One of the flaws of this approach is you have to trace through the behavior of your function by hand to determine what the outcome of your function is with your chosen seed.

Another approach to testing with randomness is by using mocking. Mocking refers to creating an imitation module to replace the behavior of :rand with something predictable. For this approach, you'd have to create a module to replace :rand at test time with predictable behaviors. This approach is common when testing the behaviors of functions that interact with some API offline. It doesn't work as well with randomness.

Writing Property Tests with ExUnit

Elixir makes testing a breeze using it's testing framework ExUnit. ExUnit is a framework for writing unit tests that's built in to every Elixir project. Every time you create a new project using mix new, Elixir will automatically create a test directory for you and populate it with a skeleton for writing unit tests for your project. ExUnit is already packaged with Elixir, so you don't need to install any dependencies.

StreamData is an Elixir library for writing *property-based tests.* Property-based tests test the properties of a function to ensure your code meets some specified properties every time. Property-based tests are especially useful when your functions contain randomness, because you can write tests that run hundreds of times and ensure your functions meet specified properties and behaviors. For example, if you had a function that generated lists of length 10 of random integers between 1 and 10, you could run the function hundreds of times and ensure that every time it ran, the list it generated contained 10 elements and all of the elements were integers between 1 and 10. StreamData offers utilities for creating streams of data that can be combined with it's ExUnitProperties module to write property-based tests.

This section will walk you through an example property-based test for Toolbox.Crossover.single_point/2. You can repeat this process with the rest of your functions in your framework. To learn more about property-based testing, check out *Property-Based Testing with PropEr, Erlang, and Elixir [Heb19]* or *Testing Elixir [LM20].*

To get started, you first need to add StreamData to your dependencies, like this:

```
defp deps do
  ...
  {:stream_data, "~> 0.5", only: :test}
end
```

The only: :test property specifies that you only need this dependency in a test environment. Run mix deps.get to ensure StreamData is loaded.

Next, create a new file in tests called crossover_test.exs. In that file, add the following:

```
def CrossoverTest do
  use ExUnit.Case
  use ExUnitProperties
  alias Types.Chromosome
end
```

Here you define a module that will contain your test and ensure it uses the ExUnit.Case suite of tools. You then use ExUnitProperties to import the macros for writing property-based tests. Finally, you alias Types.Chromosome, because you'll be creating chromosomes to test your function with later on.

Now, consider what properties the function Toolbox.Crossover.single_point/2 needs to maintain. Recall from Chapter 6, Generating New Solutions, on page 87, single-point crossover takes in two chromosomes and swaps slices of genes at a random crossover point. It maintains the size of both chromosomes, and produces two unique chromosomes at the end. Your test should check to ensure that the size of the chromosomes produced by Toolbox.Crossover.single_point/2 is the same as the input chromosomes. You can try to enforce other properties later on; for now you'll just ensure that single_point/2 maintains the size of the input chromosomes.

Define your test like this:

```
property "single_point/2 maintains the size of input chromosomes" do
  check all size <- integer(0..100),
            gene_1 <- list_of(integer(), length: size),
            gene_2 <- list_of(integer(), length: size) do
    p1 = %Chromosome{genes: gene_1, size: size}
    p2 = %Chromosome{genes: gene_2, size: size}
    {c1, c2} = Toolbox.Crossover.single_point(p1, p2)
    assert c1.size == size and c2.size == size
  end
end
```

Here you define a property using the property macro. You then use the check all macro to generate some data to test your function with. StreamData comes with a number of helpful generators that make creating data easy. In this example you use them to generate genes for two parent chromosomes. In the body of the test, you define two parent chromosomes and then run Toolbox.Crossover.single_point/2 to get two children. Finally, you assert that the size of the children is equal to the original size of both of the original sets of genes.

Next, run mix test, like this:

```
$ mix test
...
Finished in 0.08 seconds
1 property, 1 failure
```

After running, your test might have failed; but why? If you inspect the output of the test, you'll notice that the function doesn't behave well when running on chromosomes with empty genes. While it's not likely you'll run into this problem in practice, you should fix your function to handle empty genes just in case. Open up crossover.ex in toolbox and add the following above single_point/2:

```
def single_point(c1 = %Chromosome{genes: []},
                 c2 = %Chromosome{genes: []}), do: {c1, c2}
```

This function uses pattern matching to check if c1 and c2 are empty. If they are, it returns the original chromosomes. Now, run mix test again:

```
$ mix test
...
Finished in 0.08 seconds
1 property, 0 failures
```

And your problem is fixed. Property-based testing is a useful tool for quickly identifying bugs in your code, especially when trying to test stochastic functions. You may have written a test to explicitly handle the case of empty chromosomes, but the property-based test here caught it for you automatically. You can implement tests like this example for most of the functions in your framework to identify any similar bugs in your code.

Now that you know how to test, in the next section you'll learn how to clean up your code using the static analysis tool, credo.

Cleaning Up Your Framework

Part of good development practice is making sure your code is consistent, clean, and concise. Keeping your code clean and consistent is important to the long-term maintenance of your framework. You, and any future developers who improve your code base, will benefit by ensuring your code is easy to build upon in the future.

In this section, you'll use two tools: credo and the Elixir formatter to improve the structure and style of your code.

Using the Elixir Formatter

Following the coding style of a particular programming language is important to ensuring your code is readable to you and any other developers that work on your project. Fortunately, Elixir comes with a formatter that will help you enforce the formatting standards of the language.

If you take a look at your framework, the genetic directory should contain a file .formatter.exs. This file contains configurations for the mix format task. It looks like this:

```
# Used by "mix format"
[
  inputs: ["{mix,.formatter}.exs", "{config,lib,test}/**/*.{ex,exs}"]
]
```

You can configure the formatter from this file; however, you don't need to for your framework. You just need to run mix format in the terminal in your genetic directory, like this:

```
$ mix format
```

The formatter will run for a bit and then exit without any output. The formatter ensures your code meets the Elixir Style Guide.[5] For the most part, your code shouldn't be much different, minus a few additional newlines here or there.

This step isn't entirely necessary, but it's beneficial to the readability of your code and your development moving forward.

Using Credo

credo[6] is a static code analysis tool for Elixir. It will analyze your code for you and offer suggestions for refactoring, improving readability, and avoiding warnings. You'll run credo and address some minor issues in your framework.

To get started, add credo to your dependencies:

```
{:credo, "~> 1.4", only: [:dev, :test], runtime: false}
```

You only need credo during development and testing, so you specify that here. The runtime: false option tells Elixir that credo doesn't need to be compiled at runtime.

Now, run mix deps.get. After you've successfully pulled down the credo package, you'll be able to use the credo mix tasks. To do that, run the following in the base directory of your genetic framework:

```
$ mix credo --strict
...
Analysis took 0.07 seconds (0.00s to load, 0.07s running 54 checks on 12 files)
55 mods/funs, found 1 refactoring opportunity, 10 code readability issues.
```

The task might take awhile to run. Once it's complete, you'll see some output related to the issues credo finds with your project. In this example, all of your modules will be tagged for not including a @moduledoc tag. That's OK; you can add documentation later. credo also identified a refactoring opportunity in toolbox/selection.exs. This is because the function body of Toolbox.Selection.roulette/2 is nested too deeply. As a general rule, functions should only do one thing—the level of nesting in your function is usually an indication that your function is doing more than it's supposed to. The warning is telling you that you could possibly break the function into smaller pieces that would make your code cleaner and easier to test.

Take a look at the function Toolbox.Selection.roulette/2 in selection.ex:

---

5. https://github.com/christopheradams/elixir_style_guide
6. https://github.com/rrrene/credo

```
def roulette(chromosomes, n) do
  sum_fitness =
    chromosomes
    |> Enum.map(& &1.fitness)
    |> Enum.sum()

  0..(n - 1)
  |> Enum.map(fn _ ->
    u = :rand.uniform() * sum_fitness

    chromosomes
    |> Enum.reduce_while(
      0,
      fn x, sum ->
        if x.fitness + sum > u do
          {:halt, x}
        else
          {:cont, x.fitness + sum}
        end
      end
    )
  end)
end
```

You defined this function in Chapter 5, Selecting the Best, on page 71. Remember, roulette selection simulates the spinning of a roulette wheel to select chromosomes where each chromosome occupies a percentage of the wheel based on its fitness. The offending part of the function occurs in the body of the anonymous function in Enum.reduce_while/3. The function is meant to simulate the spinning of a roulette wheel. To fix it, replace the call to Enum.reduce_while/3 with a call to a private function spin/2, like this:

```
def roulette(chromosomes, n) do
  sum_fitness =
    chromosomes
    |> Enum.map(& &1.fitness)
    |> Enum.sum()

  0..(n - 1)
  |> Enum.map(fn _ ->
    u = :rand.uniform() * sum_fitness
    spin(chromosomes, u)
  end)
end
```

Then implement spin/2 like this:

```
defp spin(chromosomes, u) do
  chromosomes
  |> Enum.reduce_while(
    0,
```

```
    fn x, sum ->
      if x.fitness + sum > u do
        {:halt, x}
      else
        {:cont, x.fitness + sum}
      end
    end
  )
end
```

Notice you've broken your code down into separate functions that are easier to read and, in theory, easier to work with. Now if you run mix credo again, the warning should disappear:

```
$ mix credo --strict
...
Analysis took 0.1 seconds (0.00s to load, 0.1s running 54 checks on 13 files)
58 mods/funs, found 10 code readability issues.
```

Again, this step isn't entirely necessary, but it can help you identify possible issues with your code and clean up your code so it's easier for you and others to work with. You should perform checks with credo as you develop.

Writing Type Specifications

While Elixir isn't a statically typed language, it does give you the ability to specify types using *typespecs*. Typespecs are specifications that communicate the intended use of a function. For example, a function add/2 that adds two numbers a and b might have the following specification:

```
@spec add(number, number) :: number
def add(a, b) do
  a + b
end
```

Notice the syntax used to declare a specification. You use the @spec attribute to indicate you're defining a specification and then declare the parameter types and the return type of the function. The syntax is similar to the syntax you used in Chapter 3, Encoding Problems and Solutions, on page 33, to define callbacks for your Problem behaviour and to define your Chromosome type.

Defining typespecs for your functions won't do anything to improve the performance of your code; however, it does serve to enhance the readability of your code and can be used by dialyxir to find bugs and other problems with your code. In this section, you'll define typespecs for the functions in the Toolbox.Crossover module and analyze them using dialyxir. You can extend this method to the other functions in your framework to identify problems and inconsistencies and improve your code base overall. You can also check out the Elixir typespec documentation[7] to learn more about typespecs and how to use them.

Crossover Typespecs

To get started, open up crossover.ex in toolbox. You'll write typespecs for all of the functions in the Toolbox.Crossover module. Your file should contain four functions: single_point/2, uniform/3, whole_arithmetic/3, and order_one/2.

Every function takes at least two parameters which are two parent chromosomes and returns a tuple of two child chromosomes. uniform/3 and whole_arithmetic/3 take an additional parameter. uniform/3 takes a float between 0 and 1, representing the uniform crossover rate. whole_arithmetic/3 takes a float between 0 and 1, representing the percentage of genes to blend in each child chromosome.

Based on the parameters and return values of each function, implement your typespecs like this:

```
@spec single_point(Chromosome.t, Chromosome.t)
      :: {Chromosome.t, Chromosome.t}
def single_point(p1, p2) do
...
end

@spec uniform(Chromosome.t, Chromosome.t, float)
      :: {Chromosome.t, Chromosome.t}
def uniform(p1, p2, rate) do
...
end

@spec whole_arithmetic(Chromosome.t, Chromosome.t, float)
      :: {Chromosome.t, Chromosome.t}
def whole_arithmetic(p1, p2, alpha) do
...
end

@spec order_one(Chromosome.t, Chromosome.t)
      :: {Chromosome.t, Chromosome.t}
def order_one(p1, p2) do
...
end
```

Here you define typespecs for every function. Notice how you can use the custom type t from the Chromosome module. Each function takes at least two parent chromosomes and they all return a tuple of child chromosomes. Your code is now a bit more expressive, and you can run it through tools like dialyxir to perform some static code analysis.

---

7.   https://hexdocs.pm/elixir/typespecs.html

Running Dialyxir

dialyzer[8] is an Erlang static analysis tool that identifies type errors, unreachable code, software discrepancies, and more. dialyxir implements mix tasks that make using dialyzer from Elixir projects easier.

You'll run your code module through dialyxir to identify any possible issues with your code. To start, add dialyxir to your dependencies, like this:

```
defp deps do
  ...
  {:dialyxir, "~> 1.0", only: [:dev], runtime: false}
end
```

Next, run mix deps.get. Once you have dialyxir installed, you can run it like this:

```
$ mix dialyzer
...
Total errors: 0, Skipped: 0, Unnecessary Skips: 0
done in 0m0.89s
done (passed successfully)
```

dialyzer will take a long time to run. Your code should have passed without any errors. To see what it looks like when your code has errors, change the specification for single_point/2 to look like this:

```
@spec single_point(Chromosome.t, Chromosome.t) :: Chromosome.t
def single_point(p1, p2) do
...
end
```

Then run dialyzer again:

```
$ mix dialyzer
...
Total errors: 1, Skipped: 0, Unnecessary Skips: 0
done in 0m0.95s
lib/toolbox/crossover.ex:6:invalid_contract
The @spec for the function does not match the success typing of the function.

Function:
Toolbox.Crossover.single_point/2

Success typing:
@spec single_point(atom() | %{:genes => _, _ => _},
  atom() | %{:genes => _, _ => _}) ::
  {%Types.Chromosome{:genes => [any()], _ => _},
   %Types.Chromosome{:genes => [any()], _ => _}}
```

---

8.   http://erlang.org/doc/apps/dialyzer/dialyzer_chapter.html

This time dialyzer should run faster. Notice how it identifies the invalid type specification for you and then tells you what the correct type specification looks like. Obviously, this error was intentional, but it's possible to make mistakes like this if your code has many different branches or if you don't stop and check your code often.

Once you change your typespec back, dialyzer will return correctly. You can implement typespecs for all of the functions in your framework and try to run dialyzer to ensure they are correct.

What You Learned

In this chapter, you learned about how to use testing and code analysis to improve your framework and identify any bugs that might negatively affect your algorithms. You started by learning a little about randomness and how randomness can be difficult to test. Then, you learned how to use property-based tests to ensure your functions maintain some specified behaviors.

Next, you used credo to analyze your code for consistency and clarity. You also learned how to use the Elixir formatter to enforce Elixir's style standards in your code.

Finally, you learned about typespecs and how to use dialyxir and typespecs to identify possible bugs in your code.

At this point, you've built a complete framework and learned how to optimize its performance and ensure your code is correct. You've learned how to solve many types of problems. In the next chapter, you'll learn about genetic algorithms in the real world and how you can use the knowledge you've learned in this book in practical settings.

## CHAPTER 13

Moving Forward

Throughout this book, you learned how to use genetic algorithms to solve optimization problems. You discovered the ins and outs of basic genetic algorithms and worked through solving difficult problems with a problem-solving framework. You designed a genetic algorithm framework from start to finish and expanded on this framework with the addition of basic tracking mechanisms and visualizations. You then optimized your framework with tools like ExProf and Benchee, and you learned how to ensure the code you implement within your framework is correct using tools like ExUnit and dialyxir.

At this point, you have a powerful suite of skills and tools in front of you that you can build upon or use to solve practically any problem with a genetic algorithm. One thing you might be wondering now is, "Where do I go next?"

In this chapter, you'll learn about some of the recent advancements in genetic algorithms and the recent innovations driven by genetic algorithms and evolutionary algorithms. Additionally, you'll get familiar with some advanced resources that you can use to continue your journey with genetic algorithms.

Learning with Evolution

Artificial intelligence (AI) and machine learning (ML) have dominated the last decade of computing. AI is experiencing its third "boom" with no signs of stopping. It seems that almost everyday there's a new revolutionary innovation in AI or another startup using AI to improve everyday life. The demand for developers who are familiar with and can solve problems using AI/ML will continue to increase over the next decade.

The latest AI boom is owed mainly to advancements in *deep learning*. Deep learning is the application of multiple layers of transformations on data to extract features from raw inputs and perform tasks like classification or regression. One area deep learning has found a lot of success is in *reinforcement learning.*

Reinforcement learning is a subset of machine learning concerned with teaching agents to take optimal actions in an environment. For example, reinforcement learning is often used to implement AI capable of playing arcade games like the Tetris playing agent you implemented in Chapter 10, Visualizing the Results, on page 157.

Reinforcement learning is all about rewards and punishments. Agents are rewarded for certain actions they take, like completing a line of blocks in Tetris, and punished for others, like losing the game in Tetris. Based on these rewards and their interactions with the environment, agents learn to optimize the decisions under certain conditions.

One area reinforcement learning is applicable is in the optimization of mechanical movement. For example, you can use reinforcement learning to teach a robot how to walk by modeling the movements and angles of a robot's limbs as a series of actions the robot has to take. Over time, the robot learns to lift its legs at a certain angle and plant them at a certain angle, and so on, until it can efficiently move forward.

So, what does this have to do with genetic algorithms? In some situations, genetic algorithms are a viable alternative to reinforcement learning. One of the drawbacks of reinforcement learning is that it relies on deep learning techniques to train. These techniques can be expensive, difficult to optimize, and ultimately may take a long time to converge on effective solutions. That's where genetic algorithms come in.

OpenAI proved that in many circumstances evolution strategies[1] were a better alternative to reinforcement learning, as they converged faster and were far less expensive to train. If you recall from previous chapters, evolution strategies are a subset of evolutionary algorithms that very closely resemble genetic algorithms. Evolution is an excellent alternative to reinforcement learning for many of the same tasks because they're much easier to train and are far less computationally expensive.

Designing with Evolution

NASA is responsible for perhaps the most famous application of genetic algorithms, as they used them to evolve the design of an antenna for maximum

---

1. https://openai.com/blog/evolution-strategies/

efficiency aboard their ST5[2] mission. They were able to produce a number of viable designs in a short amount of time—replacing the usual labor intensive work of designing by hand. Their algorithms also produced a number of unique designs that likely would never have been considered by human designers.

The concept of evolving designs extends to other fields as well. For example, game designers use artificial intelligence to develop unique levels. As you learned in the previous section, you can use evolution as a viable alternative to other machine learning approaches. Imagine you were a game designer tasked with designing new levels for a new puzzle game. Your task is to design 500 unique levels. Using a genetic algorithm, you could evolve levels from a collection of a few hand-designed levels to be sufficiently different from one another, adding in penalties for levels that are invalid or impossible to complete.

Researchers[3] in 2018 experimented and outlined an approach to evolutionary game design and developed a fitness function that rates evolved levels based on their playability. They also created recombination methods that enforced creativity between levels and ultimately proved that evolution is a viable approach to level design.

Designing anything from games to antennas to websites is a practical application of genetic algorithms. As you've learned in this book, genetic algorithms are capable of intelligently searching through a large space of solutions to iteratively produce better and better solutions. One advantage of genetic algorithms in this space is they're not bottlenecked by the limits of human design philosophy. It's often difficult for human designers to break away from convention to come up with truly unique and revolutionary designs. Genetic algorithms don't have these same limitations.

Trading with Evolution

In Chapter 4, Evaluating Solutions and Populations, on page 51, we briefly introduced portfolio optimization using genetic algorithms. In that chapter, you learned a little about how genetic algorithms can be used to balance risk and reward in financial portfolios. The best portfolio with respect to risk and reward is called the *efficient frontier*.

Genetic algorithms can also be used to make trades. Institutional quantitative traders use genetic algorithms to evolve the parameters that help them decide

---

2. https://www.nasa.gov/mission_pages/st-5/main/index.html
3. https://www.semanticscholar.org/paper/EAI-Endorsed-Transactions-on-Creative-Technologies-Connor-Greig/
   2624416bea5b3ccab0f53e64b470efaaef1bf8db

which assets to trade. They can also be used to identify which parameters most significantly impact the price of a given asset.

Financial trading has used genetic algorithms for almost as long as genetic algorithms have been around. The abundance of available financial information coupled with the power of genetic algorithms to find useful solutions in a sea of information makes the combination incredibly powerful.

Networking with Evolution

The world today is undoubtedly more connected than it has ever been. In one way or another, the majority of people are connected all around the world virtually and physically through social networks and trade. In an increasingly connected world, network science has become more and more relevant.

Initially, genetic algorithms might not seem like a relevant tool for network science, but if you dig deeper, you'll find plenty of practical applications of basic genetic algorithms being used in network science. One relevant example is in *epidemic mitigation.*

Epidemic mitigation is the study of how to effectively prevent the spread of disease in a social network. Ideas surrounding epidemic mitigation are increasingly relevant in today's world with the proliferation of COVID-19. As early as 2017, researchers[4] showed that genetic algorithms could be used to mitigate epidemics by removing, especially, the most impactful relationships in a social network. Disease spreads through contact between individuals. The paper shows how you could use genetic algorithms to remove key relationships to prevent the spread of a disease. This repository[5] shows an Elixir example of this application using libgraph[6] and genex.[7]

Another relevant application of network science is mapping and understanding social networks. In the same respect as the process of identifying relevant nodes in a network to mitigate the spread of disease, you can use genetic algorithms to identify the most influential nodes in a social network. The process of identifying and understanding influential nodes helps advertisers identify the most influential people on a platform. Identifying influential nodes can also help you understand the spread of information in a social network.

---

4. https://arxiv.org/pdf/1707.05377.pdf
5. https://github.com/seanmor5/covid
6. https://github.com/bitwalker/libgraph
7. https://github.com/seanmor5/genex

Evolving Neural Networks

As you learned in the first section, advancements in deep learning have fueled unprecedented advances in AI. You've seen instances throughout this chapter where genetic algorithms are a viable alternative to neural networks; however, genetic algorithms are also a viable tool for designing neural networks.

In Chapter 2, Breaking Down Genetic Algorithms, on page 15, you learned about hyperparameters. Remember, hyperparameters are the settings you choose, such as selection rate, crossover rate, and mutation rate, and not the parameters your algorithm learns. When designing neural networks, you can choose from a number of hyperparameters, such as how many neurons are in each layer or what the learning rate of an optimizer is.

Genetic algorithms are a great choice for *hyperparameter optimization*. Hyperparameter optimization in the context of neural networks is the practice of maximizing the performance of a neural network by tweaking the combination of hyperparameters. As you've seen in this book, genetic algorithms work well for optimization tasks. You can use genetic algorithms to intelligently search through a set of hyperparameters for the best combination of hyperparameters. The process of hyperparameter optimization can be long and tedious to perform by hand—so genetic algorithms are a smart choice, as they automate the process and are proven to work effectively with optimization problems.

Another application of genetic algorithms to neural networks is the field of *neuroevolution*. Neuroevolution is different from hyperparameter optimization in that it involves evolving not only the hyperparameters used in the neural network but also the weights and structure of the network. The *NEAT algorithm* is an example of this use case. NEAT stands for NeuroEvolution of Augmented Topologies. The NEAT algorithm is an algorithm for evolving a neural network using genetic algorithms.

Compared to more traditional deep learning approaches, neuroevolution is relatively understudied. Uber[8] proved in 2018 that genetic algorithms can significantly reduce the training time of neural networks.

One of the most significant works on genetic algorithms on the BEAM is Gene Sher's *Handbook of Neuroevolution Through Erlang [She12]*. Sher firmly believes the BEAM is the best platform for the development of neuroevolutionary algorithms because the interaction of processes so closely mirrors the interaction of neurons in the brain.

---

8. https://eng.uber.com/accelerated-neuroevolution/

Where to Go Next

As you continue your journey with genetic algorithms, you'll inevitably need to seek out more advanced resources related to the theory and application of genetic algorithms. *Genetic Algorithms in Search, Optimization, and Machine Learning [Gol89]* by David Goldberg, while published in 1989, offers some excellent insights into the theory and practice of genetic algorithms. You'll also find numerous other books on evolutionary computing and evolutionary algorithms in general.

The field of evolutionary algorithms is large. A logical next step would be to research the more nuanced differences between genetic programming, evolution strategies, and genetic algorithms. You might also want to learn more about other algorithms inspired by nature. Many people believe that algorithms derived from nature, such as particle swarm optimization, ant colony optimization, and so on, will have a significant role in the advancements of computing over the next few decades. The Springer Natural Computing Series[9] offers a number of textbooks on the theory behind evolutionary algorithms and natural computing.

If you want to continue developing genetic algorithms in Elixir and need something a bit more mature than the framework you designed in this book, you can check out Genex,[10] a framework for writing genetic algorithms in Elixir. The implementation of problems in Genex is nearly identical to how you implemented problems in this book, and it contains a number of other useful tools for the development of genetic algorithms.

Overall, this book was designed to be a stepping stone into the world of genetic algorithms for Elixir programmers. You might not choose to continue working with genetic algorithms, but hopefully you learned a thing or two that you otherwise may not have been exposed to in a traditional Elixir book.

---

9. https://www.springer.com/series/4190?detailsPage=titles
10. https://github.com/seanmor5/genex

Bibliography

[Gol89]   David E. Goldberg. *Genetic Algorithms in Search, Optimization, and Machine Learning.* Springer, New York, NY, 1st, 1989.

[Ham20]   Tony Hammond. *Using Elixir for Graphs.* The Pragmatic Bookshelf, Raleigh, NC, 2020.

[Heb19]   Fred Hebert. *Property-Based Testing with PropEr, Erlang, and Elixir.* The Pragmatic Bookshelf, Raleigh, NC, 2019.

[LM20]   Andrea Leopardi and Jeffrey Matthias. *Testing Elixir.* The Pragmatic Bookshelf, Raleigh, NC, 2020.

[She12]   Gene I. Sher. *Handbook of Neuroevolution Through Erlang.* Springer, New York, NY, 2013, 2012.

[Tho14]   Dave Thomas. *Programming Elixir (out of print).* The Pragmatic Bookshelf, Raleigh, NC, 2014.

[Wen20]   Jay Wengrow. *A Common-Sense Guide to Data Structures and Algorithms, Second Edition.* The Pragmatic Bookshelf, Raleigh, NC, 2020.

Index

SYMBOLS

& for partial application, 134

? (question mark), for Boolean functions, 41

μ+λ in generational replacement, 131

μ,λ, in generational replacement, 131

A

abstractions, 38, 41

accumulators, 11

add_edge (Graph), 153

add_vertices (Graph), 152

adopting behaviours, 39

advertising, 202

age, tracking chromosome, 35, 37, 42

Agents
    defined, 181
    parallelism with, 181
    starting, 164
    Tetris example, 164–168

aggressiveness, mutation, 115, 118

AI, *see* artificial intelligence

ALE (Arcade Learning Environment), 162, 164

ALEx (Arcade Learning Environment in Elixir)
    installing and compiling, 163
    Tetris example, 162–168

Alex module, 164

Alex.Interface module, 164

algorithm, for recursion, 7, 12

algorithms, genetic, *see* genetic algorithms

algorithms, optimization, 2

aliasing
    modules, 40
    structs, 41, 115

alleles
    chromosome structure, 35
    converged, 107

alpha parameter for whole arithmetic recombination, 100

apply, 76–77, 116, 130

Arcade Learning Environment (ALE), 162, 164

Arcade Learning Environment in Elixir (ALEx)
    installing and compiling, 163
    Tetris example, 162–168

arguments, passing functions as, 18

artificial intelligence, 2, 199, 201, 203

async (Task), 179

Atari 2600 Tetris ROM, 165

await (Task), 179

B

base case, 7, 24, *see also* termination criteria

BEAM
    about, 169, 171
    neuroevolution and, 203
    parallelism and, xvi, 177–178, 181
    performance and, 169
    resources on, 169, 171, 177

The BEAM Book, 169, 177

behaviours
    as abstraction, 41
    adopting, 39
    as a contract, 38
    defining, 38
    modeling problems with, 37–43
    One-Max problem with, 46

bench directory, 171

Benchee, 171–174

benchmark.exs file, 171

benchmarking, 170–174, 180

bias, 68

biased sampling, 73

binary genotypes
    class schedule example, 127
    crossover strategies, 97, 99
    defined, 44
    flip mutation and, 118
    tiger evolution example, 140
    XOR cipher example, 110

bit flip mutation, *see* flip mutation

bitstring sum problem, *see* One-Max problem

bitstrings, *see* binary genotypes

Bitwise, 110, 118

Boltzmann selection, 85

Booleans, 40

bottlenecks, 170, 174

brute-force search, 3, 5

C

callbacks, *see also* behaviours
defined, 38
restricting, 40

cargo loading example, 52–
57, 59, 61

Case (ExUnit), 190

check all macro, 191

children, *see also* crossover;
mutation; reinsertion; replacement
genealogy trees, 150–155
in genetic algorithm
structure, 6
reproduction diagram, 20

chromosomes, *see al-
so* crossover; fitness functions; mutation; reinser-
tion; replacement; selection
age, 35, 37, 42
defaults, 36
defined, 16
enforcing with keys, 36
fields for tracking, 35–
37, 42
genealogy trees, 150–
155, 157–162
generating random, 18
in genetic algorithm
structure, 5, 15–16
IDs, 150
inserting into graphs, 152
neighborhoods, 136
number of in a popula-
tion, 6, 17, 24
vs. populations, 17
property-based testing,
190
repairment, 91, 103
size, 35, 37, 42
size and binary geno-
types, 127
size and testing, 190
structs for, 33–37
structure of, 35
treating as processes,
181–183
typespecs, 36

chunk_every (Enum), 10, 25, 103

ciphers, *see* XOR cipher example

class schedule example, 126–
129, 133

cmake, 163

code breaking example, 108–
113

code quality, *see also* optimizing code
code analysis with credo,
187, 193–195
code analysis with dialyxir,
187, 195–198
typespecs and, 195–198
writing efficient code,
175–177

combinatorial optimization
problems
N-queens problem, 87–
95, 104
permutation genotypes
and, 45
traveling salesman prob-
lem, 1, 35, 45

*A Common-Sense Guide to
Data Structures and Algo-
rithms*, 175

Compiler API (Mix), 184

compilers
credo and, 193
NIFs and, 184

compound types, 36

concurrency
vs. parallelism, 178
with Task module, 179

configuration
files, 22
hyperparameters, 27

constraint satisfaction problems
cargo loading example,
55–57
defined, 53
knapsack, 53
N-queens problem, 87–
95, 104
penalty functions, 55–
57, 127

constraints
cargo loading example,
55–57
defined, 53
local populations, 137
on population growth
rate, 136

contracts, behaviours as, 38

convergence, *see also* premature convergence
elitism selection and, 78
generation-based termina-
tion criteria, 58
improvement-based termi-
nation criteria, 60–61
population size and, 17
selection pressure and,
74
selection rate and, 74
time to in examples, 49
visualizations, 160–162
whole arithmetic recombi-
nation, 101

convex functions, 69

convex optimization, 69

cooling rate, 61

credo, 187, 193–195

crossover, *see also* order-one
crossover; permutation
genotypes; single-point
crossover
about, 95
balancing genetic diversity and fitness, 122
benchmarking setup, 172
chromosome repairment
and, 91, 103
crossover points, 11, 97
cycle, 102
default strategy, 94
defined, 3, 10, 87
genealogy trees, 152–155
genetic algorithm frame-
work with behaviours,
42
genetic algorithm frame-
work, customizing, 93–
95
genetic algorithm frame-
work, setup, 19, 25
in genetic algorithm
structure, 19
messy single-point, 102
multi-point, 102
with multiple parents,
102
N-queens problem, 87–
95, 104
with NIFs, 183, 185
One-Max problem, 8, 10
order-one, 91–95, 196
performance and, 93, 95,
97, 99, 101
property-based testing,
190
rate, 94, 97–99

real-value genotypes, 67, 99
reinsertion and, 77
selection rate, 74, 76
strategies, 11, 91–102
transforming populations into tuples for, 19, 77, 103
typespecs, 196
uniform, 97–100, 122, 196
whole arithmetic recombination, 100, 196
writing efficient code, 176
:crossover_type parameter, 94
custom types, 37, 196
cycle crossover, 102

D
Darwin, Charles, 71
data
formats and transformations, 33
generating test data, 191
in interactive optimization, 68
types and memory usage, 171
Davis order, see order-one crossover
debugging
with dialyxir, 195–198
property-based tests, 192
typespecs and, 195
decay, exponential, 136
decryption, XOR cipher example, 108–113
deep learning, 199
defmodule, 36
defstruct, 36
dependencies
adding, 150, 160
Mix exs file for, 22
test-only environment, 190
designing
with genetic algorithms, 200, 203
web design optimization, 67
dialyxir, 187, 195–198
dialyzer, 197
difference (MapSet), 77

directed graphs
defined, 150
genealogy trees, 150–155, 157–162
directories, creating, 5, 22
:display_screen (ALEx), 164, 167
documentation tags, 193
Don't Repeat Yourself (DRY) principle, 16
DOT files, 159
drop (Enum), 176
(DRY) Don't Repeat Yourself principle, 16
dummy_population, 172
dummy_selected_population, 172

E
edges, adding to graphs, 153
efficient frontier, 201
elitism selection
about, 19, 71
limitations of, 78
performance and, 79
tournament selection and, 81
elitist reinsertion/replacement, 132, 134–135
Elixir
about, xiv
advantages, xvi
formatter, 192
resources on, xiv, 7, 150, 175
Elixir for Graphs, 150
Elixir Guides, xiv
Elixir School, xiv
elixir-statistics, 148
encodings, 43, see also genotypes
encryption, XOR cipher example, 108–113
@enforce_keys, 36
enforcement
with behaviours, 38–43
with keys, 36
property-based testing, 190
Enum library
about, 7
advantages, 35
polymorphism with, 16–17
enumerables
defined, 7

limits of, 33
polymorphism with, 16–17
resources on, 7
epidemic mitigation, 202
episodes (ALEx), 166
:eprof, 174
erl_nif.h error, 163
Erlang Scheduler, 177, 183
erlang-dev, 163
ETS (Erlang Term Storage), 144–150, 161–162
evaluation, see also fitness; fitness functions
defined, 9
in genetic algorithm structure, 18, 51
lazy, 177
need for, 51–52
evolution strategies
binary genotypes and, 45
history, 2
vs. reinforcement learning, 200
research on, 204
evolutions, see also crossover; fitness functions; termination criteria
defined, 8
genealogy trees, 150–155, 157–162
genetic algorithm framework with behaviours, 41
genetic algorithm framework, selection, 77
genetic algorithm framework, setup, 23, 26–29
real-time visualizations, 157, 162–168
statistics with ETS, 144–150
exploitation, see also crossover
defined, 3
vs. exploration, 3, 87, 114
exploration
vs. exploitation, 3, 87, 114
mutation as, 114
exponential growth/decay, 136
ExProf, 174
exs file, 22

ExUnit, 187, 189–192
ExUnitProperties, 190

F

factorials, 1
Fast Elixir, 175
feasibility problems, 69
filtering duplicate values, 90
fitness, *see also* fitness functions; selection
  average, 57
  balancing with diversity, 72, 114, 122
  calculating total population fitness, 84
  chromosome field, 35, 37, 42
  defined, 9, 63
  elitism selection, 78
  elitist reinsertion, 132
  fitness landscapes, 65
  fitness-based insertion, 131
  fitness-based selection, 75
  fitness-based termination criteria, 57, 59
  fitness-proportionate selection, 82–85
  maximum, 57
  mean fitness, visualization of, 160–162
  minimum, 57
  random selection, 79
  reinsertion and, 129
  roulette selection, 82–85
  selection pressure, 74
  sorting by, 10, 18, 24
  statistics, 147
  temperature, 60, 85
  tournament selection, 80–82
fitness functions, *see also* fitness
  benchmarking setup, 172
  cargo loading example, 54
  class schedule example, 127
  defined, 9
  genetic algorithm framework with behaviours, 40
  genetic algorithm framework, setup, 24
  genetic algorithm framework, using, 51

in genetic algorithm structure, 18, 26
  as heuristics, 64
  interactive optimization, 68
  N-queens problem, 89
  novelty search, 80
  One-Max problem, 8–9, 30, 46, 68
  profiling setup, 174
  schemas and, 63
  spelling example, 48
  Tetris example, 166
  tiger evolution example, 141
  treating chromosomes as processes, 182
  understanding, 51, 62–65
  with weighting, 127
  XOR cipher example, 110
fitness landscapes, 65
fitness-based insertion, 131
fitness-based selection, 75
fitness-proportionate selection, 82–85
flip mutation, 116, 118, 188
floats, 37, 46, 101
format (Mix), 192
formatter, using, 192
framework, genetic algorithm
  as abstraction, 38, 41
  behaviours, modeling problems with, 37–43
  benchmarking, adding, 171
  chromosome setup, 16
  chromosome structs, 33–37
  code quality with credo, 192–195
  crossover with behaviours, 42
  crossover, customizing, 93–95
  crossover, setup, 19, 25
  fitness functions, modeling with behaviours, 40
  fitness functions, setup, 18, 24, 26
  fitness functions, using, 51
  genealogy tree, 154
  genotypes, modeling with behaviours, 40
  genotypes, setup, 24, 26
  hyperparameters, 27
  Mix setup, 22–27

mutation with behaviours, 42
  mutation, customizing, 115–117
  mutation, reinsertion strategies and, 131
  mutation, running without, 112
  mutation, setup, 20, 26
  One-Max problem, 29
  outlining, 23
  population, initializing, 17, 23, 26
  population, setup, 16–19
  recursion, setup, 24
  reinsertion strategies, 130–133
  selection, customizing, 75–78
  selection, setup, 19, 24–25
  spelling example, 47–50
  statistics tracking, 146–150
  structure, 15–22
  termination criteria, modeling with behaviours, 40
  termination criteria, setup, 21, 24
  typespecs, 195–198
functions
  applying, 76
  convex functions, 69
  parallel map functions, 179–181
  passing as arguments, 18
  penalty functions, 55–57, 127
fundamental theorem of genetic algorithms, 63

G

games
  designing with genetic algorithms, 201
  Tetris example, 162–168
Gaussian mutation, 120–122
GCC, 184
genealogy trees, 150–155, 157–162
generational replacement, 131
generations
  generation-based termination criteria, 58, 61, 128, 159

generational replacement,
131
in genetic algorithm
structure, 5, 15
visualizations, 160–162
genes
in chromosome structure,
35
enforcing, 36
format for, 35
genetic algorithms
advantages, xiii
balancing exploration
and exploitation, 3, 87,
114
defined, 2
designing with, 200, 203
flow of, 7
fundamental/schema
theorem, 63
history of, 2
informed search and, 3
learning about, 204
learning with, 199, 203
multi-population, 137
outlining, 23
overview of, 2–5
as recursive, 7, 12
as stochastic, 188
structure, 5, 7, 15–22, 51
uses, xiii, 199–204
*Genetic Algorithms in Search,
Optimization, and Machine
Learning*, 204
genetic diversity
balancing diversity and
fitness, 72
elitism selection and, 78
mutation and, 73, 114,
122
premature convergence
and, 107
random selection, 79
reinsertion and, 129, 132
roulette selection, 83
selection pressure and,
74
tournament selection, 81
uniform reinsertion and,
132
genetic programming, 46, 204
Genex, 202, 204
genotypes, *see also* binary
genotypes; permutation
genotypes
benchmarking setup, 172

cargo loading example,
53
crossover strategies and,
95, 97, 99
defined, 43
genetic algorithm frame-
work with behaviours,
40
genetic algorithm frame-
work, setup, 24, 26
graph genotypes, 46
mutation strategies, 119
N-queens problem, 88
One-Max problem, 29,
44, 46
vs. phenotypes, 44
profiling setup, 174
spelling example, 48
Tetris example, 165
tiger evolution example,
140
tree-based, 46
understanding, 43–47
XOR cipher example, 110
GenServers
creating, 144
genealogy trees, 151–154
starting, 144–145, 152–
153
tracking statistics with
ETS, 144–146
get (Keyword), 29, 76, 147
get (Mix), 150
Gnuplot, 160
gnuplot-elixir, 160–162
Goldberg, David, 204
graph genotypes, 46
Graph module, 152
graphs
creating, 152
DOT files, 159
edges, adding, 153
epidemic mitigation exam-
ple, 202
exporting, 159
genealogy trees, 150–
155, 157–162
resources on, 150
serializing, 159
vertices, 152, 155
Graphviz, 159
growth, exponential, 136

H

*Handbook of Neuroevolution
Through Erlang*, 203
handle_call, 153
handle_cast, 152
hd function, 24
head in scramble mutation,
120
hi in scramble mutation, 120
Holland, John, 2, 118
hyperparameters
defined, 27
genetic algorithm frame-
work setup, 27
mutation rate, 115–117
mutation strategies, 115
neural networks and, 203
optimization, 203
passing, 28, 77
selection rate as, 75
selection strategy as, 75

I

IDs, chromosomes, 150
@impl keyword, 39
improvement-based termination criteria, 60–61
influential nodes, 202
information spread and social
networks, 202
informed search, 3
initializing
genealogy tree, 152, 154
GenServers, 144–145,
152
populations, 17, 23, 26
populations for genealogy
trees, 154
treating chromosomes as
processes, 182
insertion, *see also* reinsertion
fitness-based, 131
inserting chromosomes
into graphs, 152
tracking statistics with
ETS, 145
interactive optimization, 67
Interface module (ALEx), 164
invert mutation, 122

J

jaro_distance (String), 48, 111

K

keys, 29, 145
Keyword module, hyperparameters, 28
knapsack problem, 53, *see also* cargo loading example

L

lazy evaluation, 177
learning
  deep, 199
  with genetic algorithms, 199, 203
  machine, 199
  reinforcement learning, 199
legal_actions (ALEx), 165
lib directory, 22
libgraph
  epidemic mitigation example, 202
  genealogy trees, 150–155, 159
  serializing graphs, 159
libsdl1.2, 163
lists
  chromosomes as, 17
  converting to strings, 111
  cycle crossover, 102
  hyperparameters, 28
  Keyword lists, 28
  order, 176
  populations as, 17
  transforming into tuples, 10
lo in scramble mutation, 120
load_nif (Erlang), 185
lookup functions with ETS, 145
loops, 7

M

machine learning, 199
map (Enum)
  about, 10
  chromosome repairment, 104
  class schedule example, 128
  crossover, 101
  mutation, 117
  vs. parallel maps, 180–181
  performance and, 176

MapSet
  chromosome repairment, 104
  order-one crossover and, 92
  selection and, 77, 82
Matrex, 183
max_by, 58
max_fitness, 26, 30
mazes, 2
mean, in Gaussian mutation, 121
mechanical movement and reinforcement learning, 200
memory
  benchmarking usage, 170–174
  parallel maps, 181
  resources on, 171
:memory_time option (Benchee), 173
messy single-point crossover, 102
metrics, *see* tracking
mid in scramble mutation, 120
min_by, 58
MingW, 184
Mix
  about, 22
  ALEx, adding, 163
  Benchee, adding, 171
  compiler for NIFs, 184
  dependencies, adding, 150, 160
  dialyxir, adding, 197
  directories, creating, 22
  formatter, using, 192
  genetic algorithm framework setup, 22–27
  projects, creating, 22
  projects, running, 30
  property-based tests, running, 191
mkdir (Mix), 22
mocking, testing and, 188–189
__MODULE__ keyword, 37
modules
  aliasing, 40
  defining, 36
  defining behaviours, 38
mu variable, 122
multi-objective optimization, 65–67, 75

multi-point crossover, 102
multi-population genetic algorithms, 137
mutation, *see also* mutation rate
  aggressiveness, 115, 118
  benchmarking setup, 172
  chromosome repairment, 104
  default strategy, 116
  defined, 4, 113
  flip, 116, 118, 188
  Gaussian, 120–122
  genealogy trees, 152–155
  genetic algorithm framework with behaviours, 42
  genetic algorithm framework, customizing, 115–117
  genetic algorithm framework, reinsertion strategies, 131
  genetic algorithm framework, running without, 112
  genetic algorithm framework, setup, 20, 26
  in genetic algorithm structure, 20
  genetic diversity and, 73, 114, 122
  invert, 122
  need for, 4, 13, 20
  with NIFs, 183, 185
  One-Max problem, 13–14
  permutation genotypes and, 45, 119
  quantifying, 114
  with rand.uniform, 13
  random slices, 120
  real-value genotypes, 67
  reinsertion and, 77, 131
  scramble, 119
  as stimulating change, 113
  strategies, 115–122
  swap, 122
  toolbox folder, 115
  understanding, 113–115
  uniform, 122
mutation aggressiveness, 115, 118
mutation rate
  defined, 114
  elitist reinsertion, 134
  genetic algorithm framework, 26, 115–117

tiger evolution example, 143

typical, 20

:mutation_rate parameter, 116

N

N-queens problem, 87–95, 104

NASA, 200

Native Implemented Functions (NIFs), 183–185

natural selection, *see* elitism selection

NEAT algorithm, 203

negative numbers and performance, 176

neighborhoods, 136

nesting, 193

network science, 202

networking with genetic algorithms, 202

neural networks, 203

neuroevolution, 203

NeuroEvolution of Augmented Topologies (NEAT) algorithm, 203

new (Graph), 152

new (MapSet), 77

new (Mix), 22

NIFs (Native Implemented Functions), 183–185

no-objective optimization, 69

normal (Erlang rand module), 121

normal distribution in Gaussian mutation, 120–122

novelty search, 79

number type, 37

O

objectives, evaluating, 51–52

One-Max problem
  basic algorithm for, 5–14, 21
  with behaviours, 46
  fitness function, 8, 46, 68
  with genetic algorithm framework, 29
  genetic diversity in, 73
  genotypes, 29, 44, 46
  population, defining, 6
  termination criteria, 7, 21, 30, 46, 58–59, 61
  user input, 68

only: :test property, 190

OpenAI, 168, 200

optimization, *see also* optimization algorithms; optimizing code; performance; performance portfolio optimization
  cargo loading example, 52–57, 59, 61
  combinatorial optimization problems, 45
  convex optimization, 69
  defined, 2
  hyperparameter optimization, 203
  interactive, 67
  multi-objective optimization, 65–67, 75
  neural networks, 203
  no-objective optimization, 69
  problems as search problems, 2
  shape optimization, 69
  web design optimization, 67

optimization algorithms, 2, *see also* genetic algorithms

optimizing code
  benchmarking, 170–174, 180
  lazy evaluation and, 177
  with NIFs, 183–185
  parallelization, 177–183
  profiling, 170, 174
  treating chromosomes as processes, 181–183
  when to, 170, 173
  writing efficient code, 175–177

opts
  crossover, customizing, 93–95
  mutation rate, extracting, 116
  mutation strategies, 116
  One-Max problem, 30
  passing hyperparameters, 28, 77, 116
  selection rate, extracting, 77
  statistics option, 146

order, *see also* sorting
  invert mutation, 122
  using map and reduce, 176

order-one crossover, 91–95, 196

outlining algorithms, 23

P

parallel map functions, 179–181

parallelism
  BEAM and, xvi, 177–178, 181
  vs. concurrency, 178
  defined, 177
  Elixir advantages, xvi, 177
  multi-population genetic algorithms, 137
  optimizing code with, 177–183
  with processes, 181–183
  with Task module, 179–183
  tournament selection, 81

parents, *see also* crossover; fitness functions; mutation; reinsertion; replacement; selection
  duplicate parents in selection, 81–82
  genealogy trees, 150–155
  in genetic algorithm structure, 6
  length of, 26
  reproduction diagram, 20
  using more than two, 102

pattern matching
  accessing statistics, 147
  in crossover, 10, 102
  property-based tests, 191

penalty functions, 55–57, 127

performance, *see also* optimization
  BEAM and, 169
  benchmarking, 170–174, 180
  crossover strategies, 93, 95, 97, 99, 101
  elitism selection and, 79
  in examples, 49
  lazy evaluation and, 177
  negative numbers and, 176
  neural networks, 203
  NIFs and, 183–185
  order-one crossover, 93
  parallelization, 177–183
  processes, treating chromosomes as, 181–183
  profiling, 170, 174

reinsertion strategies, 131–132, 135
resources on, 175
roulette selection, 83, 85
selection rate and, 74
single-point crossover, 97
tournament selection, 81
uniform crossover, 99
whole arithmetic recombination, 101
writing efficient code, 175–177
permutation genotypes
creating, 89
defined, 45
mutation strategies, 45, 119
order-one crossover and, 91–95
single-point crossover and, 91, 97
uniform crossover and, 99
phenotypes, 44
plotting, visualizations, 160–162
pmap, 179–181
polymorphism, 16–17
populations, *see also* crossover; evaluation; fitness functions; mutation; reinsertion; replacement; selection; sorting
benchmarking setup, 172
calculating total fitness, 84
vs. chromosomes, 17
defined, 17
defining, 6
diversity and premature convergence, 108, 114
genetic algorithm framework, setup, 16–19
in genetic algorithm structure, 5, 15–19
initializing, 17, 23, 26
local, 136
monitoring with statistics, 148–150
One-Max problem, 6
size hyperparameter, 29
size of, 6, 17, 24
size, adjusting in crossover, 94
size, convergence and, 17
size, default, 29
size, growth/decay of, 135

size, premature convergence and, 6, 113
size, survival rate and, 132
transforming into tuples for crossover, 19, 77, 103
portfolio optimization
efficient frontier, 201
fitness landscapes, 65
multi-objective optimization example, 66
termination criteria and fitness threshold, 57
ports, 183
precision and real-value genotypes, 46
premature convergence, *see also* mutation
avoiding with randomness, 7
crossover and, 122
defined, 4, 107
elitism selection and, 79
genetic diversity and, 108, 114
One-Max problem, 12
population size and, 6, 113
replacement and, 122
selection strategies and, 122
XOR cipher example, 112
PRNG (pseudo-random number generation), 188
probability
flip mutation, 118, 188
roulette selection, 83
selection pressure and, 74
testing and, 188
in uniform crossover, 97
processes, 179–181
profile macro, 175
profiling, 170, 174
Programming Elixir, 179
projects
configuration files, 22
creating in Mix, 22
running in Mix, 30
property macro, 191
property-based testing, 188–192
Property-Based Testing with PropEr, Erlang, and Elixir, 190

protocols, 16
pseudo-random number generation (PRNG), 188
pure reinsertion, 131, 133, 135

Q

question mark (?), for Boolean functions, 41

R

rand module, 13, 188
random (Enum)
streaming, 48
Tetris game, 166
using, 7
random replacement, 132, 134
random selection, 79
:random_seed (ALEx), 164
randomness, *see also* mutation
avoiding premature convergence with, 7
crossover points, 11
with Enum.random, 7, 48, 166
with Enum.shuffle, 13, 26, 89, 120
property-based testing and, 190
pseudo-random number generation (PRNG), 188
with rand.uniform, 13, 26, 84, 97
random number generators, 183–185, 188
random replacement, 132, 134
random selection, 79
scramble mutation, 119
seeding and, 164, 188
in single-point crossover, 96
solutions and, 62
testing and, 188–189
true, 188
uniform, 11
Ranges, 7
rank selection, 85
real-value genotypes
crossover strategies, 67, 99
defined, 45
Gaussian mutation, 120–122
scramble mutation, 119

recursion
    with algorithm, 7, 12
    base case, 7, 24
    genetic algorithm frame-
        work setup, 24
    genetic algorithms as, 7,
        12
    recursive case, 7
    tail-recursion, 82
    tournament selection, 82
recursive case, 7
reduce (Enum)
    crossover with multiple
        parents, 103
    N-queens problem, 94
    performance and, 176
    Tetris game, 166
    using, 10
reduce_while (Enum), 84, 194
reinforcement learning, 199
reinsertion
    basic, 77
    class schedule example,
        126–129, 133
    customizing strategies,
        130
    default strategy, 133
    defined, 125, 129
    elitist, 132, 134–135
    local vs. global, 136
    performance and, 131–
        132, 135
    pure, 131, 133, 135
    vs. replacement, 125, 135
    strategies, 130–133
    toolbox for, 131
    uniform, 132, 134
:reinsertion_strategy parameter,
    130
repair_chromosome, 104
repair_helper, 104
repairment, chromosome, 91,
    103
repeatedly (Stream), 48, 177
replacement
    avoiding premature con-
        vergence, 122
    class schedule example,
        126–129, 133
    defined, 125
    elitist, 132, 134–135
    generational, 131
    performance and, 131–
        132, 135
    random, 132, 134
    vs. reinsertion, 125, 135
    strategies, 130–133

reproduction, *see* crossover
resources for this book
    BEAM, 169, 171, 177
    Elixir, xiv, 7, 150, 175
    enumerables, 7
    genetic algorithms, 204
    graphs, 150
    memory, 171
    testing, 190
    typespecs, 195
    writing efficient code, 175
rewards-based selection, 75
RNGs (random number gener-
    ators), 183–185, 188
robots and reinforcement
    learning, 200
ROM files, 164–165
roulette selection, 82–85, 193
run (Mix), 30
runtime: false option, 193

S
sampling
    biased, 73
    stochastic universal
        sampling, 85
scenario generation, 79
schedulers, parallelization
    and, 177–178, 183
schema theorem, 63
schemas, 3, 63
scores
    determining, 141
    Tetris example, 166
    tiger evolution example,
        141
scramble mutation, 119
screenshot (ALEx), 167
scripts directory, 22
search
    brute-force search, 3, 5
    informed search, 3
    looking up statistics with
        ETS, 145
    novelty search, 79
    optimization problems as,
        2
seeding
    in ALEx, 164
    testing and, 188
    Tetris example, 164

selection, *see also* elitism se-
    lection; fitness; fitness
    functions; selection rate
    balancing genetic diversi-
        ty and fitness, 72, 122
    as biased sampling, 73
    Boltzmann selection, 85
    changing strategies, 76
    customizing, 75–78
    default strategy, 76
    defined, 9, 71
    fitness-based selection,
        75
    fitness-proportionate se-
        lection, 82–85
    genetic algorithm frame-
        work, customizing, 75–
        78
    genetic algorithm frame-
        work, setup, 24–25
    in genetic algorithm
        structure, 19
    leftovers, 77
    One-Max problem, 8–10
    performance and, 74
    random selection, 79
    rank selection, 85
    rewards-based selection,
        75
    roulette selection, 82–85,
        193
    selection pressure, 74
    stochastic universal
        sampling, 85
    strategies, 10, 78–85
    toolbox folder, 75
    tournament selection,
        80–82
    understanding, 71–75
selection pressure, 74
selection rate
    adjusting, 76, 94
    benchmarking setup, 172
    defined, 74
    in genetic algorithm
        framework, 75–76
    performance and, 74
    reinsertion strategies,
        132, 134–135
    tiger evolution example,
        143
:selection_type key, 76
serializing, graphs, 159
servers
    creating, 144
    genealogy trees, 151–154

starting, 144–145, 152–153
statistics, 144–146
shape optimization, 69
Sher, Gene, 203
shuffle (Enum), 13, 26, 89, 120
sigma variable, 122
simulated annealing, 60
single-point crossover
    code analysis with dialyxir, 197
    defined, 96
    limitations, 91
    with multiple parents, 102, 104
    with NIFs, 185
    One-Max problem, 11
    performance, 97
    premature convergence and, 122
    property-based testing, 190
    typespecs, 196
slice (Enum), 93
slicing, 93, 96
SMP (symmetric multiprocessing), 178
social networks, 202
solutions, see also crossover; visualizations
    assigning variables to, 12
    outputting, 30
    randomness and, 62
    scripts directory, 22
sort_by (Enum), 9, 25
sorting, see also fitness functions; order
    elitism selection and, 78
    in elitist reinsertion, 132
    with Enum.sort_by, 9, 25
    fitness, 10, 18, 24
:sound (ALEx), 164
@spec attribute, 195
speed, see performance
spelling example, 47–50
split (Enum)
    in order-one crossover, 93
    single-point crossover, 97
    using, 11, 25
splitting
    with Enum.split, 11, 25, 93, 97

in order-one crossover, 93
in single-point crossover, 96
ST5 mission, 200
standard deviation, in Gaussian mutation, 121
start point for scramble mutation, 120
starting
    Agents, 164
    GenServers, 144–145, 152–153
    Tetris game, 166
statistics, see also tracking
    accessing, 147
    benchmarking, 173
    default suite, 146
    with ETS, 144–150
    libraries, 148
    tiger evolution example, 148–150
    visualizations, 157–162
step (ALEx), 166
stochastic universal sampling, 85
stocks
    portfolio optimization, 57, 65–66, 201
    trading with genetic algorithms, 201
stopping, see termination criteria
Stream
    lazy evaluation with, 177
    spelling example, 48
StreamData, 187, 190–192
strings
    converting lists to, 111
    measuring similarity between, 111
structs
    aliasing, 41, 115
    creating, 35
    using, 33–37
sum (Enum), 30
sum_fitness, 84
sums, weighted, 66
supervision tree, 144
survival rate, 132–135
suspect sketches, 68
swap mutation, 122
symmetric multiprocessing (SMP), 178

T
t custom type, 37, 196
tab2list, 161
tables
    converting ETS tables to tuples, 161
    exporting, 161
tail in scramble mutation, 120
tail-recursion, 82
take (Enum), 78, 176
take_random (Enum), 80, 133
Task module, 179–181
tasks
    concurrency with, 179
    parallelization with, 179–181
temperature, 60, 85
termination criteria
    about, 52
    benchmarking setup, 172
    cargo loading example, 54, 59, 61
    class schedule example, 128
    defined, 7
    fitness-based, 57, 59
    generation-based, 58, 61, 128, 159
    genetic algorithm framework with behaviours, 40
    genetic algorithm framework, setup, 21, 24
    in genetic algorithm structure, 21
    goals of, 57
    importance of, 57
    improvement-based, 60–61
    N-queens problem, 90
    One-Max problem, 7, 21, 30, 46, 58–59, 61
    profiling setup, 174
    spelling example, 48
    temperature, 60
    Tetris game, 166
    tiger evolution example, 142, 159
    XOR cipher example, 111
test (Mix), 191
test directory, 22
test-driven development, 187
testing
    generating test data, 191
    importance of, 187

memory benchmarking, 173

mocking and, 188–189

property-based, 188–192

randomness and, 188–189

resources on, 190

seeding and, 188

test directory, 22

test-driven development, 187

Testing Elixir, 190

Tetris example, 162–168

Tetris ROM, 165

tiger evolution example, 139–144, 148–150, 157–162

to_list (MapSet), 77, 104

tournament selection, 80–82

tracking

advantages, 139

chromosome fields, 35–37, 42

genealogy trees, 150–155, 157–162

statistics with ETS, 144–150

tiger evolution example, 139–144, 148–150, 157–162

visualizations, 157–162

transformations

data formats, 33

in genetic algorithm structure, 5, 15

population size and, 17

replacing with processes, 181

transforming populations into tuples for crossover, 19, 77, 103

traveling salesman problem, 1, 35, 45

tree-based genotypes, 46

tuples

converting ETS tables to, 161

returning with Enum.split, 11

statistics, 147

transforming populations into for crossover, 19, 77, 103

transforming values into, 10, 25

zipping and unzipping, 98, 101

@type attribute, 36

types

compound types, 36

custom types, 37, 196

typespecs, 36, 195–198

U

Uber, 203

uniform (Erlang rand module)

parent length and, 26

probability rate, 13

roulette selection, 84

single-point crossover, 97

using, 11

uniform crossover, 97–100, 122, 196

uniform mutation, 122

uniform reinsertion, 132, 134

unzip (Enum), 98, 101

use Bitwise, 110, 118

user input in interactive optimization, 68

utilities directory, 144, 151

V

values

ETS, 145

filtering duplicate, 90

Keyword.get, 29

transforming into tuples, 10, 25

variables, assigning to solutions, 12

vertices

accessing, 155

adding, 152

visualizations

convergence, 160–162

evolutions in real time, 157, 162–168

problem dependency in, 68

tiger evolution example, 157–162

tracking, 157–162

W

web design optimization, 67

Webgraphviz, 159

weighted sums, 66

weights

class schedule example, 126–127

in multi-objective optimization, 66

tiger evolution example, 141

whole arithmetic recombination, 100, 196

X

XOR cipher example, 108–113

XOR-Shift RNG, 183–185

XOR96 random number generator, 184

Z

zip (Enum), 98, 101, 128

Thank you!

How did you enjoy this book? Please let us know. Take a moment and email us at support@pragprog.com with your feedback. Tell us your story and you could win free ebooks. Please use the subject line "Book Feedback."

Ready for your next great Pragmatic Bookshelf book? Come on over to https://pragprog.com and use the coupon code BUYANOTHER2021 to save 30% on your next ebook.

Void where prohibited, restricted, or otherwise unwelcome. Do not use ebooks near water. If rash persists, see a doctor. Doesn't apply to *The Pragmatic Programmer* ebook because it's older than the Pragmatic Bookshelf itself. Side effects may include increased knowledge and skill, increased marketability, and deep satisfaction. Increase dosage regularly.

And thank you for your continued support,

Andy Hunt, Publisher

A Common-Sense Guide to Data Structures and Algorithms, Second Edition

If you thought that data structures and algorithms were all just theory, you're missing out on what they can do for your code. Learn to use Big O Notation to make your code run faster by orders of magnitude. Choose from data structures such as hash tables, trees, and graphs to increase your code's efficiency exponentially. With simple language and clear diagrams, this book makes this complex topic accessible, no matter your background. This new edition features practice exercises in every chapter, and new chapters on topics such as dynamic programming and heaps and tries. Get the hands-on info you need to master data structures and algorithms for your day-to-day work.

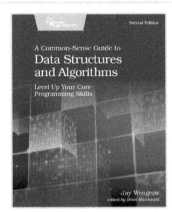

Jay Wengrow
(506 pages) ISBN: 9781680507225. $45.95
https://pragprog.com/book/jwdsal2

Build Location-Based Projects for iOS

Coding is awesome. So is being outside. With location-based iOS apps, you can combine the two for an enhanced outdoor experience. Use Swift to create your own apps that use GPS data, read sensor data from your iPhone, draw on maps, automate with geofences, and store augmented reality world maps. You'll have a great time without even noticing that you're learning. And even better, each of the projects is designed to be extended and eventually submitted to the App Store. Explore, share, and have fun.

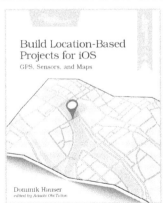

Dominik Hauser
(154 pages) ISBN: 9781680507812. $26.95
https://pragprog.com/book/dhios

iOS Unit Testing by Example

Fearlessly change the design of your iOS code with solid unit tests. Use Xcode's built-in test framework XCTest and Swift to get rapid feedback on all your code — including legacy code. Learn the tricks and techniques of testing all iOS code, especially view controllers (UIViewControllers), which are critical to iOS apps. Learn to isolate and replace dependencies in legacy code written without tests. Practice safe refactoring that makes these tests possible, and watch all your changes get verified quickly and automatically. Make even the boldest code changes with complete confidence.

Jon Reid
(358 pages) ISBN: 9781680506815. $47.95
https://pragprog.com/book/jrlegios

Become an Effective Software Engineering Manager

Software startups make global headlines every day. As technology companies succeed and grow, so do their engineering departments. In your career, you'll may suddenly get the opportunity to lead teams: to become a manager. But this is often uncharted territory. How do you decide whether this career move is right for you? And if you do, what do you need to learn to succeed? Where do you start? How do you know that you're doing it right? What does "it" even mean? And isn't management a dirty word? This book will share the secrets you need to know to manage engineers successfully.

James Stanier
(396 pages) ISBN: 9781680507249. $45.95
https://pragprog.com/book/jsengman

Build Websites with Hugo

Rediscover how fun web development can be with
Hugo, the static site generator and web framework that
lets you build content sites quickly, using the skills
you already have. Design layouts with HTML and share
common components across pages. Create Markdown
templates that let you create new content quickly.
Consume and generate JSON, enhance layouts with
logic, and generate a site that works on any platform
with no runtime dependencies or database. Hugo gives
you everything you need to build your next content
site and have fun doing it.

Brian P. Hogan
(154 pages) ISBN: 9781680507263. $26.95
https://pragprog.com/book/bhhugo

Practical Microservices

MVC and CRUD make software easier to write, but
harder to change. Microservice-based architectures
can help even the smallest of projects remain agile in
the long term, but most tutorials meander in theory
or completely miss the point of what it means to be
microservice based. Roll up your sleeves with real
projects and learn the most important concepts of
evented architectures. You'll have your own deployable,
testable project and a direction for where to go next.

Ethan Garofolo
(290 pages) ISBN: 9781680506457. $45.95
https://pragprog.com/book/egmicro

Real-Time Phoenix

Give users the real-time experience they expect, by
using Elixir and Phoenix Channels to build applications
that instantly react to changes and reflect the application's true state. Learn how Elixir and Phoenix make
it easy and enjoyable to create real-time applications
that scale to a large number of users. Apply system
design and development best practices to create applications that are easy to maintain. Gain confidence by
learning how to break your applications before your
users do. Deploy applications with minimized resource
use and maximized performance.

Stephen Bussey
(326 pages) ISBN: 9781680507195. $45.95
https://pragprog.com/book/sbsockets

Programming Machine Learning

You've decided to tackle machine learning — because
you're job hunting, embarking on a new project, or
just think self-driving cars are cool. But where to start?
It's easy to be intimidated, even as a software developer. The good news is that it doesn't have to be that
hard. Master machine learning by writing code one
line at a time, from simple learning programs all the
way to a true deep learning system. Tackle the hard
topics by breaking them down so they're easier to understand, and build your confidence by getting your
hands dirty.

Paolo Perrotta
(340 pages) ISBN: 9781680506600. $47.95
https://pragprog.com/book/pplearn

Competing with Unicorns

Today's tech unicorns develop software differently. They've developed a way of working that lets them scale like an enterprise while working like a startup. These techniques can be learned. This book takes you behind the scenes and shows you how companies like Google, Facebook, and Spotify do it. Leverage their insights, so your teams can work better together, ship higher-quality product faster, innovate more quickly, and compete with the unicorns.

Jonathan Rasmusson
(138 pages) ISBN: 9781680507232. $26.95
https://pragprog.com/book/jragile

Programming Flutter

Develop your next app with Flutter and deliver native look, feel, and performance on both iOS and Android from a single code base. Bring along your favorite libraries and existing code from Java, Kotlin, Objective-C, and Swift, so you don't have to start over from scratch. Write your next app in one language, and build it for both Android and iOS. Deliver the native look, feel, and performance you and your users expect from an app written with each platform's own tools and languages. Deliver apps fast, doing half the work you were doing before and exploiting powerful new features to speed up development. Write once, run anywhere.

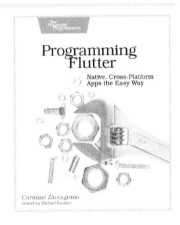

Carmine Zaccagnino
(368 pages) ISBN: 9781680506952. $47.95
https://pragprog.com/book/czflutr

The Pragmatic Bookshelf

The Pragmatic Bookshelf features books written by professional developers for professional developers. The titles continue the well-known Pragmatic Programmer style and continue to garner awards and rave reviews. As development gets more and more difficult, the Pragmatic Programmers will be there with more titles and products to help you stay on top of your game.

Visit Us Online

This Book's Home Page
https://pragprog.com/book/smgaelixir
Source code from this book, errata, and other resources. Come give us feedback, too!

Keep Up to Date
https://pragprog.com
Join our announcement mailing list (low volume) or follow us on twitter @pragprog for new titles, sales, coupons, hot tips, and more.

New and Noteworthy
https://pragprog.com/news
Check out the latest pragmatic developments, new titles and other offerings.

Save on the ebook

Save on the ebook versions of this title. Owning the paper version of this book entitles you to purchase the electronic versions at a terrific discount.

PDFs are great for carrying around on your laptop—they are hyperlinked, have color, and are fully searchable. Most titles are also available for the iPhone and iPod touch, Amazon Kindle, and other popular e-book readers.

Send a copy of your receipt to support@pragprog.com and we'll provide you with a discount coupon.

Contact Us

Online Orders:	*https://pragprog.com/catalog*
Customer Service:	*support@pragprog.com*
International Rights:	*translations@pragprog.com*
Academic Use:	*academic@pragprog.com*
Write for Us:	*http://write-for-us.pragprog.com*
Or Call:	+1 800-699-7764

Milton Keynes UK
Ingram Content Group UK Ltd.
UKHW010415100924
448100UK00007B/105